‘Diversion is a vital and yet strangely neglected and often misunderstood concept in youth justice discourse. By reclaiming diversion and by historicising, theorising and applying the concept, Roger Smith makes an indispensable and timely contribution to youth justice scholarship. His book is rigorous, challenging and provocative. It sets an agenda for new thinking and it will be widely read.’

– **Professor Barry Goldson**, *Charles Booth Chair of Social Science, Department of Sociology, Social Policy and Criminology, The University of Liverpool*

‘*Diversion in Youth Justice* provides definitive overview of a key aspect of youth justice, bringing a critical, incisive and informed perspective to the subject, presented in Smith’s inimitably accessible and dynamic writing style.’

– **Stephen Case**, *Professor of Criminology and Director of Studies, Department of Social Sciences, Loughborough University*

‘*Diversion in Youth Justice* focuses on important questions: why do we need to prosecute? Why don’t we divert more children and young people away from a system if it is ultimately damaging to them? Or is diversion from formal prosecution a mistake? Analysing shifts in thinking about diversion across time, Roger Smith offers us an account which has, at its heart, a quest for progressive social and criminal justice for children and young people who find themselves in conflict with the law, concluding that diversion itself can be transformational. The author offers deep critical reflection and analysis, and a book which is both candid and searching. An essential read!’

– **Professor Loraine Gelsthorpe**, *Director of the Institute of Criminology, University of Cambridge*

Diversion in Youth Justice

Diversion in youth justice is a subject of enduring interest. It concerns the processes by which decisions are made about whether or not to prosecute young offenders, and this book explores the continuing debates and historical developments which shape these processes. The treatment of young offenders is a contentious subject, and this book provides a comprehensive review of out of court decision-making in the context of wider arguments about how we should deal with the crimes of the young.

This book follows a broadly historical structure, exploring the development of ideas and approaches to agency decision-making at the point of prosecution. This leads to the identification of a number of distinctive 'models' of diversion, reflecting both specific periods of time and particular philosophies of intervention with young people in trouble with the law. Based on this classification, this book explores the implications for wider debates about childhood, crime and punishment and how these relate to theories of social control. This, in turn, leads to the conclusion that diversionary ideas and practices act as a kind of barometer for wider developments in the governance of youth.

This is one of the very few books that focuses exclusively on diversion as a feature of youth justice, and it provides a range of original and contemporary insights into this subject area which remains of considerable interest in this field, both academically and in practice. The ideas outlined here will contribute to new thinking in youth criminology, as the discipline responds to a prolonged period of apparent liberalisation in the treatment of young offenders which has yet to be fully understood or properly theorised.

Roger Smith is Professor of Social Work at Durham University, UK. As a practitioner, and in a senior policy role, he specialised in youth justice, and he has pursued this area of interest in his academic research and writing (including the well-known book *Youth Justice: Ideas, Policy, Practice*). He has also been involved in research and publications on a wider range of subjects, including childhood (*A Universal Child*), social work and power (*Social Work and Power*), participatory methods and social work education, and he retains a continuing interest in researching and promoting children's rights in practice (*Social Work with Young People*).

Routledge Frontiers of Criminal Justice

A full list of titles in this series is available at: https://www.routledge.com/Routledge-Frontiers-of-Criminal-Justice/book-series/RFCJ

Recently published titles:

43. **Young Offenders and Open Custody**
    Tove Pettersson

44. **Restorative Responses to Sexual Violence**
    Legal, Social and Therapeutic Dimensions
    Edited by Estelle Zinsstag and Marie Keenan

45. **Policing Hate Crime**
    Understanding Communities and Prejudice
    Gail Mason, JaneMaree Maher, Jude McCulloch, Sharon Pickering, Rebecca Wickes and Carolyn McKay

46. **The Special Constabulary**
    Historical Context, International Comparisons and Contemporary Themes
    Edited by Karen Bullock and Andrew Millie

47. **Action Research in Criminal Justice**
    Restorative Justice Approaches in Intercultural Settings
    Edited by Inge Vanfraechem and Ivo Aertsen

48. **Restoring Justice and Security in Intercultural Europe**
    Edited by Brunilda Pali and Ivo Aertsen

49. **Monitoring Penal Policy in Europe**
    Edited by Gaëtan Cliquennois and Hugues de Suremain

50. **Big Data, Crime and Social Control**
    Edited by Aleš Završnik

51. **Moral Issues in Intelligence-led Policing**
    Edited by Nicholas R. Fyfe, Helene O. I. Gundhus and Kira Vrist Rønn

52. **The Enforcement of Offender Supervision in Europe**
    Understanding Breach Processes
    Edited by Miranda M. Boone and Niamh Maguire

53. **Diversion in Youth Justice**
    What Can We Learn from Historical and Contemporary Practices?
    Roger Smith

Diversion in Youth Justice

What Can We Learn from Historical and Contemporary Practices?

Roger Smith

Routledge
Taylor & Francis Group
LONDON AND NEW YORK

First published 2018 by Routledge

2 Park Square, Milton Park, Abingdon, Oxfordshire OX14 4RN
52 Vanderbilt Avenue, New York, NY 10017

Routledge is an imprint of the Taylor & Francis Group, an informa business

First issued in paperback 2019

British Library Cataloguing in Publication Data
A catalogue record for this book is available from the British Library

Library of Congress Cataloging-in-Publication Data
A catalog record for this book has been requested

ISBN: 978-1-138-69728-7 (hbk)
ISBN: 978-0-367-22764-7 (pbk)

Typeset in Times New Roman
by HWA Text and Data Management, London

Contents

Introduction

Getting into diversion

This book is an account which draws on two interlinked journeys. One is mine, in that I have been involved professionally with youth diversion in a number of guises for over thirty years. In travelling this road, though, I have also become increasingly familiar with the path followed over a much longer period by the various practices which have fallen under the heading of youth (or juvenile) diversion, constituting the process of out of court or pre-prosecution decision-making and intervention in respect of young people who are officially identified as offenders. I hope that my own multi-faceted experience of this process and its outcomes will provide a helpful backdrop to a wider discussion of the histories, ideas and practices which it represents.

I first came into contact with diversion as a probation officer in Northamptonshire when the second of the county's Juvenile Liaison Bureaux (JLBx) was established in the area where I worked. Along with many others in the probation service at the time, I viewed this innovation with considerable suspicion. Constituted as it was, with an apparently dominant role for the police, I did not believe that it had much chance of changing pre-court decision-making practices for young offenders; and that, if anything, the need to justify its role would lead to an expansion of unnecessary and potentially stigmatising intervention into areas of minor delinquency and nuisance (or anti-social rather than criminal behaviour). Subsequently, though, I was seconded to work in the multi-agency bureau (in 1984), and began to get a much better picture of its operation, from the inside. In fact, as the evidence has amply demonstrated over the years, the JLBx were highly effective in establishing the county as one of the leading examples of effective practice in diversion, extending the use of cautioning to displace court appearances, even in the case of offences which appeared relatively serious (including domestic burglary, robbery and knife crime, for example). At the same time, the bureaux were successful in achieving an extension of police use of informal action in respect of a wide range of offences; in introducing a variety of reparative interventions (as a pre-cursor to restorative justice); in encouraging partner agencies (in education and the youth service) not to exclude young people from mainstream services; and in maintaining a broad range of support for their work. This experience convinced me that diversion could have a part to play in a progressive youth justice system, without necessarily contributing to net-widening, or the unnecessary and harmful labelling and institutionalisation of young people with which it had previously been associated.

Subsequently, I took on a policy development role with The Children's Society, and in this capacity continued to contribute to arguments for decarceration and less intrusive problem-solving approaches to youth offending. By this point, though, the mood was changing, and from a position of apparent strength, with the end of youth custody in sight, the reversals of the 1990s, as we shall see, had a very dramatic effect on the terrain within which I was operating. Nonetheless, I may have contributed in a small part to the thinking of the politicians and officials associated with the development of multi-agency models of intervention (Youth Offending Teams), and the formal recognition of pre-court disposals in legislation (as provided for by the Crime and Disorder Act 1998).

Later still, I moved into an academic role and in that capacity I have continued to write and research on the subject of youth diversion, providing at various points, a detailed analysis of the practice of diversion in Northamptonshire, an overview of the emergence and development of youth offending services, an account of the place played by reparation in diversionary practice, and a discussion of the experience and implications of the revival of diversion from 2007–8 onwards.

Over the period of time in which I have been involved with diversion, I have observed what appears from close at hand to be a series of quite dramatic changes in practice and underpinning rationale, linked undoubtedly to similar reversals and re-orientations within the wider field of youth justice, and this has prompted a belief that it is important to try and make sense of the dynamics and implications of these shifts, both to shed light on our wider understandings of criminal and youth justice; and also, hopefully to provide what will, in the end, be a clearer rationale and justification for the kind of progressive and socially just practice to which I aspired when I started on my own journey.

The context for this analytical project will be the rather longer journey followed by diversionary practices themselves, similarly punctuated with periods of calm progress, considered debate and review, controversy and challenge, recurrent uncertainty and rapid change. Whilst it appears that some doubters have always been with us, diversion does seem to have become established as a feature of youth justice, and it has provided the seed bed for other innovations such as the development of restorative justice in England and Wales, for example. Beginning, at least in a more or less 'official' sense, with the introduction of modern policing, the exercise of discretion over whether or not to bring charges against alleged young offenders has been incorporated into routine practice, becoming almost a *fait accompli* of policing practice. At the same time, however, as we shall see, it is a form of practice which arouses strong opposition and controversy, especially concerning its extra-judicial and discretionary character. There is something apparently questionable about the agglomeration of powers to one agency to determine whether or not to arrest, process and then prosecute (or report for prosecution) young offenders, and thus the extent of police powers in these matters has come into question. Is their use of wide-ranging powers sufficiently fair, proportionate and free from arbitrary and discriminatory judgement? Does this prevent proper exercise of due process and scrutiny of the evidence and levels of responsibility of the perpetrator? And, how are other interests (such as those of victims) to be protected in the context of the unaccountable exercise of discretionary powers? How are the rights of children and families to be protected from excessive demands in the name of informal justice? And, on the other hand, does 'letting off' young offenders too readily bring the justice system into disrepute? Does diversion, in fact, encourage crime? Do localised models of informal decision-making lead to unacceptable geographical variations?

All these key questions, and more, have featured consistently throughout the history of youth diversion, certainly, but it is also a form of criminal justice intervention which raises wider questions. The tendency for diversion to be seen as more acceptable in use with children identified as offenders, for example, seems to suggest that it is also bound up with our ideas and assumptions about childhood, for example. The answers to this question undoubtedly also have a bearing on the precise form that diversion takes in any given context. Perhaps our response to the low-level offending of children and young people might be grounded in assumptions about the 'normality' of errant behaviour, and the value of a simple admonition to warn them of the error of their ways. But, similarly, it might be thought that a child's offending is merely symptomatic of wider needs and problems, and that diversion *from* the criminal justice process ought also to mean diversion *into* appropriate preventive services to promote future well-being. Others might argue that addressing the specific issues arising from the offence, perhaps through some sort of restorative intervention, is an important vehicle for ensuring that the child or young person acquires a better sense of their own social obligations.

Behind these considerations, too, lies the matter of the relationship between diversion and social control. The immediate construction and delivery of diversionary interventions is a form of material practice which itself is related to deeper belief systems and wider forms of social organisation. Is diversion, then, a reflection of wider liberalising tendencies in criminal justice? Or, is it perhaps a manifestation of an informal means of social control, using a 'light touch' approach to extend moral messages and informal control into the lives of children, families and communities, especially in the sense that it is tied up with notions of conditionality or penalisation of non-compliance?

My aim in what follows is to open up some of these questions for exploration, to develop a detailed account of the emerging practices of youth diversion and their underlying justifications, and to reflect on the implications of these observations for our wider understandings of criminal justice. The book's structure broadly follows these objectives, being divided into three, unequal sections. The first chapter, then, provides a theoretical backdrop to the following substantive account. Here, I will explore ideas of crime, justice and childhood, exploring the connections between these and drawing out the potential implications for diversionary practice. This focus is important because, as I have already observed, children and young people are treated as a separate category by the criminal justice system, and although many of the formal grounds for this distinction appear arbitrary (such as the age of criminal responsibility), their distinctive treatment does derive from underlying and interacting assumptions with their own logical basis.

The following chapter explores the translation of changing ideas about childhood into the specific context of the emergence of modern policing and the changing shape of practice in relation to young people's offending. Here, the emerging formalisation of practice, and the development of a distinctive rationale for dealing with children's crimes can be shown to have shaped the exercise of police discretion and legitimised a differential approach to their reported wrongdoings. As a consequence of this accommodation, a ready basis was established for the rapid expansion in the use of cautions for juvenile offenders with the implementation of the post-war welfare state.

Chapter 3 brings into focus the apparent periodisation of diversion in youth justice, with the emergence of substantial criticism of its impact with linked evidence indicating a significant 'net-widening' effect. Far from reducing the number of children and young people being formally processed, an expansion in the use of cautioning appeared to have contributed to a demonstrable encroachment of formal systems into the lives of children and families who would not previously have been subject to such close attention, whether for reasons of need (welfare) or deed (justice). The limits of diversion seemed to have been reached by this point.

By contrast, Chapter 4 provides an account of the effects of the 'back to justice' movement of the early 1980s, and of a much better informed body of agencies and practitioners whose approach was grounded in principles of minimum intervention and offence-based problem solving, supported by a wider strategy of reducing the size and scope of state involvement in the lives of children and families. During this period, then, a mood of renewed optimism became apparent, with practitioners expressing a widespread belief in their capacity to change systems to positive effect, despite the persistence of some critical voices, who saw vestiges of institutionalised social control in the new multi-agency delivery models of the time.

Although overall I am cautious about presenting too neat a picture of pendulum swings, or discrete phases in policy and practice, what follows in Chapter 5 is a reflection on the 'punitive turn' of the early 1990s, and the consequences for diversion, with the re-emergence of dangerousness and the 'risky child'. This period, as I note, extends beyond a change of government, and the introduction of new terminology (cautions being replaced by reprimands and final warnings), since the ethos of risk management and micro-level correctional intervention did not significantly alter despite claims of radical innovation. Here, then, is concrete support for the argument that the relationship between superficial change, often at the level of policy and rhetoric, and substantive, material practices is not linear or one-directional; and both sit within a wider framework of ideology and structures which shape the networks and practices which constitute the mechanisms of social control.

However, following another period of system expansion, the era of austerity, accompanied by a growing realisation of the effects of a renewed period of net-widening, led to another rapid reversal, in the mid-late 2000s, and the emergence of a range of diversionary initiatives. The combined effect of these changes was a substantial reduction in the number of young people entering the criminal justice system, although the diversity of the new practice models put in place suggested a distinct lack of clarity of ideological focus or practice objectives associated with this phase in the ongoing journey of youth diversion. Indeed, it may well be that this period is more indicative of the dominance of financial imperatives (cost cutting and the rolling back of the neo-liberal state) than of the ascendancy of principles of substantive or social justice.

In the final part of the book, I turn again to consider the ideological and theoretical contexts of diversion. In Chapter 7, the idea of distinct phases and models of diversion is revisited; and clear distinctions are made between the objectives and practices of the different periods identified. Welfare, rights, risk and responsibilisation are identified as the underlying qualities of each form of practice, albeit in somewhat idealised form. This should not, however, obscure continuities which seem to permeate and, indeed, structure debates about the extent and purposes of out-of-court interventions in youth justice; the notions of a tariff of disposals, and individual responsibility, for example, are central to most diversionary schemes, even where the aim is to provide genuine 'alternatives' to conventional criminal justice processes.

The final chapter broadens the focus to consider diversion within wider discussions of the dynamics and structures of social control, drawing specifically on three alternative narratives developed by Cohen (1985) which seek to account for the emergence and institutionalisation of criminal justice systems and practices over time. Each of these can be applied to diversion, accounting for it either in terms of linear growth, periodic re-evaluation and rupture, or sustained hegemonic control; but, as I conclude, each is limited in its capacity to account for the insight and intentions of those directly engaged in understanding and enacting the critical form of practice which it represents. Diversion, I will conclude, is a form of critical practice (praxis) which is best understood as a continually active and unsettling representation of alternative, transformational models of intervention which are (or can be) a vehicle for achieving inclusive and socially just outcomes for young people 'in trouble'.

1 Theorising youth diversion

Unpacking basic assumptions

When reflecting on how to start this book, it occurred to me that the central concept of youth (or juvenile) diversion itself relied on a number of important assumptions; and these assumptions, in turn, were grounded in a number of key debates associated with significant theoretical domains, namely, childhood, deviance and punishment. It thus began to make sense to try to explore these important areas of discussion and controversy as a way of setting the scene for subsequent chapters outlining the emergence and development of diversion as a form of practice.

If we reflect on the idea of youth diversion itself, it becomes apparent that this does in fact incorporate a series of implicit assumptions which, themselves, are grounded in the theoretical domains indicated. For someone to be 'diverted' for something, for example, that implies a default position or norm which would apply in the absence of the diversionary process. In the present case, that would in effect consist of the standard or routine disposal (prosecution leading to punishment) for a crime. Inherent in this supposition, though, is the concept of 'crime' or infringement, which is clearly defined by law and popular consent, and which must have been committed by an offender in order for him/her to be considered for diversion. Here, too, there may be embedded assumptions about the definition of guilt or culpability for a crime committed. We must presumably assume a level of intent or responsibility in order for an action to be treated as criminal; and whilst such considerations might apply to the population in general (in the sense of 'mental capacity' perhaps), it seems that children and young people constitute a distinctive category in this respect. Some are deemed insufficiently mature (or responsible) to be able to form criminal intent, and are thus presumed not to be capable of assuming criminal responsibility. Others, however (10–17 year olds in England and Wales, for example), are deemed to be capable of acting criminally, but at the same time, their age qualifies them for distinctive treatment by the justice system, in the form of both criminal processes and subsequent disposals (special forms of custody, for instance). Decisions, then, to divert children/young people from the justice system are inevitably grounded in the situated assumptions made about their level of culpability for crimes which conventionally merit a particular form of judicial intervention.

So, the decision to divert a specific child/young person from the justice system is both contingent on the circumstances and constructions placed on the particular behaviour under consideration; and at the same time, grounded in a series of generalised assumptions brought to bear by decision makers about childhood, criminality and criminal justice. In order to gain a sound insight into the former, therefore, we not only need to know what went on in the 'case' in question, but also what are the theoretical and normative resources on which those party to the decision will be drawing. I will therefore, begin here by introducing a brief overview of key ideas and assumptions about these three conceptual domains, in order to provide a basis for evaluating what follows. Space does not allow for a comprehensive discussion of any of them, but it will be possible to introduce essential elements of each, and also to reflect on the ways in which they interact and inform the specific subject of youth diversion.

Constructing crime and punishment

Much has been written about theories of crime and punishment, spanning a range of disciplines; and it is clearly a subject area which has engendered a great deal of intense discussion, not least because it does seem to bring a light to shine on essential questions of humanity, such as the origins of good and evil, how these attributes should be assessed and what our responses should be.

So: 'What is Crime?' (Michalowski, 2015). As Michalowski observes, for many of us, this may seem a relatively straightforward question. Crime can be seen as a 'value-neutral' term, which operates as a means of classifying actions prohibited by laws, which in turn are the product of consensual deliberation, and therefore unproblematic. This is certainly the conventional and often implicit understanding which applies when most of us begin to think about criminal behaviour. The law and the thresholds it represents act as a powerful dividing line between what is socially and morally acceptable and forms of activity which cannot be tolerated in the public interest. For those approaching the question from a legal standpoint, this is fundamental to the operation of systems of justice and punishment. So, for Hart (1968, p. 6), the reason for 'certain kinds of actions' being forbidden by law is simply and uncontroversially: 'To announce to society that these actions are not to be done and to secure that fewer of them are done'. Some forms of behaviour are defined as crimes so that they can be discouraged, prevented or punished; and if we did not have this mechanism for defining conduct as unacceptable, then clearly there would be no justification for penalising such offences. By contrast, societies are typically characterised by a range of problematic behaviours which meet widespread disapproval and sometimes moral condemnation, such as cheating at cards, lying or infidelity, although these are not routinely made the subject of criminal sanctions.

This, in turn, leads us to consider the underlying purposes of defining certain behaviours as criminal and the implications of pursuing those objectives. We can assume, perhaps, that the aim is to obtain a degree of certainty in the task of securing and maintaining social order and conformity; and that both the implicit moral statement of defining something as a crime and the direct response to criminal activity are intended to put a stop to it. According to Hart (1968, p. 9), though, pure retribution, in the sense simply of applying 'the pains of punishment to an offender' is also a potential 'Justifying Aim' of the form of justice to be imposed on someone who breaks the law.

Establishment of the principled basis for classifying crimes and legitimising the use of sanctions against them is thus the first step in constructing a coherent framework for systems of law and criminal justice. Beyond this, though, lie a further series of assumptions about the capacities and intent of those actors who are identified as breaching the requirements of the law. Thus, for example, we are introduced by legal scholars to the concept of *mens rea*, the Latin term taken to represent the idea of 'being of sound mind', and therefore capable of forming independent intent to carry out a given act. It is by now well-established that intent is a necessary pre-requisite for determining that an action which may be prohibited by law is in fact criminal:

> Few today would disagree with the maxim; the criminal law has long since rejected the idea that causing harm should be criminal regardless of the defendant's subjective culpability.
>
> (Heller, 2009, p. 317)

Thus, we are assured that the idea of absolute or strict liability for an action does not apply across the board (although in some contexts this is not the case, such as motoring offences). By implication, then, it is widely accepted that to be defined as an offender and thus to be subject to some sort of penal sanction, the individual is defined as fully and solely responsible for his/her actions. The attribution of responsibility is therefore a core principle informing the operation of the justice system; and a crucial trigger for state intervention of one kind or another in response to an offence. Of course, the principle of *mens rea* is not restricted in its application to those circumstances where the offender deliberately intends to commit a crime; there are also cases where it could be deemed that any reasonable person could and should have been able to foresee the consequences of their actions and could have taken steps to avoid them. So it is that Hart (1968, p. 140) argues in support of the extension of the concept to 'include the capacities and powers of normal persons to think about and control their conduct'. Crimes of omission thus become as culpable as crimes of commission, in light of this. As we shall see subsequently, the capacity to foresee what might happen as a result of an action is one of those attributes which might be seen as subject to variation according to the characteristics of the individual concerned.

These considerations lead Hart to formulate an important set of pre-conditions for the administration of sanctions to those who are found to have offended:

> What is crucial is that those whom we punish should have had, when they acted, the normal capacities, physical and mental, for doing what the law requires and abstaining from what it forbids, and a fair opportunity to exercise these capacities.
>
> (Hart, 1968, p. 152)

The formal construction of notions of crime and criminality along these lines also requires certain other expectations to be met, such as the standards of proof to be applied, both to the commission of the offence and the extent to which it was an intentional or wilful act. Here, too, the formulation of conventional understandings of crime, guilt, due process and justice depend on assumptions about our capacity to achieve measurability and certainty in determining what has happened, who is responsible and to what extent, and what should be done about it.

Given that this is the case, space is therefore created for considered applications of the principle that criminal responsibility can be modified in various ways. That is to say, there will be cases where intent and culpability are not absolute, and there may be grounds for modifying our approach to the offender and his/her offence. Historic precedents for this have been established by cases such as that of Daniel M'Naghten, where a specific legal test for insanity was developed by the court, whereby defendants could be acquitted on the grounds of diminished responsibility. In that case, the test was developed partly to restrict the use of this kind of defence, but it also by implication also confirmed that the defendant's liability to be held responsible for an offence could be modified in certain circumstances. Although as time has passed, the nature and extent of circumstances which could justify claims of diminished responsibility has been highly controversial, it has become increasingly well-established that children constitute a special case, simply on grounds of age and maturity. As we shall see, this presumption has been associated with the progressive development of a distinctive 'youth justice system', from the point of apprehension and pre-court decision-making, through judicial processes, to the sentencing framework and institutional regimes to which convicted children are subject. Thus, from the early 19th century in Britain, there is evidence of growing concern about the position of children in relation to the justice system, and whether or not they should be treated differently by the justice process, simply by virtue of their status (Muncie, 2009, p. 53, for example).

So, within the broad framework of a system of justice which relies on individualised notions of guilt and responsibility for its justification, there is scope for modifying this, depending on certain pre-set conditions, of which 'being a child' is one. This, as we shall see shortly, is inevitably bound up with our assumptions and understandings of childhood as a distinctive life stage. However, it is also important at this point to acknowledge alternative (critical) perspectives on the place of crime, law, punishment and individualised notions of guilt which call into question the kind of assumptions we have sketched out here. In this light, those aspects of the subject which appear 'natural' and uncontroversial are called into question. The idea of crime, for example, can be reframed in terms of the context within which it is applied, and the structural relationships and inequalities which lie behind conventional understandings, and lead to the criminalisation of some sections of the population rather than others. So, for instance, Michalowski (2016, p. 195) outlines a complex set of interacting relationships between 'power, domination and consciousness' which are complicit in determining what forms of harm are determined as criminal, and which are not. In a specific case of the 'social construction of reality', crime and criminality are similarly products of an interactive process whereby specific interests and assumptions come to shape what might be seen as common sense views about law and justice.

As Rafter (1990, p. 376) has put it, there has been a relative reluctance to question the certainty with which established categories of crime and assumptions about justice have been imbued, partly linked to what she describes as the criminological 'field's adherence to a fairly narrow, scientific positivism that conceives of social facts as inert and independent, like fragments of ancient pottery'. An alternative view is that crime is not a fixed entity, but is rather a function of processes of rule-making and enforcement, which are unevenly distributed in society. As Becker (1963, p. 9) asserts, deviance 'is created by society'. By this he does not mean simply that it is the product of social factors impacting on the offender, but that '*social groups create deviance by making the rules whose infraction constitutes deviance*' (his emphasis). In other words, it is the holders of legitimised power who are able to determine the rules by which the boundaries of acceptable behaviour are defined. By extension, as Becker also acknowledges, the deviant (or criminal) only becomes defined as such through the application of the abstract rules devised; and so, the determination of criminality depends also on the differential exercise of judicial and administrative powers. Those who become defined as offenders are selected to fulfil that role, and again as Becker (1963, p. 9) points out, 'we cannot assume that these people have actually committed a deviant act or broken some rule, because the process of labelling them may not be infallible; some people may be labelled deviant who in fact have not broken a rule', and at the same time 'many offenders may escape apprehension…'.

For Michalowski (2016, p. 194), the processes by which some forms of activity are defined as unlawful and some people come to be criminalised on the basis of transgression are not arbitrary and depend on a combination of 'economic, political, social and cultural forces' which lead in turn to 'the construction of what a society imagines to be its "crime problem"'. And, further, when we come to ask questions about the operation of the criminal justice system, these should always be couched in terms of an 'understanding that the acts, events or conditions' concerned are intertwined with a range of 'wider social, economic and political arrangements' which determine how they are dealt with. Here, then, we have a contrasting view of crime and criminality to that which casts these as neutral features of a social landscape shaped by an underlying and consensual view of right and wrong and just deserts.

This is a critically important point; for if we cannot take the neutrality of law and criminal justice processes as simply a 'given', then we have to open up the question of what is the basis on which it is established, and why? Those features of abstract theories of law which are embedded in the assumptions informing the everyday operation of the justice system such as equality before the law and individual responsibility are now problematised; as are the specific aspects of the system with which we are concerned, such as the exercise of discretion and out of court decision-making procedures. We can perhaps distinguish here between what may be a more or less coherent internal logic of law and criminal justice, and the wider and more contingent relationships between these entities and the social and structural realities which frame their construction and routine practices. So it is that even provisions which seem in one sense to involve setting aside the normal expectations of the judicial process can only operate (or be permitted to operate) according to the prevailing logic of the process itself. In other words, the rules and requirements to be met before a decision not to prosecute can be made are framed in terms of the prevailing legal framework. Hence, exemptions can only be applied in terms of recognised characteristics, for which there is clear and unequivocal evidence, such as mental health issues, or reduced responsibility on grounds of age and maturity.

On the one hand, such mechanisms for disapplying the requirements of the judicial process might appear to call the rule of law into question; but on the other, because they are applied on its own terms, they actually contribute towards the maintenance of its underlying legitimacy. Its strict application in all other cases is thus justified to the extent that it is capable of demonstrating flexibility, and accommodating exceptions. Importantly, then, the law can be seen as carrying out what Gramsci (1971, p. 242) has described as a 'civilising' or educative function, operating in a logical, coherent and authoritative manner under the auspices of the state, in order to support the prevailing form of social organisation. Similar arguments have been developed by those such as Garland (2001, p. 30) who refer to a process of modernisation and systematisation of law and the machinery of social control which brought a sense of uniformity and inevitability to a previously disparate field of the dispensation of justice. The rule of law then becomes one vehicle by which a particular form of social structure achieves and sustains its internal justification.

On this basis, then, we can also begin to map out the basis on which specific exemptions might apply. The place attributed to children and childhood in the organisation of society thus also confers a certain status in relation to law and justice. Children, by their nature it is assumed, are less responsible and thus less culpable for their actions than adults responsible for similar behaviour. Thus, in the same way as there is an inherent default logic to the way we understand and apply legal principles and processes, so too, there appears to be an equivalent basis on which childhood is understood. We will explore this further in what follows.

Framing childhood

Childhood is very often conceptualised as a linear developmental life stage, whereby younger members of the population gradually acquire the levels of knowledge, understanding and maturity to take an accepted and responsible position as fully-fledged citizens, contributing productively to the common good. Growing up is essentially a process of socialisation, whereby unformed and unconstrained temperaments are shaped according to the conventions of normality and responsible behaviour. As in the case of the legal framework, embedded in these presumptions of normality is the implicit belief that this is the only way in which acceptable behaviour can be defined and that any deviation represents a form of faulty programming of one kind or another. So, to a greater or lesser extent, there is a default view of childhood and what would constitute a natural and expected process of growing and moving towards a state of adult maturity.

In recent times, theories of childhood and youth have become quite widely debated, and to some extent this has involved a considerable loosening of the prior conceptual straitjacket; but nonetheless, developmental assumptions remain a powerful element of our understanding of what it means to be a child or adolescent. Hendrick (2003, p. 13) interestingly attributes the emergence of contemporary assumptions about 'normal' childhoods to the changes associated with modernity, shifting patterns of employment, and the 'anxieties' of the late 19th and early 20th centuries. Concerns about apparently growing social problems such as criminality, family breakdown, poor health and poverty prompted serious consideration of the factors contributing to 'abnormal' forms of childhood.

Others, too, have reflected on the impetus behind attempts to define and distinguish the elements which constitute a 'normal' childhood; and, by extension the basis on which children might be seen as different by nature from adults. Corsaro (1997), for instance, has provided an authoritative account of the kind of assumptions about childhood which prevailed before it was 'rediscovered' by sociology. As he puts it, there was little interest in theorising childhood for a very long time, precisely because it was treated as a more or less natural state of being, through which individuals could be expected to pass in consistent and predictable fashion. Models of childhood were developed which assumed a standard pattern of biological and cognitive development, constituting a series of predictable stages, and to which social systems and educative practices would need to adapt to ensure that children were prepared for the demands of conventional society. The normal child 'must be appropriated and shaped to fit in' (Corsaro, 1997, p. 9). Jenks (1996, p. 36), too, highlights the idea of 'development' as 'the primary metaphor through which childhood is made intelligible'. Children's development is understood as 'a wholly 'natural' process' which 'echoes' (p. 37) the deterministic strand to be found in some sociological accounts of social functioning and social change. For Jenks, this kind of schema is associated with the ideas of Piaget (1959), in particular, whose observations of children's activities provided the basis for the formulation of a systematic model of cognitive growth, according to a series of clearly defined stages. Although Corsaro (1997, p. 12) warns us against oversimplifying Piaget's work, it is nonetheless most often associated with a fairly prescriptive model of children's development according to a series of developmental phases. According to these, children can be seen to make progress as their problem-solving capacity becomes more sophisticated and they became more aware of the complexities involved in understanding the world and acting on what they know or believe.

Corsaro (1997, p. 15) goes on to make an important distinction between what he describes as Piaget's 'nativistic' assumptions that development is essentially linear and driven by internal and natural attributes of the child, on the one hand; and the socially-determined dimensions of collective sense-making and intellectual development, on the other, as articulated notably by Vygotsky (1986).

Developmental accounts grounded in depictions of psychological maturation are also mirrored in increasingly prominent explanations of children's progressive acquisition of capabilities grounded in the biological sphere and particularly viewed in terms of neurological changes. So it is that we are led to believe that genetic and physiological factors play a very substantial part in defining the dynamics and nature of children's transitions through a series of fixed phases of development. Thus, for example fMRI (functional magnetic resource imaging) techniques have been progressively utilised to demonstrate distinct and changing patterns of brain activity which are believed to reflect thought and behavioural patterns as they also change over the lifespan, and especially during childhood. Similarly, changes in the size and composition of the brain are also now believed to be associated with specific patterns of information processing and decision-making. It has been argued for example that: 'Notably late to reach adult levels of cortical thickness is the dorosolateral prefontal cortex [of the brain], involved in circuitry subserving control of impulses, judgement and decision-making' (Lenroot and Giedd, 2006, p. 723), with the associated implications for the capacity to reach 'mature' conclusions about the implications of one's actions. So it is that studies have tried to isolate the influence of particular changes in certain aspects of brain functioning concerned with 'impulse and inhibitory control' (Blakemore and Robbins, 2012, p. 1,189), to account for a 'peak' in risk-taking behaviour in adolescence.

Such neurological accounts of child and adolescent development find themselves in accord with those which are grounded in more established psychological explanations which also view adolescence as a clear and discrete phase with very specific attributes. Erikson's (1995) influential work, for example, charted 'eight ages of man', of which youth was identified as a period in which the search for a coherent sense of identity would be threatened by the possibility of an emerging sense of 'role confusion' (p. 235). But in Erikson's model of life stages, it is also clear that childhood and adolescence are essentially the precursors of a fully formed adult state: 'Adolescence is the age of the final establishment of a dominant positive ego-identity. It is then that a future within reach becomes part of the conscious life plan' (Erikson, 1995, p. 277). Here, too, we find a close alignment with other approaches to the study of youth and adolescence which have characterised this as a time of 'storm and stress' (Arnett, 1999). In one sense, certainly, it is the very persistence of these ideas of child development which is persuasive; it is a powerful paradigm:

> The concept of childhood progressing through a series of stages is not a contemporary device or construction. The division or categorisation of human life into different periods, which incorporate childhood as well as adulthood, are to be found in writings as far back as the seventh century…
>
> (Rose et al., 2006, p. 163)

Much of the practice literature which shapes professional involvement in the lives of children is also informed by these largely consensual assumptions; and it is particularly pertinent as we shall see subsequently that an influential school of thought amongst practitioners at one point began to make explicit calls for the organisation and delivery of youth justice to be based on the principle of children 'Growing Out of Crime' (Rutherford, 2002).

Interestingly, too, these standard assumptions about the progressively emerging capacities of children and young people were for a time incorporated into the law in the form of the assumption of the principle of *doli incapax*. According to this doctrine, criminal responsibility would become attributable progressively, rather than at a fixed point in time.

Similarly, developmental assumptions are embedded in the range of practices concerned with child welfare, child protection and child care provision, with decisions based on models such as that articulated by Fahlberg (1994) to facilitate placement decisions on behalf of 'looked after' children. So, too, it has been widely argued (Scott and Grisso, 1997, for example) that a developmental perspective offers the best lens for understanding and responding to the crimes of the young. According to this line of argument, children and young people are 'naturally' less well advanced than adults across a range of characteristics (biological, social or psychological) which thus predisposes them to committing criminal acts; for example, because they are more prone than their elders to seek instant gratification, without considering the social and moral constraints which might apply (Scott and Grisso, 1997, p. 178). In essence, then, there seems to be a widely held view that there are certain characteristics and behavioural traits which are specific to childhood, irrespective of the context and nature of individual experiences; and these in turn can be associated with certain types of activity which may vary from that to be expected in adulthood. Additionally, these forms of behaviour may be inherently anti-social to a greater or lesser degree.

By contrast, critiques of developmental assumptions about childhood draw attention to a number of areas which are not well explained by this kind of standardised model, notably the diversity of children's experiences and their 'agency'; that is their capacity to interpret their own experiences and make the world, rather than simply following predetermined maturational pathways. Accepting the biological basis of maturation (James and James, 2004, p. 18), and certain features of their experiences which children are likely to have in common (Smith, 2010), we are still confronted with the challenge of accounting for diversity, and the influence of the adult world on the constitution of childhood as a concept. James and James (2010, p. 58), for example, elaborate a fourfold framework for understanding children's lives, which clearly moves us away from a linear notion of growth and change towards the 'finished' state of adulthood. Thus, the 'tribal child' seeks to capture the sense in which children 'actively construct' their own worlds (p. 59), and develop their own shared meanings, moral frameworks and forms of expression. These may or may not be viewed as 'anti-social' from outside, but importantly, they are grounded in the everyday lives and sense making of children themselves, and so are not simply natural or predictable consequences of age or limited understanding. Extending this line of reasoning further, James and James (2004, p. 59) go on to formulate the idea of children as a 'minority' group, which is 'separated and often discriminated against by the very institution of childhood itself'. Here, then, children's perceptions, and indeed their actions are shaped by their collective experiences of 'lack of citizenship status' and lack of 'political, economic and social rights'. This, it might be argued, is actually to invite the kind of irresponsibility and absence of concern for the consequences of their actions which are held to be inherent attributes of children. There is a sense here in which their transgressions, if this is what they are, actually take place in the very spaces (metaphorical or physical) where these are expected and in some respects perhaps permitted.

Set against this, according to the fourfold model offered by James and James (2004, p. 60) are the models of childhood by which the 'social space' which children inhabit is marked out. By this they mean, on the one hand, the broad and essentially uncontested presumption that there is something like 'childhood' in every social system, and that this provides the basis for broad-based frameworks according to which childhoods can be studied comparatively, and common instruments can be developed for promoting their interests (such as the UN Convention on the Rights of the Child).

The final perspective on childhood articulated by James and James (2004, p. 60) is the one which they suggest is 'diametrically opposed to the perspective offered from within developmental psychology', precisely because it problematises the 'discourses through which the idea of both "the child" and "childhood" is produced'. Here the concern is very much with articulating the specific and contextual structures and processes according to which childhood is defined, organised and understood. In other words, the very basis for any assumptions about normal trajectories through childhood and adolescence is questioned, however well-established or strongly held they may be.

As Lee (2001) amongst others has pointed out though, the underlying consensus that informs much thinking and practice with children is that they are in a state of development towards completeness in the adult life stage. Importantly here, in the same way that there is a default position according to which the rule of law and criminal justice are understood, so too there appears to be a conventional perspective on childhood. This exhibits a tendency to view behaviours as intelligible according to a set of pre-existing and age-specific characteristics or behavioural predictors, rather than contingent and actively negotiated. This, as we shall see, provides one lens through which children's delinquencies might be viewed; and correspondingly, this then also offers a potential rationale for a distinctive decision-making framework in juvenile or youth justice.

Understanding deviance

The third arm of our initial theoretical framework will involve an exploration of the explanations and meanings of deviance or anti-social behaviour amongst children and young people. Once again, the first and perhaps most telling observation is that this is very much contested terrain, and depends greatly on the starting point from which analysis progresses. Typically, children's delinquencies have been explained according to either biological, psychological or social disciplinary perspectives; and in some cases, attempts have been made to integrate these, at least to the extent of describing those who become offenders.

Importantly, explanations of deviance will have a relationship with our assumptions about childhood; and these, in turn, will impact on the further positions we take on the appropriate role of law and criminal justice in responding to young people's infractions.

So, it perhaps makes sense to begin here with those explanations which simply see delinquency as a natural and predictable feature of childhood, deriving from the initial untamed state of being a child. To an extent, this perspective is consistent with the developmental assumption of the child as different, unformed and somehow in a less advanced state than adult members of society. Children, by definition, do not know how to behave, and it is only through the experience of growing and being socialised that conventional expectations and conformity can be promoted. In some cases, these processes fail to take effect and children remain in a natural state of 'savagery' (Jenks, 1996), or are characterised as 'devils' (Fionda, 2005), acting out a natural state of predatory instincts and aggression. In this way, children's crimes are attributed to the failures of socialisation to curtail and re-focus their natural qualities and instincts onto pro-social goals along acceptable developmental pathways. This provides us with a convenient and relatively neat explanation of extreme forms of behaviour which are both shocking and, because of this, difficult to accept and potentially problematic when we begin to seek out explanations. Both Jenks (1996) and Fionda (2005) refer to the death of James Bulger at the hands of two relatively young boys, and the challenges of accounting for their behaviour in terms other than those of evil or devilry (Jenks, 1996, p. 128).

However, such responses, perhaps predictable in such dramatic and tragic cases, could not in themselves offer anything more than a superficial explanation. As is quite clear, once the scope of behaviour under consideration is widened, so, too, is the challenge of providing a more complete account of the origins and drivers of children's behaviour when it is unacceptable.

Failure of socialisation may offer a plausible and potentially attractive explanatory frame, but it cannot account alone for the considerable variety of behaviours manifested by children and young people which are defined as unlawful. Thus, we need to know not just what is absent, but also what is present in terms of providing the impetus and motive for children's crimes. Nonetheless, it must be acknowledged that many explanations of offending by the young rely on an implicit and sometimes explicit 'deficit' model of their behaviour. Thus, for example, their apparent impulsiveness stems from a lack of capacity to make rational judgements about the consequences of their behaviour. Of course, in the very way the question of deviance is framed, the assumption is made that we are in the business of seeking explanations for problematic behaviour, and so attributes which in other contexts might be viewed positively ('hesitate and you're lost', as the proverb puts it) are imbued with negative connotations ('look before you leap' appears to be the default position here). As I have observed elsewhere, the issue here is a definitional problem in essence:

> In short, there is an analytical disjuncture between the socially constructed nature of youth crime and young offenders, on the one hand; and attempts to explain these as if they are specific and exclusive characteristics of certain individuals, on the other.
>
> (Smith, 2011, p. 51)

Instead, Muncie argues, the key question to be asked is: 'who says this is a social problem – and why do they say so?' (Muncie, 2009, p. 3).

Despite these reservations, it is clear that much effort has been devoted to identifying and classifying the causes of offending by children and young people. These explanatory accounts have often been categorised as pertaining to one of the following: individual characteristics; psychosocial features; or population-wide influences (Rutter et al., 1998). Others have sometimes sought to identify causal factors according to a number of distinct 'domains', in particular the family, the school, the community or the personal; and, indeed, a number of analyses have sought to attribute each of these as a causal role in the genesis of youth crime.

Thus, for those who seek to identify inherent qualities which predispose young people to offend, the likely origins of these are to be found in genetic influences, biological differences, the impact of behaviour changing conditions (head injuries, for example), or patterns of psychological development which are embedded in the make-up of the individual concerned. In one of these examples, we can observe a continuing interest amongst researchers in the 'adolescent brain'. As technology has itself become more sophisticated, we have in turn increasingly been able to 'fine tune' our understanding of the neurological processes which underpin the choices made by young people. Blakemore and Robbins (2012, p. 1,184), for example, argue that it is possible to distinguish a number of 'component processes, including the representation of value, response selection (including inhibitory control), learning and socio-emotional factors' in the act of decision-making. In particular, in this discussion, they argue that it can be determined that there is a 'dissociation' between the rate of development of 'impulse control and response inhibition during adolescence' and the less predictable pattern of change in the 'reward system'; by which I think they mean that there are neurological developments in the adolescent years which reflect the apparently greater propensity of young people to seek instant gratification than those at other points in the life span.

For these authors, this observation alone is not enough to account for criminality amongst young people; the 'social brain' is also important, and may actually be a crucial dimension of the adolescent developmental map, since this concept, and the findings associated with it, allow for differential responses and choices depending on the context within which decisions are made, such as the varying nature of 'peer relationships' and mutual perceptions (Blakemore and Mills, 2014, p. 191).

For some, of course, it may not be social factors so much as genetic predispositions that account for differential patterns of behaviour, and deviance. These are linked in some accounts to an argument that criminality is associated with certain innate traits common to all, which are the product of evolutionary processes. Thus, what may be seen as common patterns of behaviour, such as represented by the 'age-crime curve' – the greater preponderance of offending amongst adolescents – reflect the outcome of the evolutionary process to this point: 'Because developing organisms face different adaptive challenges at different stages of their life history we should, therefore, expect… the proximate mechanisms that underpin human behaviour to be calibrated to specific developmental contexts' (Durrant and Ward, 2012, p. 17). Certain types of behaviour, including offending by young people, should therefore be seen as the natural products of an evolutionary process that promotes certain types of behaviour which suit the longer-term adaptation of the species to its environment. So, for example, risk-taking and competitive behaviour (which may thus fall into the category of 'crime') is perhaps a predictable feature of 'a crucial period of development in which dominance hierarchies are being established and competition over mates and mating is heightened' (p. 18); at least to the extent that it is predictive of male criminality, it might seem.

This is by no means an exhaustive list of potential explanations of youth crime which rely on innate or inbuilt characteristics, but it does help to illustrate some of the assumptions behind this sort of categorisation, such as the deterministic nature of these accounts, and their tendency to universalise, so that their ability to account for differential outcomes is relatively limited or schematic.

Other explanatory frameworks for youth offending rely on what might be described as psychosocial theoretical models, still based on individualised characteristics, but rooting these in the interface between standardised developmental processes and personal experience. These might well, for instance, be seen as offering the basis of plausible accounts of the kind of 'storm and stress' (Arnett, 1999) experienced by young people going through a series of more or less unsettling transitions in their lives. So, for example, the hormonal changes associated with puberty are believed to prompt significant upheaval in young people's sense of self and relationships with those around them; but the precise nature and effects of these changes will also depend on individual variations in these universal experiences.

For those interested in psychosocial explanations, the concept of 'maturity' seems to be important (Prior et al., 2011; Steinberg et al., 2015). Here, we are offered an idealised view of the 'finished' adult citizen, who is able to act as a normal and responsible member of conventional society, against which children and young people are to be judged in terms of their progress and acquisition of the desired attributes associated with this ideal. So, there is seen to be an interactive process whereby a 'criminogenic environment' (social factors) interacts with an individual's 'propensity to offend' to generate criminal behaviour, but both elements need to be present (Prior et al., 2011, p. 19). This type of explanation is on the face of it rather more helpful than those which rely simply on common features of adolescence or singular causal factors, since neither of these accounts for differential effects or variable outcomes dependent on contingent and contextual factors.

As we move along the spectrum from individualised to social and more diverse 'causes' of crime amongst the young, so a wider range of potential contributing factors opens up. This takes us into the realm of 'risk factors' which are multidimensional and operate on a whole range of levels to predispose young people to get involved in anti-social activities. Over the years a rich and diverse literature on the risk factors associated with youth crime has emerged, as documented by Case and Haines (2009) in their critical review of this literature. Typically, this has led to the development of extensive lists of those factors associated with offending by young people. The Youth Justice Board (2005) has provided an overview of 'risk and protective factors', for instance, which lists no fewer than 26 factors believed to be associated with a greater likelihood of offending or reoffending, under the headings: family, school, community, and personal. There appears to be a multiplier effect of these factors as well, so that they work across category boundaries to intensify the possibility of young people becoming offenders:

> It is... clear that risk factors cluster together in the lives of the most disadvantaged children; and the chances that these children will become anti-social and criminally active increases in line with the number of risk factors. Young people who have been exposed to the greatest risk are between five and 20 times more likely to become violent and serious offenders than those who have not.
>
> (Youth Justice Board, 2005, p. 4)

By agglomerating all these various categories and indicators, the 'risk factor' explanatory model has arguably created a kind of catch-all which in one sense is almost bound to be able to account for offending in some way. It is, though, also to a greater or lesser extent more extensive than other approaches, in that it has granted space to explanations which go beyond the individual and the immediate family to offer wider and sometimes structural explanations. For instance, Case and Haines (2009, p. 150) refer to the contribution of the 'Teesside Studies' of young peoples' lives and transitions to adulthood, which are seen as more broadly based in the sense that they highlight the influence of neighbourhood factors and disadvantage, as well as contingent events and individual biographical narratives.

As we move onto the terrain of structural accounts of crime, explanations become more readily oriented towards the social context, and the contribution of poverty and disadvantage towards offending patterns. Here, then, we also begin to see at least implicit acknowledgement of the place of choice and agency in determining whether or not particular actions are undertaken. Whilst choices may well be constrained, there certainly appears to be a degree of rationality and autonomy in the decision to steal, say, in order to augment an inadequate family budget. Theorists such as Merton and Matza may, in different ways, be associated with this perspective on youth crime. Merton (1957) developed what is effectively an adaptive framework, which locates the decisions made by young people within a network of social and structural influences which shape the behaviour choices they make; whilst Matza (1969) tries to set out the dynamic context within which young people make active choices about how they respond to the 'invitation' to offend. Thus, for Matza (1969, p. 110), it is important to understand that offending is not pre-ordained, and that there is a conscious process which takes place at what he calls the 'invitational edge' where the possibility of offending is translated into an explicit intent, followed by the action itself.

The matter of children's agency and its relationship to criminality will be a recurrent issue throughout the book, but we should also at this point acknowledge another theoretical perspective on the 'production' of offenders, drawing on labelling theory (Lemert, 1967), notions of 'othering' and the criminogenic behaviours of agents of the state themselves. Here, young people's criminality is effectively initiated or exacerbated (amplified) by the actions of criminal justice practitioners of one kind or another, or others concerned in the process of defining who is to be deemed an offender. Here, of course, we are moving into the area of the social processes according to which certain behaviours in certain contexts are defined as criminal; and, in turn, certain people and groups of people are deemed to be offenders. For those taking a radical or critical approach, these issues should be of more concern than the antecedents of those who become labelled as offenders. So, Garland (2001), for example, refers to the process of 'othering' by which certain groups become seen as threatening outsiders, and therefore more plausible as a focus for social control activities than the law abiding bulk of society. Here, too, of course, the issue of ethnicity and the disproportionate representation of Black and minority ethnic groups in the population of officially-sanctioned offenders becomes salient. We know that young people from some minority ethnic backgrounds are disproportionately likely to come into contact with the justice system, and that this flows through into an extremely high custody rate amongst these groups (May et al., 2010) – suggesting that they are being criminalised because of their particular characteristics, rather than because of any objective factor predisposing them to higher levels of criminality.

Children's deviance and youth diversion – more questions than answers?

So we can perhaps conclude that attempts to explain the criminality of children and young people are diffuse, and ultimately unresolved. These uncertainties are further compounded when we try to integrate our insights into the theoretical frameworks surrounding law and justice, on the one hand; and childhood, on the other. Essentially, there are a number of key oppositions and tensions, which are of practical significance in that they manifest themselves in the continuing debates about how children and young people should be treated in practice by the justice system.

Thus, for example, the question of children's 'agency' is critically linked to the question of whether or not they should be held partly, fully or progressively responsible for their actions when in breach of the law. As we have seen, this issue often appears as an afterthought in discussions of deviance, because so much attention is paid to antecedent factors and 'causes', across the spectrum of explanatory perspectives, from the deterministic individualised accounts to the social structural analyses at the other end of the spectrum. This too, of course, is another deeply embedded tension in alternative and often opposing accounts of the underlying dynamics behind the criminalisation of young people.

For now, though, our rather more limited concern is with the interface between these generalised theoretical perspectives and arguments, and the idea of 'diversion' as it is applied to young people reported for offences; and the underlying assumptions and values which inform decisions not to go ahead with formal proceedings against them. As we have already acknowledged, the basis of the system of law and due process depends on the notion of crime as a rational self-interested act carried out by a fully responsible perpetrator. It is only under certain quite specific conditions that this principle can be modified and procedures adapted accordingly. In the case of children, then, the conventional understanding of developmental pathways towards maturity and acquisition of full (adult) responsibility provides just such a rationale for the modification of decision-making procedures in criminal justice. Incomplete development is associated with a 'deficit' in the sense of a less than fully-established capacity for rational thinking – linked, as we have seen, to notions of plasticity and the immature brain.

This, in turn, can be associated quite neatly with a narrative that attributes deviance to the consequences of development, with irrational thinking and imperfect judgement being associated with deficiencies in children's capacities, which may indeed be 'self-righting', in the sense that this is simply a phase, and a natural feature of the normal transitions of childhood. In this sense, then, youthful misbehaviour is to be expected, and can be accounted for and managed within established frameworks of socialisation and moral education. In cases of more extreme or disruptive wrongdoing, additional explanatory weight is required, and here the developmental narrative must be modified, to take account of what might be described as skewed or corrupted pathways through the later stages of childhood. Importantly, though, the developmental frame still accommodates notions of bad influences, poor parenting, trauma and poor socialisation, as potential outcomes of the journey towards adulthood, and as understandable within this theoretical discourse.

Following this narrative to its conclusion in the context of youth justice, it seems to provide a ready-made justification for the application of diversionary principles to children and young people who infringe the law, especially if this is regarded as 'low level' and early offending. However we view the processes of development in adolescence, we are offered a basis for recognising these as incomplete, and therefore modifying the formal legal procedures which would be expected under conventional assumptions about adults, rational thinking and culpability. Children and young people can be assumed, by nature, not to have acquired the capacities to act in a fully rational way, or to take account of the implications of their behaviour in a completely responsible manner. This frame of understanding is also sufficiently broad to encompass differences of view about the nature of developmental processes themselves, and indeed children's capacity to exercise 'agency'. Thus, the idea of the child as 'noble savage' provides an intuitive explanatory model by which 'wilful' behaviour can be accounted for, and, indeed, excused in the sense that 'they didn't know any better'. Children's errant behaviour can thus be seen at the same time as innocent or naïve, intentional, harmful and excusable, on the basis that their incomplete development means that they lack the judgement to be able to distinguish right from wrong in the same way as adults. As we have already observed, the principle of *doli incapax* was established as a common law principle precisely in order to capture this sense of progression from a state of innocence towards full rationality, and absolute accountability for one's behaviour.

Diversion, then, appears to have a natural place in the array of disposals available to the agents of the criminal justice system when making decisions about how to proceed when children and young people are reported for offences, because it is attuned to the prevailing assumptions about the progressive acquisition of the capacities of a fully formed adult. Notwithstanding the apparent paradox of the recent abolition of the presumption of *doli incapax* for children aged 10–13 in England and Wales, alternatives to prosecution are generally held to be a legitimate and indeed desirable outcome for young offenders. There are certain corollaries of this position of course: the assumption of progression towards a state of full responsibility means that diversion becomes less appropriate as young people move towards adulthood, for example. Similarly, the educative function of a diversionary disposal may be seen to have failed if young people continue to offend – there is no sign of progressive maturation or the acquisition of proper levels of self-control in the case of those who become recidivists. So, it might be assumed, diversion has both temporal and structural boundaries, consistent with the wider discourse on which it draws for its justification. The case for further discretion and continuing leniency can then only be made if we are to argue that the individual's development is skewed, halted or disrupted in some way – and in such cases it is evidence of abnormality which must be relied on to warrant alternatives to formal proceedings.

Interestingly, whilst what might be termed conventional assumptions and belief systems such as these may support the case for youth diversion, so too do critical arguments, which focus on the failings of the justice system and wider structural factors which might contribute to the criminalisation of the young, or certain segments of the younger age group. Thus, the negative potential effects of labelling may well be viewed as a powerful argument for keeping children and young people out of the justice system altogether, and avoiding the stigmatising and amplifying effects of formal contact with criminal justice agencies; an argument strongly supported by McAra and McVie (2007), for example, who found empirical support for the suggestion that system contact is itself associated with an increased likelihood of subsequent encounters with the police. Thus, for those who see the criminalisation of youth as nothing to do with the turbulence associated with developmental change, but rather to do with systemic factors, such as young people's increasing visibility and susceptibility to forces of social control as they undergo progressive socialisation, the argument for diversion from the justice system to avoid such criminalisation remains persuasive.

This interesting coincidence of disparate arguments in favour of a less punitive approach to young people in trouble with the law suggests that diversion should be able to call on a wide range of supportive opinion, albeit that there are a number of divergent understandings associated with this common point of agreement. However, even in face of this general consensus, a further argument yet would ground the principles and practice of youth diversion within a more extensive hegemonic project, whereby the forms and functions of the exercise of leniency also serve to sustain a particular set of social relations. In a kind of mirroring effect, the presumptions and procedures on which diversion is based also serve to provide further justification for the wider project of responsibilisation and the establishment of a common notion of the rules and limits of conformity. Children may be expected to operate outside this framework because they are children, but our exercise of leniency on this basis acts itself as confirmation that this is a legitimate lens through which we may account for the trajectories and destination of human development beyond childhood. According to this line of argument, then, we would expect to find a logical basis for the 'limits of diversion', the exculpatory explanations which are available to justify it, and the 'responsibilising' processes associated with it. So, young people can only be spared the full rigours of the judicial process if they, voluntarily or otherwise, demonstrate their compliance with a more or less specific narrative of diminished responsibility, attributable to one or another cause.

For those who adopt the middle ground, of seeking to pursue youth diversion because of its criminalising potential, this may be an uncomfortable line of reasoning. Is it perhaps the case, that well intended and indeed effective strategies which seek to minimise the negative impacts of the justice system at the same time only serve to support and indeed reinforce the embedded logic which actually offers justification for the (limiting and potentially oppressive) rationale on which that system is based? So, for example, an effective and progressive model of diversionary practice, such as we have observed in operation from time to time, might at the same time provide implicit confirmation of the legitimacy of unequal outcomes, such as the disproportionate representation of some ethnic groups in criminal justice processes and outcomes.

As we shall see in subsequent chapters, the history and practices of youth (or juvenile) diversion are now extensive and varied. However, at each moment, we should be able to discern an underlying logic and embedded theoretical assumptions; it is these which inform competing approaches, and provide the basis for changes in policy and practice. But at the same time, we should also be mindful of the commonalities in ways of seeing and thinking about children's criminality, and how we should respond to it. Here, in particular, we might expect to be able to make out what might be described as the deep logic and embedded rationalities which may otherwise go unnoticed in that they infuse every aspect of our thinking and activities with 'natural' common sense beliefs. So, we should examine closely our assumptions about what *all* children and young people have in common, because it is these which provide the starting point for making judgements about innate qualities, vulnerability, maturity and responsibility; and it is on this edifice that constructs such as guilt, culpability and mitigation are based, determining the shape and effects of formal decisions and interventions, whether diversionary or otherwise.

2 The origins and emergence of diversion

The starting point: modern childhood and youth justice

As we have observed in the previous chapter, there is a close relationship between ideas about childhood and the construction of the youth justice system. Thus, for instance, assumptions about the age of criminal responsibility, and the need for special treatment of those under the age of 18 (usually), are rooted in a range of prior presumptions about child development and maturity, or its absence, supported by what we have also seen to be a copious body of evidence. At the same time, however, there has been a persuasive line of argument to the effect that these ideas and this knowledge of childhood are essentially recent phenomena, at least for some, such as Ariès (1962), for whom the very concept (of childhood) did not exist in medieval society, and is only a relatively recent development. Although, undoubtedly, this claim has been the subject of extensive criticism subsequently (Pollock, 1983, for example), there is still some support for the idea that modern societies do share a distinctive view of childhood as a critical life stage, in which the preparation for full and responsible adult citizenship is expected to play a central part (Hendrick, 1994; Smith, 2010).

Hendrick's study of the development of child welfare in England certainly takes this sort of view, highlighting the Factory Acts of the early 19th century as a key marker of the trend towards treating children as a special case, requiring both protection and a period of preparation for their adult responsibilities as workers. During this period: 'We see the emergence of the view that children should not work at all (or do only the minimum necessary for "educational" purposes); that childhood should be quite separate from wage earning' (Hendrick, 1994, p. 25). In similar vein, Cunningham (2005) discusses the contemporary framing of concerns about young people's behaviour in terms of lost childhoods. He describes a number of influential 'middle-class' observers expressing fears about children behaving like 'barbarians' or 'savages'. The lack of any form of constraint or social organisation meant that street children enjoyed a form of freedom which encouraged irresponsible and delinquent behaviour. These young people had, in fact, never had the opportunity to enjoy the advantages of being children: 'This was not simply sentimentalism, a regret for childhoods that had not been allowed to happen…; it was also the outcome of an internalisation of the romantic belief that the enjoyment of a proper childhood was the only foundation for a tolerable adult life' (Cunningham, 2005, p. 148). In parallel with these emerging concerns, we can observe a new focus on the problem of 'juvenile delinquency' and how to deal with it (Shore, 1999). Although, undoubtedly there had been earlier concerns about the misbehaviour of young people (Smith, 2014), these appeared to become progressively intensified in the early part of the nineteenth century. As childhood itself became more clearly conceived as a distinct life phase and as an important precursor to the adoption of responsible adult roles, so children who did not meet the stereotypical expectations of innocence, passivity and educability became a much more acute object of inquiry.

Attention has been drawn, for example, to the deliberations of the graphically titled Committee for Investigating the Causes of the Alarming Increase of Juvenile Delinquency in the Metropolis, whose report was published in 1816. The committee had previously met around 800 supposedly 'delinquent children' in Newgate and other prisons (Shore, 1999, p. 20), and claimed to identify a series of principal causes of children's crimes, including the 'improper conduct of parents', 'the want of education' and 'the want of suitable employment' (Smith, 2015, p. 49). Also cited as possible reasons though were the inadequate state of policing at the time and the prevailing 'system of prison discipline' (Shore, 1999, p. 20).

Shore observes that this list of purported causes of delinquency quickly became accepted wisdom, and concern was especially directed towards the supposed deficiencies in parenting and lack of constructive opportunities available to many young people in unsuitable living environments. Similar kinds of explanation, of course, are still to be found in common sense understandings of youth crime in the contemporary era. However, Shore (1999, p. 21) also points out that there were others who sought more nuanced explanations of the supposed increase in delinquency which had been so alarming to the committee and many others. Indeed, it was one of the committee members who speculated about what might be seen as an early form of 'net widening': 'I am inclined to think not so much as is generally supposed; I apprehend they [young offenders] are more known from being more investigated' (James Miller, quoted in Shore, 1999, p. 21). In other words, the greater attention being given to the crimes of the young, increasing criminalisation of their behaviour, and a more active role for the police may have combined to ensure that more children in this period came to the attention of the authorities for behaviour which would not previously have been sanctioned.

Similarly, a number of pieces of legislation at around that time, including the Vagrancy Act 1824, had the effect of drawing into the net a considerable number of children who were simply 'on the streets' (Johnston, 2015). Perhaps predictably, in parallel with these criminalising developments, there was also an emerging concern to protect children from the consequences, with fears of 'contamination' and 'corruption' of the young should they be institutionalised with other, older and apparently more hardened offenders (Shore, 1999, p. 31): 'When a boy is taken into custody, though he is innocent, he loses his character, and it is with the greatest difficulty possible that he can ever come into society again; he then falls into crime as a matter of necessity' (John Ousby, Evidence to the Select Committee on Metropolitan Police Officers, 1837, quoted in Shore, 1999, p. 34).

Exercising discretion?

It may well be that the very severity of the justice system in the early 19th century contributed to a willingness on the part of the police (and possibly also victims of crime) to exercise discretion, and to administer 'summary' justice instead. As one of the witnesses to the 1828 Select Committee on Metropolitan Police observed: 'I do really think a more domestic and summary process against a juvenile offender would be much the best mode of proceeding against him, to let him be punished on the spot and discharged…' (Mr Serjeant Pell, quoted in Shore, 1999, p. 81).

Certainly, by the time of the formal establishment of the Metropolitan Police, the use of warnings in the place of prosecution had become an established practice (Lee, 1998, p. 7). As police forces were progressively established in other areas beyond London, so, too, did the potential to identify and apprehend offenders, often for relatively minor, but highly visible forms of anti-social activity (p. 13). On the other hand, as Lee notes, the police did not have the capacity to investigate every suspected crime, and in some cases, the incentives to do so were not great – with arrests leading to bureaucratic processes and additional calls on their time.

As time went on, the relationship between the 'new police' and the local population was often tense, given that they had not at this point clearly established their legitimacy; and at the same time, the nature and scope of the criminal law and the justice system seemed to bring them into contact with particular neighbourhoods and certain forms of problematic behaviour in particular. This brought the police routinely into conflict with young people, in connection with a range of 'misdemeanours – for instance, street gambling in the form of pitch and toss, loitering youths, the bicycling "scorchers"' and young boys throwing stones from the bridges of London (Lee, 1998, p. 15).

However, changing views of children and young people, the influence of social reformers and adaptation by the justice system to what was seen as the excessive criminalisation of young people, led to a modification in perspectives on juvenile crime. So, as Parsloe (1978) has acknowledged, concerns were expressed during the mid-nineteenth century about the excessive nature of the punishments imposed on child offenders; and a growing interest in developing specific processes and forms of intervention for them was evident. The principal concern was to provide them with forms of 'moral training and discipline' and to avoid 'contamination' by virtue of time spent in adult prison (Parsloe, 1978, p. 113).

Gradually, then, legislation and practice began to make increasingly broad exceptions for children and young people. The Larceny Act 1847, for example, made provision for 'justices to deal summarily with offenders under fourteen who were charged with stealing' (Parsloe, 1978, p. 114), thereby modifying the justice process to allow for their youth, and presumably, lesser degree of responsibility than adult criminals. And, subsequently, the Youthful Offenders Act 1854 provided for children to be sent to reformatories to serve custodial sentences, again in preference to adult prisons. These developments are attributed in large part to the energetic efforts of Mary Carpenter and other prominent reformers of that era. They were disappointed, though, to find the 1854 Act amended before completing its passage through parliament, to the effect that 'a child must spend fourteen days in prison before going to a reformatory. This is a nice illustration of how the criminal justice approach, which demanded punishment for wrongdoing, was balanced against the child's need for training and reform' (Parsloe, 1978, p. 119). Indeed, as we shall see again, the tension between a needs-based approach to children's offending and expectations that they should be held to account for any wrongdoing has in many ways remained a constant feature of debates about how children should be dealt with by the justice system.

Divergent paths – the treatment of young offenders

These early moves to promote distinctive treatment of young people in trouble, and to establish specific criteria for intervention began to gather momentum, with a number of further reforms during the latter part of the nineteenth century, which culminated in the passage of the Children Act 1908. In Parsloe's (1978, p. 133) view, there was 'little that was new' in this piece of legislation, but what it did achieve was the consolidation of a number of reforms put in place over the previous fifty years or so, and it made juvenile courts mandatory. The Act also made specific provision for the juvenile courts to take action in non-criminal matters where children appeared to be in need of care. In some instances, this appeared to blur the boundaries between what might be seen as offences, and merely indications of disadvantaged circumstances, such as begging or being 'in the company of thieves' (p. 134). Whilst the 1908 Act did not make any particular pronouncements about the policing of juvenile crime, it did appear to represent an important symbolic milestone, in that it gave parallel weight to social circumstances and welfare needs as it did to unlawful behaviour: 'it decided the direction in which juvenile justice was to develop for the next seventy or more years' (Parsloe, 1978, p. 135).

It seems, too, that the police had begun to incorporate a 'welfare' element into their role, according to Lee (1998, p. 17): 'In the 1890s, the Liverpool Police introduced a system of clothing and licensing juvenile street pedlars…'.

The Molony Committee and beyond: recognising diversion?

By the 1920s, considerable work had been undertaken to try and understand juvenile crime and its causes. Much of this work is credited to Cyril Burt (1945), who developed a very extensive analysis of the causes of crime, which he attributed to a wide range of factors, including heredity, environment and psychological factors: 'Crime is assignable to no single universal source, nor yet to two or three: it springs from a wide variety, and usually from a multiplicity of alternative and converging influences' (Burt, 1945, p. 599). As Lee (1998) acknowledges, this conclusion points towards a requirement to treat every 'delinquent' as unique. Therefore, in each case, there would appear to be a parallel need to understand the unique individual and her/his circumstances, in order to gain insight into the underlying factors shaping her/his behaviour. Interventions should similarly be tailored to the needs of each identified offender, with a view to changing both internal and external predisposing factors. From these origins stemmed the increasingly influential 'treatment' philosophy as a key element in the organisation of responses to the crimes of the young (Lee, 1998, p. 20).

Although this emerging consensus on the origins and treatment of juvenile offending did not lead to decriminalisation, it was certainly influential in policy debates of that period. The Home Office Committee on the Treatment of Young Offenders (the Molony Committee) undoubtedly 'reflected the prevailing concerns and assumptions about the treatment of juvenile delinquents…' (Lee, 1998, p. 20). However, its deliberations and conclusions in the end reflected an uneasy compromise between the new emphasis on welfare and support to meet the needs of children, on the one hand; and a more established and unbending commitment to ideas of responsibility, justice and due process, on the other. The Molony Committee thus saw the juvenile court as the natural site for the dispensation of justice, but also as a suitable place for resolving children's welfare needs.

As a result, these assumptions tended to frame the committee's thoughts about the exercise of police discretion and non-prosecution of young offenders in certain cases. Due 'respect for the law' was to be maintained (Home Office, 1927, p. 19). However, some exceptions were acceptable:

> In trifling cases, especially when it is a first offence, a police officer may properly prefer to turn a blind eye. Many police forces adopt a system of warning youngsters who appear to be getting into trouble. The warning is usually administered in the presence of the parents by the Chief Constable or a superior officer – a practice which seems to us to be a wise method of dealing with minor offences if applied with judgement and good sense.
>
> (Home Office, 1927, p. 22)

Significantly, and as a precursor of subsequent arguments of a similar nature, the committee's endorsement of the practice of exercising police discretion in favour of non-prosecution was heavily qualified: 'undue leniency is apt to be misunderstood, and to allow a child to continue habits of petty thieving may be fraught with grave danger' (Home Office, 1927, p. 23). A warning in lieu of prosecution was only to be applied in cases which involved a minor, usually first offence; and it should be treated as an occasion of great substance, with a ceremonial admonishment 'in the presence' of parents, underpinning both the gravity of the situation and the significance of the parental role in maintaining their children's good behaviour.

The committee did seem, however, to be acknowledging and accepting the emergence of the practice of issuing warnings of this kind as a *fait accompli*, since there did not appear to be any legal basis for the exercise of discretion not to prosecute. At the same time, there was a clear resistance on the committee's part to the extension of any kind of decision-making forum beyond the sphere of the courts; matters of guilt or innocence were clearly not to be delegated elsewhere. Criticisms were made of the apparent usurping of the court's role by the Glasgow City Police from 1905 onwards, where provision was made for a full scale conference to take place in the Chief Constable's office, with the child, parents, police officer involved and possibly even the probation officer present. Whilst this might be seen as prefiguring the children's hearing system in Scotland, interestingly, for the Molony Committee, such developments (others involved schools assuming authority for resolving minor offences) were to be 'strongly deprecated' because 'any such proposal … could not be so satisfactory as a juvenile court' (Home Office, 1927, p. 22).

Here, indeed, the Molony Committee reflected a number of perennial faultlines in debates about the extent and legitimacy of diversion in youth justice. Embedded in the committee's reasoning are a number of assumptions about due process, the authority of the court, a notional tariff of disposals, equitable treatment and the problem of undue leniency.

Although the legislation which was substantially based on the committee's conclusions, the Children and Young Persons Act 1933, is largely regarded as a significant step towards enhanced recognition of children's welfare needs, a reluctance to allow these to supersede the authority of the criminal law, its structures and processes was plainly evident.

It does not seem that the committee's attempt to define limits to the use of diversionary measures actually led to any observable change in policing practices. As Lee (1998, p. 22) notes, magistrates continued to express concerns at what appeared to be a continuing increase in the use of discretionary powers not to prosecute by the police. Things seemed to come to a head with the onset of the Second World War, where it appeared that expediency might have played a part in encouraging practices viewed as completely unacceptable to some members of the magistracy. They wanted to:

> Correct mistaken ideas which are gaining ground that delinquencies by evacuees should be dealt with by the school authorities, or by the police, without the cases being reported to the magistrates for trial, a procedure which cuts right across the Probation Act and the Children and Young Persons' Act and challenges the jurisdiction of the juvenile court'.
>
> (Justice of the Peace, 27 January, 1940, p. 44 as quoted in Lee, 1998, p. 22)

Magistrates expressed deep concern about the practice, similar to that foreseen by the Molony Committee, of 'unofficial' bodies being established between education officials and the police to decide on which cases should merit a police warning. The 'Juvenile Admonition Panel' established in Rochdale for this purpose was heavily criticised by the magistracy as an 'imitation' of the juvenile court hearing, and having no standing or authority to take informal action of the kind it did (Lee, 1998, p. 23). Whilst it was clear that at least some of the hostility arose from a perceived threat to their own standing, the magistrates' objections also extended to concerns that alleged young offenders would be denied due process and the safeguards afforded by an independent trial. Like the Molony Committee, though, there was also considerable concern about the potential consequences of undue leniency: 'I do not wish to exaggerate the importance of this question, but it is beyond dispute that grave mischief may result if a boy gets the impression that if he commits an offence he has nothing to fear than a warning from the police' (from *The Magistrate*, 1943, quoted by Lee, 1998, p. 23).

Juvenile Liaison Schemes – early developments

In the post-war period there was undoubtedly a shift in emphasis in the understanding of the relationship between the state and those of its citizens experiencing personal difficulties or the consequences of social upheaval. Much of this, of course, is attributed to war time experiences of collective provision and recognition of the importance of mutuality in maximising the well-being of the community and its members. The Curtis Committee on the care of children reported in 1946, and identified a significant shortfall in the quality of care available to children identified as vulnerable and in need, some of whom would also be offenders (Hendrick, 1994). This, in turn, led to the introduction of the Children Act 1948 which established formal arrangements for the delivery of services to meet the needs of this group of children, through the establishment of children's departments. Considerable emphasis, too, was now placed on supporting families, and the importance of providing help to parents to enable them to care for their children in order to avoid the need for formal intervention. These developments of course coincided with the influential work by Bowlby on the importance of parental (and especially, maternal) attachment to children. Bowlby was particularly concerned about the impact of separation of children from their families, with obvious parallels with wartime experiences of evacuation. As Hendrick (1994, p. 219) observes: 'Predictably… Bowlby praised the new childcare service' thus re-emphasising its primary role in supporting parents to bring up their children effectively, whatever their own difficulties might be. There did seem to be an emerging consensus at this point, as to the importance of the family in promoting children's welfare, and in addressing childhood problems, including delinquency. Fox Harding (1991), for example, has identified this as a period of time when 'family support' became the prevailing ethos determining the shape and nature of interventions to meet the needs of children. Thus: 'the Children Act 1948 reflected an entirely new ethos… there was a notion of positive discrimination to compensate the deprived child…' (Fox Harding, 1991, p. 136). As this perspective gained influence, and with the establishment of a new service to address problems experienced by children, so it is unsurprising to find that interventions to address childhood delinquency should also be influenced by the same ideas. The emphasis on children's well-being, coupled with the suggestion of a stronger role for families in tackling their own problems, perhaps informed a new interest in informal measures for addressing offending in partnership with parents. By 1949, Liverpool had established a Juvenile Liaison Officer (JLO) initiative, whose purpose was to act as an effective alternative to prosecution and court appearances (Mays, 1965). The argument advance in support of the scheme was that it was an efficient way of dealing with minor infringements which would free the 'official legal apparatus to concentrate on more serious cases' (Mays, 1965, p. 185). At the same time, the avoidance of a court appearance would also significantly reduce the possibility of the offending child progressing to the point of 'accepting himself as a delinquent' or reinforcing 'this undesirable self-image' (p. 186).

From its origins, the Liverpool scheme was framed in terms of pre-empting and preventing further criminality. The first police officers to be recruited to the project were expected 'to establish their image as that of a helper rather than that of a prosecutor'; and: 'Stress was also laid on home visiting, contact and discussion with parents…' (Mays, 1965, p. 186), in support of the overall objective of discouraging children's continued involvement in offending. Additionally, as the scheme's name indicates, considerable emphasis was placed on collaborative working with other agencies and community interests to support families and children. The scheme immediately became seen as a success and expanded quickly to provide a comprehensive service across the Liverpool police area. Although other police areas such as Norwich and Swansea were known to have established 'clubs' to help to address the problem of youth crime (Lee, 1998, p. 18), Liverpool was the first force to develop anything as wide-ranging and systematic as the liaison scheme.

The scope and organisation of the scheme are of considerable interest, as they provide insights into a number of the perennial tensions associated with the exercise of discretion and the delivery of extra-judicial interventions with children and young people. In the Liverpool case, then, the scheme was very clearly police-led, being staffed exclusively by sergeants and constables from the city force. The 'liaison' element of the scheme was to be achieved by establishing relationships with key figures in the community, such as religious leaders, and social work agencies. A mode of intervention was envisaged, involving 'regular contact with children who had been cautioned and, where possible, introducing them into membership of clubs or similar youth organisations' (Mays, 1965, p. 186). So, familiar ideas about reintegrating young people into conventional organisations and activities were evident in the conceptualisation of the scheme.

The early experiences of the initiative, too, prompted another shift of emphasis which highlights what has subsequently become one of the central concerns about youth crime prevention practices. Apparently, the early contacts between juvenile liaison officers and Liverpool shopkeepers brought to light many examples of children being caught shoplifting and not being reported to the police, simply because of the demands on staff time: 'Thus, from a very early date the JLO's were concerned with a number of young delinquents who had hitherto been escaping the official net' (Mays, 1965, p. 187). And, so, one of the immediate effects of the scheme was to focus attention on a group of young people described as 'near delinquents and potential offenders', who, in fact, attracted rather more attention from JLO's than did those who had already committed offences. Here, then, might be a clear indication that the scheme was responsible as much for 'net widening' (Austin and Krisberg, 2002) as it was for actually diverting young people from the justice process. The common goal with both groups, pre-delinquents and established offenders, was to 'prevent the recurrence of bad behaviour and to try to halt the drift of youngsters into delinquent habits' (Mays, 1965, p. 187); so it could be argued that their actual known behaviour was less important than the goal of anticipating and 'nipping in the bud' any risk of future criminality. The consequences of this reasoning are evident in the reported caseloads of the scheme, with a clear reversal over time, as the proportion of those dealt with for offences declined from 93 per cent in 1952 to 58 per cent in 1960, whilst the figure for those treated as 'potential' delinquents increased from 7 per cent to 42 per cent over the same period.

In terms of practice, once those at risk were identified, the next step would be for the JLO to take over and undertake what in Mays' terms 'could only be called social work with the child and, on his behalf with the family and other interested parties' (Mays, 1965, p. 188). According to Mays, it was the capacity of the police officer to act as a strong authority figure, which often introduced a new correctional influence on the child, in the absence of effective parental discipline.

By the time of Mays' article, the Liverpool scheme was well-established, and he also noted that similar projects had been established in a number of other areas, including Leeds, Huddersfield, Birmingham, South Shields, West Ham, Manchester and Cardiff. Nonetheless, he observed that the approach to juvenile crime that it represented remained controversial, even though it was well-liked by those with the most direct experience of its work, such as teachers. Mays (1965, p. 193) noted five objections to the juvenile liaison scheme and what it represented: that it encroached on the professional domain of other agencies, such as the probation service; that the police officers responsible for its delivery were untrained and unprepared for its demands; that the scheme 'trespasses on the territory of the juvenile court and sets up the police as apprehenders of offenders, judges and agents of treatment in ways which are a threat to justice'; that it actually denied children access to the appropriate specialist service; and that it could not be seen as a legitimate role of the police.

Mays' response to these criticisms is robust, and essentially follows the line that prevention is a legitimate objective of policing, and that extending their role in a 'limited' number of cases did not represent a significant encroachment on the terrain of the courts. Further, there was no evidence of excessive intervention with young people associated with the scheme (Mays, 1965, p. 196). Positive evidence of the scheme's impact was also cited in support, with fewer than 10 per cent of those boys reported for indictable offences being convicted subsequently.

Similarly high success rates are reported by Mack (1963) in his review of the juvenile liaison scheme established by the police in Greenock in 1956, following encouragement from the Home Office based on the Liverpool experience. This scheme, reported to be the first of its kind in Scotland, saw the proportion of young offenders being taken to court decreasing substantially following its introduction. Here there seemed to be no evidence of 'net widening', and at the same time there was a relatively lower re-offending rate identified for those referred to the JLO scheme instead (Mack, 1963, p. 372). Mack's argument, like Mays', was that the 'positive' intervention offered by the juvenile liaison scheme bore encouraging comparison to 'the trivial and nugatory disposals made by the court in so many cases of very petty offending' (Mack, 1963, p. 373). Here, undoubtedly, a fault line was being established by sympathetic academics between the informal and tailored support offered by juvenile liaison officers and the formulaic and often irrelevant disposals available to the court. Again, there appears to be little fear that in exercising this function, the roles of the police would become blurred or that they would be responsible for oppressive treatment of children for very minor misdemeanours (or none at all, in some cases).

Despite the concerns expressed, and a rather uneven geographical response, it does seem that the Liverpool model became increasingly influential, no doubt partly because it appeared to have gained support from central government; and as noted previously because it coincided with the ethos of family support which characterised the post-war period.

Into the 1960s: diversion or decriminalisation?

The growing popularity of informal action to deal with the crimes of the young inevitably became the subject of more systematic interest as time passed. So, for example, it became one of the focal points of interest of the committee chaired by Viscount Ingleby which was appointed in 1956 by the Home Secretary to consider 'the workings of the law' in dealing with children's offending, as well as their protection from harm. The Ingleby Committee took a leisurely four years to complete its work, and included in its deliberations was a discussion of police cautioning and juvenile liaison schemes (Home Office, 1960, p. 49). Here again were rehearsed some of the arguments for and against the extension of the use of police discretion, although it might be thought that the dice were loaded as eight of the fourteen member committee were magistrates, with what might be thought of as vested interests.

The committee did express a degree of approval for the principle of police discretion; noting that it seemed 'unnecessary and indeed undesirable to bring a child before a court if the shock of being found out and the effect of a caution from the police are enough to make it unlikely that he will offend again' (Home Office, 1960, p. 49). At the same time, however, it was observed that only the court had the capacity and the authority to determine the right form of intervention, should more intensive input be required to address the underlying causes of a child's delinquency. Interestingly, here, the reservations are couched in terms of the court's ability to address the needs of the child for help and guidance rather than punishment. Again, this prefigures continuing debates about whether diversion is associated with excessive and unnecessary intervention on the one hand; or minimal and inadequate responses to offending, on the other.

The committee noted the evidence presented by supporters of the Liverpool scheme, including the Association of Chief Police Officers, who saw it as a 'natural development of the preventive work that the police… had been carrying out for many years with wholehearted public approval' (Home Office, 1960, p.

50). At the same time, however, evidence was received from the Metropolitan Police Commissioner to the effect that cautioning and juvenile liaison were not legitimate functions of the police, since they appeared to usurp the intentions of government in the establishment of a juvenile court system for dealing with young offenders whilst taking account of their welfare needs. These reservations were echoed by both juvenile court representatives and the probation service. Here, again, the argument was that the police should not assume roles or responsibilities beyond their remit, whether in adjudication of offences or in delivering social work services. Here too, the Ingleby Committee was positioning itself as much as an advocate for young people's welfare as it was insisting on the authority of the courts to administer effective punishments.

So, it followed that the committee's preferred option for dealing with children's offending was to institute a procedure whereby those who were brought before the courts would be dealt with 'as in need of protection or discipline instead of being charged with a criminal offence' (Home Office, 1960, p. 51). Interestingly, the broad orientation of the committee towards addressing what might now be termed the 'criminogenic needs' of children, especially those at young ages, led to a proposal, too, to raise the age of criminal responsibility from eight as it then was to twelve. Children who offended between these ages could still be brought to court because of their crimes, but they would not be criminalised. In light of that, the committee argued, diversion from criminal proceedings would become superfluous, for the youngest offenders, at least. However, the committee did suggest, in a way which pre-figured subsequent difficulties, that the court should have the power to make a 'protection and discipline' order as a non-criminal disposal for younger children, whether as a result of their offending or to meet welfare needs.

Subsequent legislation in the form of the Children and Young Persons Act 1963 did not accept all the Ingleby Committee's recommendations, but it did seem to share many of the committee's sentiments. Thus, the 1963 Act did raise the age of criminal responsibility, albeit only to 10, and Section 1 could be interpreted as a mild endorsement of pre-court preventive interventions, mandating local authorities to:

> make available such advice, guidance and assistance as may promote the welfare of children by diminishing the need to receive them or keep them in care, *or for them to be brought before a juvenile court* (my emphasis).

This seemed to offer some positive encouragement to local authorities to develop pro-active arrangements with other partners such as the police to develop juvenile liaison schemes and to provide a firmer basis for the extension of cautioning (Oliver, 1978). This move was significant as it represented the first time that the principle of widening the range of agencies responsible for pre-court intervention beyond the police and courts gained recognition in primary legislation. In effect, this pre-figured some of the influential multi-agency diversion schemes of the 1980s, although it was not initially supported by any form of official guidance, leading to subsequent concerns that the opportunity had not been taken up positively by many local authorities. By 1968, the then Commissioner of the Metropolitan Police bemoaned that:

> Our experience up to now has not… always been fortunate, as by no means all local authorities have taken full advantage of the responsibilities… entrusted to them and emphasised by Section 1 of the Children and Young Persons Act 1963
>
> (quoted in Smith, 1989, p. 15)

He did, however, speak positively of the experience of the police in one borough within the metropolitan area, emphasising the potential value of collaboration across agency boundaries. Certainly, it appears that this period (the 1960s) saw an increasing level of interest in this kind of scheme, a number of which were also evaluated (Mack, 1963; Cain and Dearden, 1966; Taylor, 1971). These schemes seemed to follow a similar model, with Cain and Dearden (1966, p. 421) noting, for example, that the project they had investigated 'was identical in its terms of reference to the Liverpool and other schemes'. So, like the Liverpool juvenile liaison initiative, it seems clear that this model was very much police led and involved a pro-active approach on their part to develop informal means of dealing with minor offences, such as a 'period of supervision' (Cain, 1968); as well as seeking a preventive role, particularly in schools. Thus, 'in-school' offences became a primary focus of the scheme, it seems (Cain and Dearden, 1966, p. 423). The majority of the schools in the area concerned changed their approach to minor offences, being more likely to report children for minor offences with confidence that they would be unlikely to be prosecuted as a result. So, the scheme does seem to have been associated with a greater degree of information sharing and reporting of young people to the police for offences. In Cain and Dearden's view then, there appears to have been a degree of cautious acceptance of the new way of working associated with this juvenile liaison scheme, although some increasingly familiar concerns were expressed: 'The main benefit appeared to [local services] to be that the young offender would be checked yet not prosecuted' (Cain and Dearden, 1966, p. 429). At the same time, concerns were also expressed by some that the scheme was 'soft' on offending; or by contrast that it might involve too intensive a level of intervention without the safeguards offered by the judicial process. Clearly, there were also boundary issues, with a number of professional interests expressing concern about unqualified police officers potentially usurping their roles: 'Eight of the social workers [interviewed] emphasised that the police were untrained and therefore the wrong people for the work' (Cain and Dearden, 1966, p. 429).

As Cain (1968) subsequently observed, the establishment of the JLO role within the police force led to some interesting challenges – for instance in deciding whether or not to formally record an offence 'as a crime' (Cain, 1968, p. 369). Often JLOs would choose not to do so, but to treat all those referred to them as cases where the prevention of future crimes was the priority rather than prosecution of past offences. This, again, is a precursor of a long-running debate about the exercise of police discretion and the tension between this and other pressures and targets to maximise prosecution and conviction rates, as in the cases of the 'offences brought to justice' measure of performance put in place in the early 2000s.

Cain notes that their close collaboration with other agencies also tended to have a bearing on JLOs perspective on youth crime, resulting in what she describes as an 'increasing welfare orientation' (Cain, 1968, p. 372). For some, this might be a value-base already adopted prior to joining the scheme, although for others it might be a more challenging adaptation to make; this indeed coincides with my own experience of working alongside police officers in a later multi-agency juvenile liaison project in the 1980s. Thus, referring back to the previous chapter, we can see constructions of childhood emerging, which are less to do with attributing agency and 'blame', and more to do with seeking external causes for their behaviour, for instance by shifting blame: 'so that now the *child's parents* were deemed the guilty parties…' (Cain, 1968, p. 373).

Despite this apparent willingness to shift towards a welfare model of intervention in practice, Cain (1968, p. 375) also notes that it was a source of role conflict for police officers taking on the juvenile liaison role. Arguably, too, this tension plays out at force and policy levels just as much as it does within the experience of individual officers:

> The JLO is an extreme example of the man (sic) operating on the boundary of his social system… and is classically subject to the conflicting sets of expectations which this entails. He is a policeman by choice and training, yet more of his contacts are with people in other systems than with members of his own.
>
> (Cain, 1968, p. 375)

So, in effect, the experience of the individual and the risk of being seen as 'soft on offenders' (p. 376) which the JLO may incur, is a representation in microcosm of some of the key tensions running through the history and conceptual framing of diversion in youth justice.

Notwithstanding these tensions at the operational level, it is also clear that the prevailing mood of the 1960s was very much to see a close connection between the offending of the young and their welfare needs, and this established a broadly consensual frame within which appropriate policy and intervention strategies were considered. Shortly after the introduction of the 1963 Act and evidently in anticipation of taking on a central role in driving policy forward, Lord Longford's committee on the subject of crime issued its report, *Crime a Challenge to us all*, which pre-figured many of the initial positions adopted by the incoming Labour government. That government's 1965 White Paper, *The Child, the Family and the Young Offender* made it a goal to: 'remove young people as far as possible from the jurisdiction of the court', and essentially to delegate power for resolving problems associated with children's crimes to local authorities, operating through the vehicle of 'local family councils' (Home Office, 1965, p. 5), which would have jurisdiction over all matters of care, truancy and offending for children under the age of 16. So, although there would still be provision for dealing with offences informally, they would effectively be removed from the judicial sphere altogether, except in extreme circumstances, such as the commission of 'grave' offences. If they had been enacted, of course, these measures would have rendered the issue of juvenile diversion irrelevant, since there would be no need to establish 'exceptional' measures for dealing with offences outside the normal judicial process. Here, then, lies an inherent challenge to proponents of the argument that diversion represents a radical alternative to the justice process; in fact, it appears to depend on the existence of that very process for its own justification. Without the formal procedures of prosecution and court hearings, diversion would not be necessary, evidently.

Welfarism and the growth of cautioning

In the event, the 1965 White Paper ran into some difficulty because of its radical objectives and because it ran counter to a series of vested interests, not least those of the courts. At the same time, however, the tacit approval of juvenile liaison schemes under the 1963 Act, and the progressive alignment of child welfare with the needs associated with delinquency clearly underpinned a growing commitment to interventions designed to support rather than punish young people. These developments undoubtedly fed the continuing increase in the use of cautioning in evidence at this point. From 1955 to 1965, the number of cautions administered to young people rose from 13,000 to 28,000 (McClintock and Avison, 1968). However, this apparently dramatic increase needs also to be viewed in the context of a continuing increase in the crime rate and in overall prosecutions. In fact the cautioning *rate* remained fairly constant over this period at around 11 per cent of all offenders proceeded against. At the same time, substantial variations in the use of cautions were also observed, with a continuing reluctance to pursue their use in the force area of the Metropolitan Police in particular. Such variations in cautioning rates persisted (Steer, 1970), providing early indications that diversionary practice is often an important contributor to the phenomenon of 'justice by geography' (Feld, 1981). Steer (1970, p. 17) concluded, however, that these variations could not be attributed to any specific characteristics of the areas concerned, except that most juvenile liaison schemes in operation by 1968 seemed to be in the North of England. Indeed, most relevant to current cautioning practice in individual police areas seemed to be the attitude of the incumbent Chief Constable.

By later in the decade, however, the Metropolitan Police area did adopt a change of direction, notes Steer (1970, p. 19). This is partly, in his view, attributable to the direction of policy change clearly signalled by the Labour government of the time, by way of the 1968 White Paper, *Children in Trouble*, and the subsequent legislation, the Children and Young Persons Act 1969. Indeed, the act itself included explicit recognition of police cautioning for the first time in law, under Section 5, alongside additional provisions to remove children under the age of 14 from the ambit of the criminal court altogether. Steer's (1970, p. 19) suggests that the introduction in 1969 of juvenile bureaux across the entire Metropolitan Police area was in direct response to this, in anticipation of the implementation of the new legislative requirement. Ironically as it transpired, this section of the 1969 Act was never implemented.

By the end of the 1960s then, there did seem to have been a sustained re-alignment in the ways in which young people, their offending and their welfare needs were conceptualised and provided for in policy terms:

> It has become increasingly clear that social control of harmful behaviour by the young, and social measures to help and protect the young, are not distinct and separate processes. The aims of protecting society from juvenile delinquency, and of helping children in trouble to grow up into mature and law-abiding citizens, are complementary and not contradictory.
>
> (Home Office, 1968, p. 4)

Certainly, the evidence of a substantial shift in decision-making processes and outcomes seemed to indicate the emergence of a new consensus, across key agencies and institutional structures. The signals sent out by *Children in Trouble* seemed to prompt organisations to pre-empt the expected legislative change to follow; so, between 1968 and 1969, the number of cautions administered to juvenile offenders rose by just over a third, from 33,703 to 44,998 (Lee, 1998, p. 26), and by 1971 this figure had increased dramatically yet again, to 70,957 (Ditchfield, 1976). As Lee (1998, p. 26) notes, the increase in cautioning rates was steeper amongst the younger age group (10–13), suggesting perhaps a relative strengthening of the underlying assumption that children below the age of 14 were more vulnerable and less likely to be fully responsible for their offending behaviour.

By this point, then, there seemed to be a well-established and progressive pattern of increasing sensitisation of the criminal justice system to the particular circumstances and needs associated with children and young people. A gradual growth in awareness during the nineteenth century had prompted a number of formal measures to modify the harshest impacts of the justice system, such as the establishment of Reformatory Schools under the Youthful Offenders Act 1854; and these developments were further reinforced in the early part of the 20th century, with the passage of the Children Act 1908. Under this legislation, importantly, a separate court was established for juvenile offenders, which at the same time would take responsibility for dealing with welfare, care and protection of children (Hendrick, 1994, p. 123). Here, then, the explicit merger of judicial responsibilities was an authoritative assertion of the widely held view that delinquency and deprivation were just two sides of the same coin.

At roughly the same time, the well-established informal police practices of dealing with minor offences by way of an admonishment were beginning to be superseded by more institutional arrangements; with the Glasgow City Police reportedly establishing a 'Superintendent's Court' in 1905 to administer formal warnings to juvenile offenders, accompanied by their parents (Steer, 1970, p. 55).

From this point, the extension of child welfare concerns into the criminal sphere was further legitimised by way of the Molony Committee report, and the subsequent Children and Young Persons Act 1933, which again deliberately incorporated provisions to address children's offending alongside their welfare needs. With the emergence of a strong preventive strand in policy debates following the second world war, the Ingleby Committee report, the 1963 Act and the subsequent flurry of government policy initiatives culminating in the Children and Young Persons Act 1969, this process of establishing a closer and closer elision between child offenders and children in need was yet further intensified.

Developments in policy and law were accompanied by an expansion in juvenile liaison schemes and the use of cautioning, driven by the same welfare led ideology; and if the 1969 Act had been implemented in full, a common endpoint might have been reached in the form of the virtual decriminalisation of children and young people, especially at the younger end of the age range. These trends demonstrate a considerable degree of consistency in the understandings of children and their crimes amongst researchers, policy makers, provider agencies and criminal justice interests. So, for example, it was possible to modify questions of guilt by reference to evidence of deprivation and, significantly, parental shortcomings, typified by Bowlby's inquiry into the circumstances and experiences of '44 thieves' (Bowlby, 1947). Children, then, were typically viewed as not capable of being fully responsible for their actions, and susceptible to adverse influences and circumstances, whilst undergoing a maturational process which would render them fully self-aware and accountable for their behaviour. Whilst there might be considerable disagreement amongst analysts and commentators on the origins and dynamics of the disadvantages they encountered, this broad explanatory framework was a matter of shared belief. Even though some would clearly have prioritised the effects of poverty over those of poor parenting as contributory factors (see the Longford Report, for example: Labour Party Study Group, 1964), there was enough common ground to support the wide ranging introduction of measures of practical, moral and emotional support and pro-active prevention to facilitate a healthy upbringing, characterised by increasing conformity and productive membership of society.

In this context, the development of the 'concept of "intermediate treatment" (IT)' (Cawson, 1985) is of particular interest, as this effectively frames a form of intervention which is designed to deliver preventive services as an alternative to more intrusive forms of intervention. Children and young people would in effect be *diverted into* this intervention framework in order to address what have now come to be known as 'criminogenic needs' (Hannah-Moffat, 2005). As Cawson indicates, the idea of IT originated in the theoretical debates about labelling of the early 1960s (eg, Becker, 1963), and was developed in response to an emerging belief in the importance of providing constructive intervention without formally identifying young people as problematic. Thus, it was framed as a form of 'diversionary' intervention; and, indeed, in its early days, IT was believed to be suitable as a preventive measure for offenders and non-offenders alike. The principle of 'normalisation' implicit in this approach suggested that the underlying aim would be to introduce (or re-introduce) children at risk of offending into mainstream 'community education and leisure programmes not intended specifically for delinquents' (Cawson, 1985, p. 675).

Despite much subsequent criticism (Pratt, 1987), this formulation of IT enabled it to achieve a number of important objectives in legitimising broadly diversionary approaches to young offenders: it blurred the distinction between offenders and non-offenders (delinquency and deprivation); it established principles of normalisation; it represented an extra-legal form of intervention; it supported notions of voluntarism and positive intervention; and at the same time, it offered some reassurance to those concerned that the simple administration of a caution meant that young criminals were 'getting away with it'.

By the end of the 1960s then, diversion from the criminal justice system had established a degree of legitimacy, and had begun to develop a form of institutional machinery to facilitate its realisation. It had a fairly clear rationale, grounded in principles of early prevention, normalisation and reintegration of children and young people at risk of becoming more persistent offenders; and it appeared to have gained widespread acceptance, if not support. Given the established reluctance of courts to relinquish their authority or scope of activity, it seems somewhat surprising that there was not more explicit opposition to the growing emphasis on diversion as a core feature of youth justice. It is certainly possible that this is attributable to the preoccupation of the magistracy and others with what was seen as a more fundamental threat to their powers, in the form of proposals, and indeed legislative provision to remove some young offenders from their remit altogether (Section 4 of the 1969 Act). This, indeed, was the focus of opposition to the decriminalising moves being made by the government of the time (Harris, 1982). Other sources of potential opposition, such as the police, appeared to have been won over to the idea of diversion:

> Organisations such as the Police Federation and the Justices Clerks' Society both argued against the [1969] Act's implementation… but both appeared to accept the growth of cautioning as a fait accompli.
>
> (Smith, 1989, p. 25)

Similarly, the Metropolitan Police Commissioner had expressed considerable concern in evidence to the Ingleby Committee about pre-empting the role of the courts: 'The police would be open to serious criticism if they took upon themselves to withdraw some children from the operation of the [court] system to be dealt with in a different way' (quoted in Steer, 1970, p. 18). However, by 1968, he had accepted that it was time to 'readjust our outlook' (Simpson, 1968, p. 125), and the police should take on 'a much fuller role' in addressing delinquency (Simpson, 1968, p. 127). They should, indeed, become 'full partners' with local authorities in juvenile crime prevention. Formal court proceedings would now only be instituted 'where necessary', rather than routinely, and in the context of comprehensive inter-agency liaison work (Simpson, 1968, p. 129). It is likely, too, that the adoption of a more pro-active policy on juvenile liaison by the commissioner directly contributed to the substantial increase in the use of cautions towards the end of the 1960s.

At this point, too, the mood of confidence in the value of pro-active welfare-led interventions was undisturbed. So, the continuation of a programme of well-intended and broadly beneficial service provision, whose aim was both to help and modify unwelcome behaviour remained uncontentious, especially at a time where the welfare state was in an expansionary phase and financial pressures on services were relatively limited.

So we can conclude this chapter with the observation that a particular model of 'welfare' based diversion had achieved pre-eminence in the ideas, policies and practices of those involved in the development and delivery of youth justice by the end of the 1960s, underpinned by a socially liberal government, a mood of optimism about the benefits of child and family support, and an expanding welfare budget. Here, we see diversion 'into' alternative services as the necessary corollary of diversion 'out of' the formal justice system; and this very conjuncture sets the terms for a number of the issues, criticisms and challenges which diversionary strategies faced in subsequent years.

3 Diversion: development and doubt

On the crest of a wave?

As we have observed, the 1960s closed on a spirit of expansionist optimism, with a welfare-oriented view of diversion very definitely in the ascendant. However, a wider view of social trends and public debates might well have helped to offset any sense of over confidence in the belief that the debate about how to respond to youth crime had been settled. As Lee (1998) reminds us, in the wider arena, young people and their behaviour were certainly generating considerable media interest, and associated with this, extensive popular concern. Amongst other issues, the 1960s was the decade of 'mods and rockers', of mass demonstrations and unrest amongst young people on an international scale, of drugs and of 'cultural revolution', prompting fears of a breakdown in the moral order and in inter-generational relations. This apparent challenge to the social order was captured effectively by Cohen (1972), of course; and this, in turn, underlined the potential sensitivity of policy and practice in criminal justice to the momentum generated by 'moral panics'. At the same time, this degree of sensitivity to the public mood also highlighted a persistent feature of the youth justice system; and this is precisely its capacity to be thrown off course by the emergence of a concerted wave of public and political pressure for change.

Here, inevitably, diversionary initiatives were particularly at risk, given their susceptibility to charges of encouraging leniency and excuse-making for harmful and anti-social behaviour. Not only would young people responsible for unpleasant acts go unpunished, but they would at the same time experience no deterrent effect, it could be assumed. Conventional arguments about 'just deserts' and discouraging re-offending could be applied straightforwardly in relation to the use of police cautions and a mere 'telling off'.

Amidst an emerging sense of disquiet about wayward youth, a number of other contextual developments helped to create the conditions for a critical response to the growing use of cautioning to deal with the crimes of the young. England's failure to beat West Germany in the 1970 World Cup has been claimed to account for the unexpected defeat of Labour in that year's General Election (Hylton, 2015); and with the return of a Conservative government, so the socially liberal trends in public policy of the time were swiftly called into question. And, as the 1970s progressed, so, too, economic growth also faltered, with the 'oil crisis' of 1972 leading to a rapid slowdown, and consequent constraints on public spending. The sense in which welfarist principles as well as expenditure came into question is significant here, and the correlation between the two can be no coincidence. These factors alone, then, undoubtedly contributed to a renewed debate about principles and priorities, both in terms of welfare state expenditure, and the ways in which young people's errant behaviour should be viewed.

For the implementation of this project of re-sensitising the wider public to fears about the problem of youth, we need only turn to the seminal contribution of Hall et al (2013) on the systematic process by which a single instance of 'mugging' became the focal point for a sustained 'law and order' campaign. As Hall et al (2013, p. 322) note, this development was also associated with a strong tendency to racialise youth crime and criminality. In parallel with this, was a campaign conducted by sections of the media and leading public figures, including the Duke of Edinburgh, apparently (Hall et al., 2013, p. 12). Thus, the evidence of an increase in crime, and especially violent crime, was linked to the emergence of 'permissive' beliefs and their influence on public policy. The only reasonable response from those charged with delivering criminal justice should be to 'get tough' and crack down on unacceptable behaviour. The success of the campaign is indicated by its achievement in generating a consensus about the threat posed by particular types of crime, notably 'mugging':

> In what we might call the common-sense view, sometime in the early 1970s British cities were visited by a dramatic and unexpected epidemic of 'mugging'. The police, reacting to these events, spurred on by a vigilant press, by public anxiety and professional duty, took rapid steps to isolate the 'virus' and bring the fever under control. The courts administered a strong inoculating dose of medicine.
>
> (Hall et al., 2013, p. 21)

In the example of the three young people from Handsworth whose case is highlighted by Hall et al (2013, p. 12), the outcomes were a period of twenty years' detention for one, and ten years' detention for the other two.

There was then (and arguably remains) a reservoir of incipient concern about the behaviour of young people, and certain groups of young people in particular, which can be readily re-awakened, and with the right combination of ingredients, orchestrated to normalise what might be termed exceptional responses to the threat that they apparently pose to the social and moral order.

Here, then, stepping back from the immediate issue of the nature and extent of youth diversion at this juncture, we may perhaps conclude that the 'mood' of the time is also an important factor in determining the predisposition held by those in influential positions towards practices which might be viewed as relatively lenient and unconcerned with holding offenders to account for their behaviour. At the conclusion of the 1960s, there were emergent concerns about the behaviour of young people; and the question for us is the extent to which they may have generated an increasing reluctance to deploy measures which might be equated with being 'soft on crime'. Lee (1998, p. 29) suggests that this was a period in which hostility between police and young people remained prevalent. And, as Parker (1974) observed at the time, there was little evidence of a conciliatory approach by the police to the young people in Liverpool whose lives he studied.

Cautioning under review: refocusing the task

Following the rapid growth in the number of juvenile liaison schemes in the 1960s, diversion naturally became a much more prominent feature of policing and decision-making in the criminal justice process. And, despite the non-implementation of the Children and Young Persons Act 1969, the option of taking a course other than prosecution was endorsed at this point. As the supporting guidance to the Act made clear, the implementation or otherwise of the relevant sections of the Act should not: 'affect the discretion of a police officer to take no action at all, or to give a child an informal warning on the spot, or to give a formal caution…' (Home Office, 1970, p. 24).

The formalisation of diversion and its increasing use did therefore perhaps prompt scrutiny, in a way in which the relatively small number of localised initiatives in existence previously did not. These were perhaps of interest and probably recognised as useful experiments; but, as such, they did not require a fundamental re-evaluation of the relationship between offending, prosecution and the courts: 'Very little official interest has been shown in the practice of cautioning offenders' (Steer, 1970, p. 56).

Subsequent to this, however, the position changed, and there was a definite upsurge in interest amongst policy makers. By 1974, the House of Commons Expenditure Committee began to show some interest (Smith, 1989). At this point, the committee's concerns mainly focused on the considerable variations in practice between police areas, which appeared to run counter to the intentions of the national guidance provided shortly before. This, of course, coincides with one of the persistent concerns about the use of police discretion; namely, the extent to which it could give rise to inconsistent and sometimes unfair treatment of those suspected of offences. Even amongst those who break the rules, equitable treatment by those responsible for upholding the law is seen as a legitimate expectation:

> It is the fact that the police themselves break the rules that makes the sense of injustice so profound. The Boys do not deny that they steal or that there's such a thing as a 'fair cop'…. But the Boys demand scrupulous fairness'
>
> (Parker, 1974, p. 164)

Inconsistently applied rules on the use of diversion do not support this, however, and the Expenditure Committee concluded that there should be an effort to standardise cautioning practice, nationally. Underpinning this, the committee believed, would be closer collaborative arrangements between police and social services departments; and particular attention should be paid to areas where such collaboration was not already well-developed. In 1976, in response, the Home Office endorsed this recommendation, setting out a fairly explicit framework for collaboration in advance of the decision whether or not to prosecute children who had offended: 'The staff of a juvenile bureau are responsible for gathering information about juveniles suspected of having committed offences from the relevant agencies.... In the light of the information gathered, the officer-in-charge of the bureau decides whether proceedings should be brought...' (Home Office, 1976, p. 10).

At the same time, however, the government also made it clear that it would not prescribe detailed arrangements for implementing this advice: 'The machinery for consultation between police, social services departments and other services concerned, is essentially a matter for local arrangement...' (Home Office, 1976, p. 10). Whilst this might have been welcomed as an attempt to avoid imposing central direction in favour of local areas and communities, it did leave open the possibility of continuing wide variations in policy and practice at the local level (Ditchfield, 1976, p. 14). It might, indeed, have been expected that the opportunity to encourage greater geographical consistency would be taken up at this point, given that a considerable body of evidence was emerging to suggest that such discrepancies were widespread, and often appeared to be dependent on the individual preferences of senior police officers. According to earlier studies, it seemed that variations in cautioning practices: 'were too great to be explained in terms of different types of crime or sex and age of offenders in the different local areas.... In particular,... sudden changes in cautioning policy by individual forces coincided in some instances with the appointment of a new Chief Constable' (Ditchfield, 1976, p. 2). McLintock and Avison (1968), for example had compared the practices of police forces nationally (England and Wales), and found very large variations between forces in 1962, which they attributed to 'different attitudes', going on to raise the question of whether this was 'inconsistent with the concept of equality before the law for all offenders' (p. 211); and this concern expressed in various forms has been associated with recurrent criticisms of excessive discretion in out of court decision-making processes.

In addition, there was little clarity in cautioning policy at this point over the precise degree of 'consultation' between police and other agencies about whether or not prosecution should go ahead; and at what point in the process this should take place, if at all. It does seem likely, nonetheless, that this broad but unspecific encouragement of local initiative by the Home Office in the mid-1970s prompted or at least paved the way for the development of progressive juvenile liaison schemes such as that in Northamptonshire which subsequently came to national prominence (Smith, 1989).

Partly prompted by the evidence of the county's relatively low cautioning rate, an inter-agency 'study group' was established with the aim of understanding the reasons for previous problems in joint working and developing possible solutions. Closely mirroring the emerging government interest in encouraging better inter-agency working (Home Office, 1978c), in youth justice and other areas of practice, the work of the study group led to proposals to take a collaborative approach to 'focus on the needs and problems of young people' (Cottrell, 1979). In the initial stages, though, the precise scope and activities of the envisaged collaboration were not clear (Smith, 1989, p. 94), and it was at least under consideration that referrals of young people experiencing problems of one kind or another could be received from a range of sources, albeit including the police. It was also suggested that the new 'bureau' would actually hold 'cases' and utilise one of a number of possible forms of intervention available to it, including, youth and community activities, individual supervision or group work, in effect building on ideas associated with Intermediate Treatment.

Only tentatively at this stage was the possibility of diversion introduced, and this was by no means the central objective of the new scheme at blueprint stage: 'As the scheme progresses, it is hoped that some young offenders would be diverted from the court process by means of the activities of the bureau' (Cottrell, 1979). Here, too, it seemed that diversion from formal proceedings would be accompanied by active intervention to address concerns about the young person and her/his behaviour; whilst some consideration was still being given to including 'pre-delinquents' within the bureau's remit (Smith, 1989, p. 97). These questions were then, and still continue to be perhaps, significant not just in operational terms, but because they relate to wider challenges for the diversionary project, to do with excessive intervention and net widening, both of which have proved problematic over the years, as we shall see.

These local developments found parallels elsewhere, as in Devon and Cornwell where the then Chief Constable was particularly noted for his 'liberal' approach to policing. As an early proponent of what came to be known as 'community policing', he oversaw the establishment of the Exeter Joint Services Youth Support Team in 1979 which developed a sophisticated framework for determining outcomes for young offenders (Pratt, 1986, p. 228), as well as being acknowledged as an early pioneer in methods of mediation and restorative justice.

Whilst these local initiatives were taking shape, so too was government policy becoming more detailed, and in some ways more prescriptive. 1978 saw the issuing of a series of official circulars (Home Office, 1978a; 1978b; 1978c) to give more precise substance to government aspirations for closer cooperation. At the same time as these documents re-emphasised the importance of close collaboration between agencies, they also began to show signs of the assertion of alternative, and to some degree more critical perspectives on the nature of out of court decision-making processes. Here, for example, there was an attempt to establish common ground on whether or not cautions would subsequently be citeable in court (that is, formally included as part of an offender's criminal record). The consensus emerging from a wide-ranging consultation process (including the Magistrates' Association) was that a caution should be citeable (Home Office, 1978a). This, in turn, appeared to incorporate the notion of a tariff of disposals into the diversionary arena, and promoted a further circular (Home Office, 1978b) setting out a series of clear criteria to be met before a caution could be administered, including: the admission of the offence; consideration of the offender's background; the seriousness of the offence; and any agency recommendations. Here, then, is evidence that alongside what might be deemed 'welfare' factors (such as the offender's circumstances), other questions to do with rights and due process should also form part of the decision-making framework. Perhaps these are the first signs of a change in the prevailing mood, and a reluctance to sanction intervention purportedly in the best interests of the young person, regardless of wider implications, such as the attribution of a deviant 'label' (Lemert, 1967).

On the basis of this attempt to regularise the cautioning process and outcomes, the government did then also reinforce its encouragement for inter-agency initiatives in diversion (Home Office, 1978c), as we have seen; and by 1980 (Home Office, 1980a) it was able to report 'live' examples of projects taking shape on the basis of this guidance. With hindsight, perhaps, we can make out the signs of a cusp, in terms of the underpinning beliefs and rationale for particular orientations to policy and practice. Whilst an array of early intervention initiatives were clearly being celebrated, so too, the early signs of concern about the impact of unconstrained 'preventive' activity began to emerge (Smith, 1989, p. 28). The Hampshire Police, for example, were by this point concerned that their own involvement might be counter-productive in the sense of giving young people a delinquent reputation at a very early stage, and without the protections afforded by due process.

So, although cautioning was becoming increasingly formalised, there remained concerns that increasingly widespread use of pre-court diversion could have 'unintended consequences' (Austin and Krisberg, 1981). Acknowledging the influence of the 1968 White Paper, and the political intent that lay behind it, Ditchfield (1976) did identify the widespread adoption of cautioning as a 'more systematic' approach to dealing with young offenders than had been in place previously:

> Before 1969, many [police] forces made little use of, or even discouraged, juvenile cautioning. Thus a decision to charge a juvenile with an offence almost always entailed an appearance at court.
>
> (Ditchfield, 1976, p. 8)

The development of more formal models of intervention, including juvenile bureaux, necessarily entailed a number of other procedural enhancements as well, such as more systematic information gathering, including that held by other departments as well as the police. Typically, the process of investigation by a bureau representative would then lead to a formal report of the findings and recommendations for consideration by a more senior police officer, in some cases replacing 'the more traditional kind of juvenile scheme under which selected offenders were given a period of close supervision by individual police officers' (Ditchfield, 1976, p. 9). Instead, the bureau would act in an essentially administrative capacity 'mostly concerned with gathering information on the offender, and recommending the action thought appropriate – chiefly either to caution the offender or to send him to court' (Ditchfield, 1976, p. 9). Thorpe at al (1980) also draw attention to the increasing formalisation of the decision-making process at this point, noting a similar process of referral by the 'beat' police officer to the juvenile bureau or its equivalent, with further information and recommendations to be sought from other agencies, and in this way, the process of making a decision which may have originally rested with the arresting officer becomes a much more prolonged and detailed exercise:

> Whilst the police will ultimately take a decision whether to take no further action, to caution or to prosecute, that decision will have been strongly influenced by the organisational structures of the force concerned and may have been further influenced by recommendations from probation or social services departments…'
>
> (Thorpe et al., 1980, p. 71)

In the event that the young person was cautioned, this 'almost invariably' took 'the form of an oral warning by a senior uniformed police officer about the offender's conduct and about the possibility of future prosecution if a further offence is committed' (Ditchfield, 1976, p. 1). Any further intervention or support for the offender or her/his family would be initiated by the newly formed social services department, rather than by the police, perhaps acting as a further encouragement of the use of cautioning since it would not entail any further work on the part of police officers themselves. Ditchfield's study also offered considerably more detail than previously available about the offending profile of those young offenders who were cautioned, noting that, perhaps unsurprisingly, most cautions were being administered for offences of theft, notably shoplifting, although there was some evidence of cautions taking place in respect of burglary ('breaking and entering'), at least in the case of juvenile offenders. In 1973, for example, just under a third of juvenile cautions were for shoplifting (Ditchfield, 1976, p. 15).

Commenting on the picture a little later, Pratt (1986, p. 212) also drew attention to the consistency with which the practice of cautioning had been adopted, contrasting this to the 'ferocity of debate' over the use of custody at the opposite end of the penal spectrum, and claiming that the routinisation of cautioning as a conventional and accepted form of practice 'had achieved a remarkable consensus', spanning a wide range of political and public interests, from Conservative governments, via liberal and progressive practitioners to 'pressure groups' promoting less punitive models of intervention. In the process, he noted the police caution had 'become, almost unnoticed in critical analysis, the predominant form of the disposition and sanction of juvenile offenders' (Pratt, 1986, p. 212).

Accounting for diversion in the 1970s: facts and figures

By the early 1970s, certainly, diversion had assumed a degree of prominence in the range of disposals applied to young people who came to the attention of the justice system for committing crimes. And, it is likely that it was this increasing role which, in turn, prompted renewed interest amongst researchers and policymakers. Undoubtedly, Ditchfield's (1976) study played an important part in generating a significant rethink of the use and impact of police cautioning, in respect of both adult and juvenile offenders. For present purposes, of course, we are principally interested in those findings relating to children and young people, but it is interesting that the study encompassed older offenders as well; and in this context, perhaps, the overall focus was more on the use of the caution as an administrative disposal than on its role in the wider sphere of early and preventive interventions with children. Despite this, the study itself certainly opened the door to subsequent consideration of these established features of youth diversion, in particular, and its interface with wider debates about children and welfare practices.

It is apparent that Ditchfield's study was prompted by two growing concerns which had stimulated the interest of policy makers. They were certainly not new, but both had increased in significance with recent changes in legislation and operational arrangements. The foreword to the study notes that following the introduction of the Children and Young Persons Act 1969, cautioning rates for 10–13 year olds had increased from one to two thirds of those subject to formal intervention by the police; whilst the comparable increase for 14–16 year olds was from a fifth to a third. At the same time, the study investigated the considerable variations between police forces, and considered the interaction between cautioning, prosecution and court outcomes. Here, then, there is some indication of a growing interest in the implications of cautioning practice on other aspects of the criminal justice process.

Ditchfield's investigation helped to give substantive support for some of the embedded assumptions about cautioning and how it was being implemented at the time (the early 1970s). He reviewed previous findings which indicated that most cautions administered by the police were for minor offences, such as theft, which had 'accounted for nearly three-quarters of all cautions in 1962' (Ditchfield, 1976, p. 1); and, as we have seen, he found that this pattern had largely been maintained by the early 1970s, despite the overall increase in the use of cautions. In fact, the overall increase in cautioning accounted for much of the combined increase in formal processing of young offenders (10–16) over the period 1964–74. Whilst the total number of those cautioned or found guilty for all types of offence increased from 132,000 to 212,000 in this time, only 12,000 of this increase was attributable to court outcomes, whilst 69,000 was the result of the increased use of cautioning (the figures do not add up due to rounding). Equally strikingly, by far the greater proportion of the increase occurred in the years from 1969–74. So, apparently, the favourable climate for cautioning indicated by the policy changes of that time could be shown to have had a clear effect on the use of the caution as a supposedly diversionary measure. As we have noted, cautioning rates did increase over this period of time: 'so that by 1973 the number of children [under 14] cautioned was twice the number being found guilty' (Ditchfield, 1976, p. 7). Although the rate for those in the 14–16 age range did not increase quite so dramatically, Ditchfield contrasts the pattern of disposals for juvenile offenders with that for adults, where the 'cautioning rates for the adult age groups… remained more or less static during the 1968–1974 period…' (Ditchfield, 1976, p. 7).

Particularly from the vantage point of the present day, this is an interesting point of divergence in the treatment of young and adult offenders; and it suggests once again that the distinctive ideas we hold about childhood are capable of translating themselves into both convergent and divergent trends when it comes to the treatment of offenders. This, as we shall see, presents analytical challenges, especially for those who may be inclined to view the criminal justice system itself as both monolithic and as performing a very specific task in maintaining social control on behalf of dominant interests.

For Ditchfield, though, the immediate concern was that:

> the large increase in juvenile cautioning since 1969 does pose the problem of whether this increase simply represents the actual number of offenders who have been diverted from court proceedings, or whether it also includes a number of offenders who previously would have been dealt with informally – i.e. by 'on the spot' warnings and 'no further action' decisions.
>
> (Ditchfield, 1976, p. 7)

This posed a clear challenge. Was the increase in cautioning rates related to a genuine shift in the policies and everyday practices of police and partner agencies; or, was it instead attributable more to a more limited adaption of procedural behaviour, with a greater use of the available formal mechanisms to deal with offences which would not otherwise have been officially recorded?

Ditchfield accepted that there had been an increase in juvenile crime in the period in question, reflecting a longstanding and persistent trend. According to Rutter and Giller (1983, p. 66), for example, the official records suggest a 'very substantial increase in crime' in the period after the First World War, with an even sharper rate of increase from the mid-1950s onwards. This pattern cannot be simply attributed to the increasing size of the population overall, since the number of crimes known to the police per 1,000 members of the population also reveals a dramatic upturn, and across all police areas alike, both urban and more rural (Rutter and Giller, 1983, p. 67). In this light, then, increased use of cautioning appears to have been an important development in limiting the potential consequences of this increase in terms of the numbers of young people potentially being prosecuted, sentenced and acquiring criminal records. However, a more problematic potential explanation might lie in the readier use of a less punitive sanction in the form of a caution, where this in itself might have contributed to the increase in the number of 'known offenders' (Ditchfield, 1976, p. 8).

The inflationary consequences of the increased use of diversion are not clear cut, however, in Ditchfield's view. It is possible, for instance, that improved procedures and closer liaison might themselves have led to a better understanding of the nature of offending and increased detection rates. In this sense, inflation of the numbers of young people coming into the justice system might simply have been a more realistic reflection of the actual levels of crime in the community.

Thus, in turn, the greater proportionate use of cautioning might in fact have mitigated the combined effects of higher crime rates and improvements in detection, which both, of course preceded the decision over whether or not to prosecute in individual cases.

On the other hand, however, Ditchfield (1976, p. 9) also argued that there was some evidence that increased use of cautioning did have an 'inflationary, as well as a diversionary effect', and this was apparent in two ways. Firstly, those police areas with the highest increases in cautioning from 1968 onwards were also those areas with the highest increases in the number of 'known offenders'. In this way, the heightened level of cautioning seems to have had a booster effect on the overall crime figures, suggesting a distinctive change of behaviour in these areas. And, secondly, some of those areas with large recent increases in the use of cautions also showed a substantial growth in the ratio of juvenile offenders to adults, which might more plausibly be associated with a change of policy towards young offenders rather than a differential shift in patterns of offending, or changing population profile. In Hampshire, the period from 1968–1973 saw an increase of 109 per cent in the number of known offenders paralleled by a decrease in the proportion of offenders 'found guilty' of 40 per cent; and similar patterns were also observable in other areas such as Devon and Cornwall and Liverpool and Bootle.

In its sheer scale, notes Ditchfield, the introduction of a new approach to juvenile liaison in the Metropolitan Police District was particularly striking. In 1965, 205 juvenile offenders received cautions in the area covered by the Metropolitan Police, but by 1973, this figure had gone up to 12,125, an almost sixtyfold rise. At the same time, the proportion of young people to adults in the overall offender population increased from 1:4 to more than 1:3. More tellingly, perhaps the sharpest gradient in this rise was to be observed between 1968–9, at just the point where the juvenile bureau system was introduced in the Metropolitan Police area. Although there was a distinct pattern to these changes, Ditchfield was relatively cautious in drawing causal conclusions, although he undoubtedly had his suspicions:

> It is not clear why some areas should have increased their known offender (and cautioning) rate more than others. However, the differences do tend to be most apparent between forces which introduced comprehensive bureau schemes during the period under review, and those which continued to make no special arrangements for dealing with juveniles.
>
> (Ditchfield, 1976, p. 10)

Pursuing this question further, Ditchfield went on to undertake a detailed analysis of regional variations in cautioning rates. He found that Suffolk had the highest overall rate in 1973 (38%), and Teesside the lowest (7%). In the case of Suffolk, and other authorities with relatively high rates, this was associated with their greater willingness to caution adults, so disparities tended to be rather less in relation to young offenders. In this case, the police force area making greatest use of cautions for juveniles was Dorset and Bournemouth (70%), although Teesside was once again the lowest (16%). When seeking out a pattern, Ditchfield noted that it was predominantly rural areas which made the greatest use of diversion by way of cautions, whilst urban areas tended to score somewhat lower. He also surmised that a narrower range for juvenile cautioning might be to do with the effects of the 1969 Act, which had 'established a more even pattern of juvenile cautioning between police forces' (Ditchfield, 1976, p. 13). Thus, by implication, the preferences of senior police officers were less influential than had apparently been the case prior to that point (McLintock and Avison, 1968). Despite this tempering of geographical variations, the range was still substantial, with the juvenile cautioning rate for Northampton and County (33%), for example still less than half that of those of Devon and Cornwall or Dorset and Bournemouth.

Even under further scrutiny, and with the introduction of further variables such as different patterns of crime, Ditchfield observed that only about half the variation in cautioning rates could be explained; for the remainder, it was most likely that force policies were responsible: 'given similar offenders who had committed similar offences, forces apparently differed as to whether or not they would be cautioned' (Ditchfield, 1976, p. 18).

Regional differences also provided more insight into the relationship between cautioning rates and courts' use of low-level disposals, with Hull having both the second lowest juvenile cautioning rates in 1973, and the third highest rate of 'discharges' at court (that is, absolute and conditional discharges). By contrast, Suffolk with the highest adult cautioning rate also had the second lowest discharge rate. Although this pattern was not universal, Ditchfield (1976, p. 20) concluded that: 'in many cases where the police decide not to caution, the courts instead assume this function by discharging – absolutely or conditionally – a larger proportion of offenders'. The possibility is raised, therefore, of a straightforward displacement effect, whereby cautioning simply displaces lower level court disposals. Of course, this again raises potential concerns about the implications of any further expansion of formal diversionary mechanisms, and particularly the displacement of informal measures by cautioning, since courts might then be inclined to impose more severe penalties on those reported and prosecuted for second or subsequent offences. Here, we get a foretaste of the potential consequences of just this sort of approach being cemented into place through policy initiatives such as New Labour's tariff-based pre-court framework of Reprimands and Final Warnings.

Ditchfield's study has come to be seen subsequently as a seminal contribution to our understanding of juvenile diversion, partly because it was more systematic and comprehensive in its analysis, partly because of its timing, shortly following the policy changes associated with the 1969 legislation, and partly because it began to raise concerns about the consequential effects of a large scale policy change such as this and the impact of system expansion. In one sense, he noted, the aims of the Children and Young Persons Act were achieved, in that the number of under 14 year olds being convicted in court fell between 1968 and 1974, by about 2,000 a year; and he also argued that the number of 14–16 year olds prosecuted would have gone up by more than it did in the absence of the changes made:

> But the Act also appears to have had some unintended consequences. For example, many forces which have recorded the largest increases in juvenile offending after 1969, also showed the largest increases in juvenile cautioning The study shows that in a number of instances these large increases in both cautioning and recorded offending accompanied the setting up of juvenile bureaux – particularly in the cities. A possible explanation is [that with] the introduction of the new policy, formal cautioning became an alternative both to prosecution and also to unofficial action. The latter possibility was certainly not intended by the Act....
>
> (Ditchfield, 1976, p. 24)

Here, then, we see early signs of a series of concerns which have played a substantial part in debates about youth diversion over the succeeding years. The impact of system expansion and the incorporation of perverse incentives (formal processes represent recordable successful outcomes, for example) certainly play a significant part in some of the critical commentaries on diversion which we shall go on to consider; and we are alerted to the more recent comment by a former Chair of the Youth Justice Board about the problems associated with organisational expectations and meeting targets:

> the police find it quite easy to meet these targets. What they do is they pick a lot of, what I call, low hanging fruit, of which the easiest are kids in groups in public places doing relatively minor things. If you arrest a child and that child gets a caution, one of the two types, or is brought before the court, that counts as an offence brought to justice.
>
> (Morgan, 2007a)

Diversion and its critics

So, at the very point where the practice of diversion, the establishment of juvenile liaison schemes and ideas associated with early welfare intervention with children in trouble had reached their peak, they became the subject of much closer scrutiny and then a period of sustained criticism. Much of this crystallised around fears of net widening, excessive intervention and uneven and discriminatory practices. Of course, the wider context, too, was epitomised by a period of increasing economic uncertainty, and growing doubts about the efficacy of pro-active welfare-based intervention with offenders ('nothing works'; Martinson, 1974). Here then was potentially fertile ground for the expression of doubts about the value and consequences of the widespread use of out of court diversion.

Prominent amongst the critiques was the work of the Lancaster University research team led by David Thorpe, which sought to provide a detailed account of the implementation of the Children and Young Persons Act 1969, and its 'aftermath' (Thorpe et al., 1980). Based on evidence of a significant expansion in 'correctional' interventions, they argued that the logic of welfare and the development of new services and disposals had led to the institutionalisation of many children and young people whose delinquencies were very minor, and the direction of many others into formal intervention programmes 'who have not even committed offences but merely come from disorderly families' (Thorpe et al., 1980.p. 16). The belief in the intrinsic value of intervention designed to improve the well-being and life chances of young people appeared to justify a range of quite intrusive, and potentially damaging forms of provision, it seemed: 'a social welfare approach provides justification for early and extensive intervention in the lives of children and their families' (Morris and McIsaac, 1978, p. 51). This, in turn, is likely to lead to differential treatment, and stigmatisation of those who become 'known' to the system, even where they have not been formally proceeded against (Morris and McIsaac, 1978, p. 147).

Morris and McIsaac were reporting on the situation in Scotland over roughly the same timescale as Ditchfield; and although the legislative framework was different, they also detected evidence of a widening of the net. Here, too, the use of police warnings had contributed to an overall rise in the number of child offenders in official statistics, whilst there had been no parallel reduction in the numbers proceeded against in court or referred to the children's reporter: 'Since one of the aims of the legislation was to deal with children informally as far as possible and to keep children out of the formal control system, such an increase must be scrutinized carefully' (Morris and McIsaac, 1978, p. 86). Although the legislative and organisational framework was different in Scotland, it did share with the rest of the UK the relative economic expansion of that period, and so can be similarly expected to have expanded the capacity of the 'system' to accommodate a greater number of children, young people and their families within formal service structures.

Further detailed analysis of patterns of offending and disposals during the period 1965–77 suggested that there were a number of dynamics in play, but that even allowing for an overall increase of crime, a 'significant proportion' of the increase in crime by young people over this period could be attributed to a net widening effect (Rutter and Giller, 1983, p. 80).

Concerns about the dynamics and implications of net widening were expressed particularly stridently by Austin and Krisberg (1981), albeit based on a review of evidence from the USA. Their argument was that a range of progressive reform movements could be identified across the criminal justice system which were all subject to processes of resistance and distortion. In the case of diversion, they argued that it was initially seen as an answer to the problems of labelling and secondary deviance which had been identified as problematic consequences of formal processing by the justice system: 'It was assumed that criminal justice was a closed and linear process in which reduced intervention at the front end, which presumably could be easily achieved, would cause reductions in more severe forms of intervention later on in the process (e.g. imprisonment)' (Austin and Krisberg, 1981, p. 170). So, avoiding arrest and prosecution would supposedly lead to reductions in the numbers in custody. However, they subsequently itemised a number of examples of ways in which this straightforward equation had come to be compromised in practice.

The suggestion they have advanced is that, far from being a mechanical, rational and essentially closed decision-making process, diversion is characterised by competing interests and acts as an 'open' system, where these interests are played out, usually to the benefit of those in more powerful positions:

> Placed under the control of the criminal justice system, diversion programmes have been transformed into a means for extending the net, making it stronger, and creating new nets.
>
> (Austin and Krisberg, 1981, p. 170)

In one instance, they refer to a review of diversion programmes which found that they had actually extended their scope to incorporate defendants who would be unlikely to be found guilty if prosecuted, and subject them to a period of supervision nonetheless. In another case, an evaluation of police-led diversion initiatives in Los Angeles found that they tended to include young people who would not otherwise have been formally proceeded against, and these findings were replicated in other similar studies. In one further example, reported by Austin and Krisberg (1981, p. 171), it was found that only 51 per cent of those participants across a number of diversion programmes had been referred as an alternative to court proceedings.

So, the first ground for criticism is that the introduction of diversion schemes can be shown to have the potential to include a greater number of young people within their remit than conventional judicial processes would have done. In addition, however, they may well compromise due process in that informal programmes might nonetheless require an admission of guilt; and might subject those diverted to specific requirements upon which their diversionary disposal would be conditional. Thus, diversion itself might involve accepting a formal record of prior offending and compliance with an intervention programme, where either the grounds for a finding of guilt are not established, or where an informal disposal could have been made as an alternative: 'As such, diversion programs represent an erosion of due process and increased formal intervention by the state. Instead of justice, there is diversion' (Austin and Krisberg, 1981, p. 171).

These and similar concerns were certainly held by UK critics of diversion as it had developed, too. The important analysis carried out by Thorpe and his colleagues (1980), tried to explore the system effects of a welfare-based approach to juvenile diversion, in the wider context of their depiction of the emergence of a twin-track model of intervention. They argued that, informed by an underlying belief in the benefits of pro-active intervention social service agencies had expanded their remit to formally intervene in children's lives, in ways which contributed to their eventual institutionalisation within the system. This, they describe as a form of 'vertical integration' (Thorpe et al., 1980, p. 21), whereby the new system becomes an adjunct to its predecessor rather than taking its place:

> Seen from a vantage point in the old system, the new system extends its scope, its range of intervention and surveillance, down through the age groups, and

> acts as a feeder mechanism for the courts and custodial institutions. One unfortunate, but apparently inevitable consequence of this arrangement is that children now coming under the jurisdiction of the old system will tend to be younger (and may tend to have fewer 'problems') than formerly.
>
> (Thorpe et al., 1980, p. 21)

The consequences of this greater readiness to recruit new entrants to the 'system' earlier and for less serious infractions are pervasive. For those working at the front end of the system, there is some incentive to problematise and work with pre-delinquents whose problems may be less deeply entrenched and thus less challenging. But at the same time, these very young people are the subject of more intensive activity and scrutiny than would previously have been the place, so any further difficulties or infractions will much more readily come to light. These again will from the system's perspective be much more likely to be seen as persistent problems of the individual concerned than evidence of practitioner or system failure. The young person thus may well attract a reputation for being difficult or intractable, and they are transferred to a more intensive regime, reputedly better equipped to deal with the persistent problems associated with them. As Thorpe and colleagues suggest, there was evidence too of the development of forms of 'social work' language which recast the needs experienced by young people in terms of more prescriptive and controlling forms of provision, typified by phrases such as the 'need for structure' (Thorpe et al., 1980, p. 21). So, failures of prevention with a new cohort of young people, potentially lead to their becoming candidates for more intrusive and, in the end, punitive interventions:

> An unfortunate consequence of this arrangement is that when children do come to court, they may be more vulnerable than they might otherwise have been since more is known about them and social work intervention has already been tried (and seen to fail).
>
> (Thorpe et al., 1980, p. 21)

Evidence of these trends is presented by these authors in the form of the pattern of court disposals over the period 1965–77, during which the rate of custodial sentences for young offenders increased substantially, whilst the use of the less punitive option of the supervision order declined as a proportion of all sentences. Indeed, as Thorpe and colleagues (1980, p. 29) acknowledge the non-implementation of key sections of the Children and Young Persons Act 1969 led to a paradox; the popular assumption of an increasingly liberal and lenient system for dealing with the crimes of the young was substantially belied by this pattern of outcomes, with the use of borstals and detention centres increasing by over 100 per cent between 1969 and 1977.

For Thorpe and colleagues (1980, p. 62) there seemed a natural link between these observations and Foucault's (1979) analysis of the emergence of modern forms of penalty. In his work, they were able to discern a number of key components of the emerging 'soft machine' for managing 'discipline' and maintaining contemporary social order (Thorpe at al, 1980, p. 63); namely, 'hierarchical observation', 'the examination' and 'normalising judgement'. By establishing a systematic, intrusive but apparently rigorous and scientific model of evaluation and judgement into the process of official intervention with young people in trouble, it was assumed that a finely-grained and precise calculation of the nature of the problem could be conducted and appropriately tailored solutions implemented, accordingly. The tendency here is therefore to seek out problems and apparent defects, and to impose external and standardised judgements to these perceived signs of deviance. Mechanisms for liaison and shared assessment in turn provide a vehicle for communicating and legitimising scientifically achieved evaluations of what is going wrong and what precise forms of response are required. Initiatives such as the juvenile liaison bureau offer just such a vehicle for intensifying concerns and underlining the assumption that something must be done to set things right, and in the case of the young offender to offer appropriate guidance, support and correction.

In light of this, Thorpe and colleagues (1980, p. 128) are led to question what by then (the late 1970s) had become established consensual assumptions: 'Will not specialist officers and specialist units simply generate more new clients?' Increased collaboration, too, might be seen as inherently beneficial and as an obvious means of achieving service improvements, but by enhancing the flow of information and enabling a wider group of providers to identify concerns, this may just lead to a greater readiness to 'label' the young person as problematic in some way; and, more worrying still, such information once shared and formally recorded becomes more widely and definitely 'known', helping to perpetuate the diagnosis of the problem.

Not only do these aspects of system expansion contribute towards a greater tendency to identify problems, and to apply indicators of concern to particular young people, but they also support the notion of a more finely graded pathway into the formal system. The insertion of additional 'rungs' in the ladder, associated with a series of differential problem definitions, may actually serve to speed up transitions towards more intensive and coercive interventions, rather than slowing the process down, as diversionary models appear to intend. Interposing 'intermediate' forms of provision at key points in the delinquent career may be intended to inhibit progress, but 'it may instead make each consecutive decision easier to take, with the result that delinquent careers are promoted, even accelerated' (Thorpe et al., 1980, p. 128). Whereas Bottoms' (1977) notion of 'bifurcation' perhaps suggests a sharpening of distinctions between minor and relatively un-troubling offences and those which were seen as particularly anti-social or serious, this does not seem to have been consistent with the direction of travel taken by agencies associated with diversion during the 1970s, with the dividing lines between lesser and more serious matters becoming increasingly less clear cut and more confused.

Commenting a little later, Pratt (1986) definitely concurred with this suggestion. He envisaged two distinct problems arising from the proliferation of stages in the process; firstly, the extension of the decision-making process 'helping it to reach out to points even further away from the juvenile court than before' (Pratt,

1986, p. 228). And, secondly, by extending its 'welcome' in this kind of non-threatening way, the system of control also provides a means by which the 'penological gradient' from low-level delinquent to serious offender' is lessened and 'this slope can be quickly traversed' (Pratt, 1986, p. 230). For Pratt, indeed, it is the very presence of 'good intentions' and the availability of less intrusive, non-punitive early interventions which combines with 'other social forces' to produce 'a new regulatory field over minor delinquency'. The issue, then, is not so much the precise form of organisation and delivery of diversionary initiatives, but their relationship to shadowy but powerful influences, geared towards the most effective means of organising social control.

This is certainly Cohen's (1985) argument, and he has no doubt that there is an effective if unfortunate alliance to be found in the proliferation of that time in the number of professionals and para-professionals with an interest in assessing, evaluating and treating the problems of the young. The increasing proliferation of personnel, and by extension criteria on which intervention decisions could be based, were indicative of a 'blurring process', according to which crime and delinquency become increasingly disparate, and 'get tangled up with other welfare, treatment and control nets' (Cohen, 1985, p. 61). And, as he implies, this allows other non-explicit criteria for taking action to become incorporated in the process, to the extent that they may be associated with the wide range of recognised indicators – institutional forms of oppression on grounds of class, ethnicity or culture may thus become routinised.

Some further weight is given to this point by a number of contributions which appeared to highlight the discriminatory effects of a discretionary out of court decision-making procedure. Institutional racism was beginning to be acknowledged (Smith and Gray, 1985), and there was some evidence available to suggest that juvenile liaison schemes were not immune to this. Several studies reviewed the changes in cautioning practice during the 1970s, with a particular focus on the impact in London and other urban areas. Farrington and Bennett (1981) sought to address the net widening question directly, and concluded that the introduction of a force wide cautioning scheme between 1968 and 1970 did contribute to net -widening. They were unable, however, to link processes or outcomes to factors such as race or class, although age and gender did appear to be linked with decisions about whether or not to prosecute; younger children and females were less likely to be taken to court (Farrington and Bennett, 1981, p. 131). Fisher and Mawby's (1982) study of cautioning in an 'inner city area' similarly suggested that age and gender were positively associated with cautioning decisions in the same way; and although young people of Asian origin were more likely to be cautioned this was largely because they were younger and less criminally experienced (Fisher and Mawby, 1982, p. 70). Although they concluded that this indicated that cautioning decisions were not influenced by ethnicity, the implication is that Asians were disproportionately more likely to be identified as offenders initially, given their offence profile. More significantly still, the study by Landau and Nathan (1983), also undertaken in London, did suggest a degree of differential treatment of young people on the grounds of their ethnicity. Mirroring earlier findings which also indicated a higher likelihood of black young people being arrested for some offences, Landau and Nathan (1983, p. 142) found that 'the chances of white juveniles receiving a caution are considerably greater than the chances of their black counterparts.... Unless alternative explanations are provided, a bias on the part of the police against blacks involved in these offences cannot be ruled out'. Importantly, too, they identified a link between these outcomes and the influence of 'non-legal variables' which might impact on the decision-making process, such as living in 'disrupted' family circumstances, or being 'latch-key children' (Landau and Nathan, 1983, p. 143). In such cases, Landau and Nathan concluded, young offenders might be viewed as 'bad risks for cautioning' due to their 'detrimental family conditions', which might themselves have been revealed as a result of a home visit, and consideration by the juvenile bureau. Of course, other young people reported for offences whose home circumstances appeared more favourable also acted as a kind of reference group against whom the more apparently problematic cases would be evaluated. In other words, this (severally) discriminatory process appeared to provide detailed evidence of just the sort of 'vertical integration' predicted by Thorpe and colleagues, with grounds for welfare intervention actually contributing to an escalation of young people into rather than away from the justice process; in this case, additionally contributing to the cumulative impact of institutional discrimination.

Ironically, at the same time as this kind of extensive critique of diversionary mechanisms was becoming widely aired, so, too, were voices heard from an altogether different perspective, complaining that diversion was, in effect, compromising due process, and limiting the authority of the courts and the wider judicial apparatus (McKittrick and Eysenck, 1984; Hullin, 1985; Kidner, 1985). Often associated with the residual reluctance to endorse diversion amongst those associated with the courts, the focus here was on the potential distortion of the justice process, the incorporation of arbitrary influences on decision-making, and lingering fears that juvenile offenders might be the beneficiaries of undue leniency.

Proper exercise of the courts' adjudicatory functions might be compromised by excessive recourse to administrative justice:

> Who is making the judgement as to whether the person arrested is guilty of the offence?... [How] can society ensure that valid distinctions between guilt and innocence are not being allowed to become blurred?
>
> (McKittrick and Eysenck, 1984, p. 379)

Although the principle of leniency in the case of minor infractions was not fundamentally questioned by these critics: ' We accept that there must be some discretion in the prosecution authorities' (McKittrick and Eysenck, 1984, p. 394), the problem of where to draw the line appeared to be of considerable significance:

> One is left wondering precisely how many offences could be made the subject of cautions before the record becomes serious enough to justify prosecution.
> (Kidner, 1985, p. 309)

And so, potentially, this may lead to a complete disregard for the rule of law and its formal apparatus:

> If offenders are enabled to commit successive offences without some penalty, this maysuggest that observance of the law is not important.
> (Hullin, 1985, p. 312)

Diversion under pressure: where next?

Although the criticisms of diversion came from different quarters and clearly represented a wide range of political perspectives their combined weight and the changing economic and political circumstances definitely contributed to an increasing sense of doubt about the frameworks and processes underpinning the cautioning of young offenders. As the 1970s came to a close, another change of government and the resurgence of a 'law and order' agenda seemed to pose some very significant threats to the whole enterprise of juvenile liaison and collaborative decision-making in the best interests of children and young people reported for crimes. If it was to survive, diversion clearly needed to adapt its rationale accordingly, and re-evaluate its previous close alignment to arguments grounded in welfarist principles of early intervention.

4 Diversion renewed

Into the 1980s – a turning point

In many ways, the prospects for youth (juvenile) diversion at the conclusion of the 1970s were not encouraging. Much criticism was being aired about the tendencies of an expansionary welfare-based system to draw into its clutches children and young people for whom such interventions were unhelpful and in many cases counterproductive. For some, this represented the 'overreach of treatment' (Morris et al., 1980, p. 57), which then acted as a precursor for further problematisation and eventually institutionalisation. There appeared to be a pathway open, whereby 'pre-delinquent' children and young people could be drawn into 'treatment-type programmes' and then further criminalised on the basis of their 'difficult' or 'troublesome' behaviour (Lee, 1998, p. 33). In this way, children could be accelerated into the justice system in the name of welfare, rather than being diverted from it into the normal range of services and support mechanisms available. A particular focus of concern regarding the effects of this elision of welfare needs and problematic behaviour was the criminal (Section 7) care order, which enabled courts and social workers to bypass conventional considerations of just deserts and tariff-based justice in order to impose an institutional solution which re-asserted 'control' at the same time as addressing identified needs, in theory at least (Taylor et al., 1979, p. 21). More generally, though, this appeared to be a symptom of a broader confusion of aims and objectives amongst key players in the justice process. For social workers, their apparently weaker position in the criminal justice arena led perhaps to a pragmatic accommodation with the language and mechanisms for exercising 'control' over young people with problem behaviour, whilst at the same time espousing and sometimes articulating explanations for their actions grounded in adverse circumstances and individualised needs. This, in turn, suggests a degree of ambiguity in their practice-informed ideologies of childhood, and a reframing of practice goals in terms of ideas such as structure, consistency of treatment, and behavioural interventions.

To the extent that, at an earlier point in the justice process, pre-court decision-making forums were also infused with similar ideas, the assumption was certainly that these contributed both to system expansion and to the problematisation, if not criminalisation of young people (Lee, 1998, p. 33). Under these circumstances, it might have been expected that the idea of diversion itself would come into question, given that in their implementation, policies based on this principle appeared to be having the opposite effect. Here, we saw the emergence of a new alliance, organised around principles of 'rights' on the one hand; and 'justice', on the other. For proponents of both viewpoints, the problem lay in the extension of discretion-based administrative decision-making processes into areas where they had no legitimacy to operate; and, indeed, where they imported unfairness and inconsistency rather than equity:

> The central arguments are that the safeguards of the formal justice process have been undermined by the rise of individualized treatment and social work's claims to specialized knowledge or expertise. The countervailing forces of legal rights have been lost in the massive expansion of discretionary powers and rehabilitative vagueness.
>
> (Lee, 1998, p. 33)

This loss of clarity may also have been linked to process issues. Priestley et al (1977) in their analysis of decision-making in Bristol and Wiltshire in 1972 shed some interesting light on the interplay between services and systems. Here, it seems, prior knowledge of a child's history was likely to predispose the police towards prosecution – suggesting perhaps that prior involvement would be likely to have a net-widening effect; and, at the same time, what might be seen as 'welfare-related items' were likely also to weight the outcome towards prosecution (Priestley et al., 1977, p. 72). Thus, tentatively, we might conclude that the development of machinery such as juvenile bureaux able to generate information, and the associated awareness of negative indicators, such as prior offending or adverse family circumstances could have an effect in escalating the level of response by the justice system. As with developments some twenty-five years later, though, we are led to the broad conclusion that the scope and capacity of the decision-making system, the escalation of access to problematic information, and the absence of limiting controls on the operation of the system, combine to generate a greater readiness to take formal action, at all points on the route into the justice system. Although this was before the idea of 'risk' began to assume a prominent place in shaping outcomes, there was already in place a tendency to seek out and draw adverse conclusions from signs of difficulty or problematic behaviour in children's lives.

Criticisms of system expansion and loss of focus were to be found across the political spectrum, too, from those who aspired to a greater liberalisation of the mechanisms for dealing with the offences of the young (eg Priestley et al., 1977, p. 106) to others who continued to express residual concerns about the diminishing powers of the courts. Morgan (1981), for instance, was one such advocate, who identified the increasing role of social workers as participants in the delivery of youth justice as a sign that the courts were losing their capacity to exercise the rule of law effectively:

> The paradox is that at the same time as there exists a mandate for unlimited intervention with extravagant ambitions, the criminal law fails to perform its most essential and irreducible role as a morally expressive and educative force which upholds and elucidates basic values.
>
> (Morgan, 1981, p. 65)

So, it seems clear that by this point a fair degree of consensus had been reached, to the effect that the existing arrangements for dealing with young people who offended were insufficiently robust or equitable; and as a result, there was widespread evidence of the phenomenon of 'unintended consequences' with two systems running in parallel but interacting, and each compounding the adverse effects of the other as far as young people were concerned.

Arguments for a change of direction

Essentially, the arguments for change which emerged at around the beginning of the 1980s and were consolidated thereafter stemmed from a belief that the Children and Young Persons Act 1969 had been critically flawed in two respects. First, the elision of delinquency and need created an amorphous space over which a range of claims and counterclaims could be advanced as to who held the professional authority to act in that domain. In this sense, the possibility of what has later become known as 'system creep' was created by the lack of precision over just what the field of practice actually was; which uncertainty was further compounded by the agglomeration of a variety of objectives, including the promotion of health, educational attainment and, of course, prevention of offending. Alongside this definitional vagueness, the 1969 Act was also critically hampered, it would seem, because key sections were not implemented, with the resulting 'vertical integration' of care and control systems articulated by Thorpe and colleagues (1980). The result, for some, was entirely predictable. In his critique of the development of Intermediate Treatment (IT), Pratt (1987) articulates these concerns. The intentions of the Act were misconceived, according to this view:

> By diminishing the specificity of the offence, by dissipating delinquency or potential delinquency across the child population rather than confining it to a single, identifiable, adjudicated segment of youth, this simply did not allow a conceptual space to be set aside for 'high risk' delinquents…
>
> (Pratt, 1987, p. 425)

At the same time, however, this reframing of children's 'troubles' did not afford the anticipated rationale for de-criminalising and de-institutionalising those who previously would have been processed routinely by the justice system. So:

> to suggest that the 1969 Act promised the possibility of diversion is also to be conceptually mistaken. It was not a question of the legislation prohibiting juvenile offenders from appearing in court; rather, it was to place them within

> a new framework of intervention – that would give priority to administrative decision-making in the first instance, with the court as part of a regulatory continuum.
>
> (Pratt, 1987, p. 425)

The air of confusion, he argued, could be further demonstrated in the aspiration of some proponents of intermediate treatment to dispense with the notion of a 'tariff' of disposals which would undercut one of the most entrenched implicit assumptions of the criminal justice system. In practice, though, what Pratt (1987, p. 426) identified was 'an *integrated* (his emphasis) rather than an abolitionist strategy', which allowed both penal and alternative (welfare) interventions to co-exist, and avoided disturbing the progressive intensification of sanctions associated with the tariff.

This kind of analysis was consistent with the interpretation of the available evidence offered by Thorpe and colleagues (1980), whose review of cautioning practices in one area indicated just the sort of co-existence of parallel systems predicted by Pratt's analysis. Here, they found that almost 60 per cent of children appearing in the local court had never received a caution, observing that this figure could be interpreted in one of two ways (Thorpe et al., 1980, p. 72). Either it was indicative of the success of cautioning, since clearly it was not a precursor to further offending in most cases leading to prosecution (and was contributing actively to young people's desistance from offending); or, alternatively, cautioning was reserved 'for a different category of juvenile – those whose offences would never have been considered for prosecution before the existence of cautioning, but for whom there now existed a "softer" option' (Thorpe et al., 1980, p. 72).

Diversion, then, was identified as problematic, not least because, far from representing a challenge to conventional means of criminalising young people, it had effectively become a complement to them, both in practical terms, but also in providing an implicit rationale for the continuing distinction between the 'deserving' and 'undeserving' amongst young people who got into trouble with the law. Failure to respond to chances offered and interventions aimed to address welfare needs would in themselves act as a justification for more intensive and coercive measures. For those concerned to reassert the principles of justice and fairness in the treatment of young offenders, clarity of purpose would be an important starting point.

Echoing the concern about the consequences of a lack of clarity of purpose, Rutter and Giller (1983) made a similar observation, this time focusing on the undoubted zeal of those who were associated with the expansion of pre-court interventions at this time:

> It is partly that the concept [of diversion] is sufficiently ambiguous to allow expansion of the judicial net, and partly that an almost inevitable consequence of enthusiasm for a new programme which is felt to be beneficial is a desire to extend those benefits to a wide range of young people thought to be at risk. The absence of legal restraints … means that there is nothing to restrict this expansion.
>
> (Rutter and Giller, 1983, p. 304)

The priority was to reinstate principles of certainty, consistency, fairness and proportionality into a system which appeared to be running out of control. Here lay the undoubted common ground between those who asserted the primacy of the courts in dealing with delinquent behaviour and those who sought to keep the use of the courts to the minimum achievable level. The starting point for Morris and colleagues (1980) was that criminal justice policy should be seen as only one part of a wider social policy field; by implication, it could not be seen as a vehicle for achieving wider changes in the lives of young people, to which ends other policy levers would be much better suited. Instead, they argued for doing as little harm as possible. Acknowledging the limitations of the justice system in preventing delinquency, and the welfare services in seeking to 'reform' the offender, they also pointed out that early and harsh treatment were more likely to be criminogenic than to reduce re-offending (Morris et al., 1980, p. 52). They argued, too, that an undue concern to consider offender characteristics rather than simple deeds would be likely to identify additional grounds for intervention rather than supporting diversion, or a reduction in the intensity of intervention. So, they concluded, with limited evidence to support active intervention: 'one is left with determining priorities as much by rejection of alternatives as by empirical investigation. We suggest that *justice* and *fairness* (their emphasis) should be key concepts in any new system. … An overriding concern, supported by empirical data, is the need to minimise the harm likely to accompany coercive intervention' (Morris et al., 1980, p. 52). This was not a simple rejection of the concept of diversion or the practice of cautioning offenders, but a statement of principle concerning the importance of proportionality and consistency of treatment.

In their view, cautioning decisions should be based on a clear, commonly agreed framework, grounded in, rather than challenging the conventionally understood sentencing tariff. There may be disagreements between more or less punitive viewpoints about the gradient of the tariff, but these principles would be widely endorsed. For first and second offences, typically, Morris and colleagues argued that cautions should be administered automatically by the police, in the form of a warning as to future conduct. From that point on, it would be a matter for police judgement as to whether or not court proceedings would be necessary. Again, the offence would be the principal determinant of subsequent action, and the child's history and circumstances would not play a significant part. Need, therefore would play a negligible part in determining what action to take. Importantly, where any kind of specialist help was to be offered to the child, this should only be on a voluntary basis, and should have no bearing on the outcome of the criminal case, they argued: 'The articulation of specific criteria limits arbitrariness in the administration of law and protects, to some extent, the rights of the young person in question. Certain criteria should be statutorily excluded; for example, the social and family characteristics of the child' (Morris et al., 1980, p. 63). And, applying the same set of principles, Morris and colleagues also argued that discretion should be constrained to the extent that any kind of intervention associated with a non-prosecution decision should be negotiated, explicit and time-limited, so as to avoid the risk of excessive intervention outside the protections afforded by the statutory legal process.

Here a very different model of diversion was being articulated which took precisely the opposite approach to earlier formulations, and excluded need from consideration as a factor either to justify or obviate the requirement for formal intervention. Here too, the existence of the tariff was not to be called into question or overlooked; but rather it was seen as the foundation on which the decision should be based, with a narrowly prescribed range of additional offence related criteria utilised to modify initial assumptions about the appropriate disposal. Crudely, we can distinguish between the prevailing welfare model of diversion and a suggested alternative grounded in notions of rights and due process.

The establishment of clear and specific grounds for police decision-making was also recommended by Taylor and colleagues (1979), who were concerned about the available evidence suggesting an escalation of intervention where juvenile bureaux were in operation. Cautions were now taking the place of 'no further action' or informal warnings, with the result that young people were acquiring criminal records where they might not have done previously. Other policing practices, such as the pre-selection of certain children for prosecution based on what was 'known' about them also gave Taylor and colleagues (1979, p. 41) cause for concern. In the face of these escalatory tendencies, they also suggested that:

> there would seem to be good arguments for the limitation of discretion in the processing of juveniles, that is for the existence of formal criteria which would ensure that in specific circumstances the police had no alternative but to caution the juvenile or to record 'no-further-action'.
>
> (Taylor et al., 1979, p. 42)

Significantly, perhaps, these calls suggested a concern about the use of discretion, and perhaps a corresponding level of doubt about the meaning of professionalism in this context. Decisions, it seemed, could not safely be left in the realms of 'expert' judgement, given that this was often grounded in unevidenced beliefs in the value and quality of the service on offer. Indeed, feedback from young people on the receiving end often seemed to throw considerable doubt on the meaningfulness of the intervention actually delivered (Morris et al., 1980, p. 48).

A more systematic approach to curtailing discretionary expansion was offered by Thorpe and colleagues (1980, p. 129), who championed the benefits of 'a general 'gatekeeping' mechanism designed to oversee, as far as possible, the entire network of policy and procedure', in relation to decision-making in child welfare and juvenile justice. Their criticisms of existing practice were not directed at diversionary principles, but rather at their imperfect application. Practitioners themselves should be armed with a better understanding of the process of which they were a part, and how different elements of the overall machinery of delivery might interact in ways which were not predictable or desirable. One possible option might be what they described as the 'informal implementation' of Section 5 of the Children and Young Persons Act 1969, 'which requires that it be demonstrated, prior to prosecution, that all possible alternatives have been tried and found wanting' (Thorpe et al., 1980, p. 129). This might, in their view, involve offering some form of informal sanction in exchange for 'a prosecution dropped' by the police, but this would be acceptable if it genuinely led to improved levels of diversion from formal processes. Importantly, such negotiations should not be distorted or compromised by the perceived need to secure a statutory basis for 'actual face-to-face work' (Thorpe et al., 1980, p. 130).

Alongside this kind of strategy, too, there should be a more conscious attempt to control the flows and uses of information, which should not be used to justify increasingly intensive forms of intervention, but rather to 'delay entry' to the formal care or justice system 'for as long as possible' (Thorpe et al., 1980, p. 130). We can see here the beginnings of the development of a detailed and systematised rationale for managing the processes of decision-making and active provision of services, in order to limit the inherent tendency of formal structures to extend their reach and draw young people in with increasing rapidity.

Rights and justice: a new policy framework?

By 1980, there was evidence of a new emergent consensus, which appeared to span the political spectrum. Frustration with the ineffectiveness of existing interventions, coupled with the harms associated with institutionalisation, concerns over the erosion of the rule of law, a changing political climate and financial constraints all seemed to point in the same direction. Active intervention in the lives of young people should be justifiable, it should have a clear rationale, and it should be based on principles of efficiency and effectiveness. From the political right then, this crystallised into a call for a return to the sense of precision offered by a rational legal framework:

> The only respectable way out of the morass is for the law to restrict itself to one narrow aspect of the individual, his [sic] criminal acts. For if it is not to become an addition to the menaces it opposes, the law must be clear and open about its contents.
>
> (Morgan, 1981, p. 64)

And at the same time, whilst advocating a similar approach, those espousing a children's rights position were clear that a return to the rule of law should not be:

> a mandate for the punitive policies of the 'law and order' lobby. Compulsory intervention in the lives of children must be limited in nature, not subject to indiscriminate intervention on the basis of current moral panics.
>
> (Morris et al., 1980, p. 8)

So the case was made and broadly agreed that the basis for intervention should primarily be the offence, rather than any other circumstantial factors or characteristics of the child concerned. Here, implicitly, a rather different view of children, their responsibilities and their 'agency' appears to be becoming predominant than had previously held sway; although some were more inclined to identify continuities in attitudes and practice. Priestley and colleagues (1977, p. 77) argued that police decision-making had never really been dominated by welfare considerations, and consistently retained a focus on the offence rather than the offender. Determinations about whether or not to prosecute would be 'much more influenced by the "seriousness" of' the reported behaviour and by their age and previous record than by what was known about their background or circumstances.

Nonetheless, policy initiatives at the beginning of the 1980s were certainly presented as a break with the past, and coincided with expectations from supporters of the incoming (1979) Conservative government of a more forceful approach to crime and punishment. It was in 1979 that William Whitelaw made his conference speech to the Tory Party announcing the introduction of the 'short, sharp shock' regime in detention centres, pronouncing emphatically that these would be 'no holiday camps'. And so, despite his apparently liberal reputation, Whitelaw aligned himself with the core message of the new Thatcher government that it would be 'resolute' on law and order (Thatcher, 1982).

Shortly after coming to power the Thatcher government introduced a White Paper, *Young Offenders* (Home Office, 1980b), which was expected to underline this strong rhetoric with a series of measures to toughen up provisions for dealing with the crimes of the young. Although the Home Office issued guidance by way of a Circular in the same year (Home Office, 1980a) which sought to encourage co-operation between police and other agencies in the form of juvenile liaison schemes, the White Paper appeared to seek to limit the expansion of welfare-based provision into the sphere of juvenile offending. The White Paper did not explicitly seek to increase the use of punitive sanctions such as custody, but sought instead to promote a range of more exacting community-based penalties, giving more explicit powers to the courts to dictate the programme content of disposals such as supervision orders, whilst also extending magistrates' powers to impose custodial sentences. Overall, Morris and Giller (1987, p. 120) consider the White Paper's proposals to have represented a 'toughening and tightening up' of provisions to deal with youth crime; but they also note an apparent contradiction, with its aspirations for an 'increased use of diversion'. In fact, it appeared to offer a clear endorsement of diversion:

> All the available evidence suggests that juvenile offenders who can be diverted from the criminal justice system at an early stage in their offending are less likely to re-offend than those who become involved in judicial proceedings. The now widespread police practice of giving a formal caution instead of instituting proceedings is therefore of particular importance.
>
> (Home Office, 1980b, p. 12)

Many commentators at the time nonetheless feared that *Young Offenders* would be the prelude to a considerable expansion in the use of harsher punishments for young offenders, despite these inherent ambiguities. Perhaps, instead, this is evidence of the acceptance of the logic of 'bifurcation' (Bottoms, 1977); with an implicit distinction being made between the many relatively minor offenders who could be effectively diverted, and those whose persistence and increasingly serious offending would qualify them for ever tougher and more demanding penalties.

Lee (1998) also reflects on the apparent paradox of a governing party with a tough 'law and order' image taking immediate action on coming into power to confirm its support for cautioning in the White Paper, commenting that: 'In effect, the punishment of young offenders has been much more ambiguous than the law and order rhetoric suggested' (Lee, 1998, p. 36). Instead, the tendency of policy-makers was to emphasise the distinction between the 'hard core' of persistent and dangerous offenders for whom more intensive punishment was required, and the remainder, whose offending should be seen as essentially 'normal'. For these young people, low-key intervention would allow them to 'grow out of crime', and would at the same time be 'cost-effective'. Lee (1998, p. 36) concludes that: 'A control model based on a redefining and redistribution of the deviant populations ... arguably allowed the government to get tough and soft simultaneously'.

Here, then, a number of factors appear to come into alignment to support an approach in which an ostensibly implausible 'twin-track' approach actually makes sense. This in turn led to an accommodation which resulted in the Thatcher years becoming associated with a significant liberalisation of youth justice. Firstly, this was undoubtedly a cost-conscious government, for whom the opportunity to reduce demands on public spending would always be welcomed, and a less intrusive and extensive criminal justice apparatus seemed to fit the bill (!) in this respect (Smith, 2003). In a context of rapidly rising crime rates, there was also pressure to 'define down' (Garland, 1996, p. 456) deviance, in order to reduce the potential for system overload. This, too, coincided with a broader *'laissez-faire'* (Fox Harding, 1997) view of the state's role, which was to intervene in the normal institutions of society as little as possible. In the case of early and minor offending by children, the family rather than the state should therefore be seen as taking primary responsibility for disciplining its members. And, framed in terms of the legal system, the distinction between different levels of offending was also consistent with a 'justice' model, where due process and proportionality were seen as more important than context and offender characteristics. Certainly for less serious offences this represented a rejection of the interventionist logic which seemed to underpin pre-emptive, welfare-based programmes such as preventive intermediate treatment.

Notably, throughout the course of the 1980s a fairly consistent message was delivered by government in respect of cautioning, and this also undoubtedly benefited from the establishment of a supportive consensus involving leading police officers in particular (Lee, 1998, p. 38). The Association of Chief Police Officers was actively involved in a working party established by the Home Office in 1984 (Home Office, 1984), which led to the explicit reaffirmation of current policy in the form of Home Office Circular 14/1985 (Home Office, 1985). For those like the present author, working in youth diversion at the time, the 1985 Circular seemed to be a ringing endorsement of the strategy of minimising formal intervention. Notably, the guidance provided encouraged the use of less formal responses to offences 'unless the circumstances of the case are sufficient to justify' a caution (Home Office, 1985, p. 4), with the implication that the notional tariff of disposals was being extended even further in the pre-court domain.

There was a clear emphasis on prosecution of juveniles being used 'only as a last resort' (Director of Public Prosecutions, 1987, p. 45), and this was supported by similar guidance provided to the newly-established Crown Prosecution Service, whose decision-making should always be governed by the principle that: 'Prosecution should always be regarded as a severe step' (Director of Public Prosecutions, 1987, p. 45), and should be initiated only when in the public interest. At these points where the direction of policy was confirmed, the rationale for taking an offence focused approach was also re-asserted. The offender must admit the offence; there must be sufficient evidence of guilt 'to give a realistic prospect of conviction' (Lee, 1998, p. 38); and parents/carers must demonstrate that they understood the significance of a caution (that is, that it would be recorded and would provide evidence of previous offending); and only once these procedural requirements had been met could the caution be administered. Clearly, the caution was viewed from within an essential legalistic frame, and its administration depended on conventional evaluations of guilt and responsibility. As such, policy documents of the time made it clear that prosecution of a juvenile would 'never' be right 'solely to secure access to the welfare powers of the court' (Director of Public Prosecution, 1987, p. 46).

The decade ended with another strong endorsement of the principle of avoiding prosecution wherever possible with the publication of Circular 59/1990 (Home Office, 1990a; see Chapter 5). Indeed, there was some suggestion at this point that what was seen as a successful approach should be extended with 'young adults' becoming included in the groups to be dealt with outside the court wherever possible (Lee, 1998, p. 39). In Northamptonshire, for instance, where cautioning was by now well established, this prompted moves to initiate the Adult Reparation Bureau, albeit with a somewhat different focus for its activities than its juvenile equivalents (Bell et al., 1999, p. 98).

The practice of diversion in the 1980s

There is no doubt that the emerging consensus of the 1980s had a direct effect, at least according to national statistics.

Figures are not strictly comparable with subsequent data because of changes in the treatment of 17-year olds, but essentially this conveys a consistent picture of a very substantial decline in the numbers of juvenile offenders formally processed over this period of time; and even more strikingly, of those processed the cautioning rate increased from 52 to 79 per cent. Although these outcomes might have been attributable to net-widening, this possibility was substantially offset by the finding that over the same period, and with the exception of females between 14 and 16, the number of young people found guilty or cautioned per 100,000 population also declined substantially. In fact, it appeared that an increased use of cautioning and other informal disposals had resulted in a progressive reduction in

Table 4.1 Young offenders cautioned or found guilty for indictable offences 1977–91 (in thousands)

	Year		
Cautioned	*1977*	*1986*	*1991*
Males 10–13	39.4	26.3	21.0
Males 14–16	31.3	43.6	41.0
Females 10–13	14.0	8.7	6.3
Females 14–16	10.5	14.9	14.8
Total	95.2	93.5	83.1
Found Guilty			
Males 10–13	19.2	6.1	2.3
Males 14–16	59.8	37.7	17.2
Females 10–13	2.4	0.5	0.2
Females 14–16	7.6	3.7	2.2
Total	89.0	48.0	21.9

Source: Criminal Statistics England and Wales 1991 (Home Office, 1992).

findings of guilt and, ultimately, the use of custody which also declined by a very substantial amount over this period (the number of custodial sentences imposed on 14–16 year olds in 1991 amounted to less than a quarter of the figure for 1981).

As indicated above, the emergence of a strong and widely-shared policy consensus certainly had a role in achieving this substantial shift in the treatment of young people in trouble. At the same time, though, there is little doubt that agency and practitioner initiatives also played a very substantial part; and of course it was in their manifestation that the direct impact of the youth justice system on young people themselves was experienced, as ever. The evidence of continuing geographical variations helps to support this suggestion, in that clear regional and local variations indicated different levels of enthusiasm for change. By 1986, for example, significant disparities in cautioning rates were apparent, with Northamptonshire's rate almost double that of Humberside (Morris and Giller, 1987, p. 149).

As I have argued previously (2003), the 'permissions' offered by the policy changes outlined were accepted enthusiastically in a number of areas, where the principles of 'minimum intervention' (Smith, 1989) and 'growing out of crime' (Rutherford, 1992) began to take hold in practice. Whilst in Hampshire, for example, efforts were concentrated on establishing an effective post-sentence strategy to provide genuine alternatives to custody, in other areas such as Devon and Cornwall and Northamptonshire, the principal aim was to turn off the tap at the point of entry to the justice system. In both cases, though, the underlying logic was to offer 'alternatives' to conventional sanctions. The project of attempting to transform the justice system from within did not necessarily represent a fundamentally different rationale for intervention, though. Certain embedded assumptions such as the idea of a sentencing tariff continued to inform practitioner strategies and justifications (Smith, 1989).

At the forefront of the newly emerging practice models were the Northamptonshire Juvenile Liaison Bureaux (and where, to declare an interest, the present author was a practitioner and manager). As outlined previously, the origins of the Northamptonshire JLBx lay in a collaboration between police and social services representatives who were jointly concerned about the relatively low use of cautions in the county in the mid-1970s, and the potential associated risks of net widening. By 1980, a clear rationale for the proposed new service had been established, with the combined objectives of: reducing re-offending; reducing the use of care orders on grounds of offending; greater involvement of young offenders in alternative 'community' provision; and at no greater cost than existing services (Northamptonshire Social Services Committee, 1 October 1980, quoted in Smith, 1989, p. 97).

Funding was acquired from a number of sources and the first JLB, in Wellingborough, began to take referrals from the police in January 1981. With little to go on but the four objectives outlined above, the incoming director of the Wellingborough team described his early days in post as having to work with a 'blank canvas' (Smith, 1989, p. 100). In these formative stages, for instance, both he and his colleague at the Corby JLB (which opened in November 1981) felt some pressure to propose 'interventions' in order to secure police agreement to the administration of a caution, even where neither felt it was justified by the circumstances of the reported offence. They felt at this point that this was necessary to earn 'credibility' (Smith, 1989, p. 101).

The structure of the bureau teams was also designed at least in part with credibility in mind. These first two JLBx were staffed by representatives of the five key agencies involved with children and young people at the time (Youth Service, Social Services, Police, Probation, Education), representing what was later described as a 'corporate' approach to pre-court decision-making (Pratt, 1986). Certainly, it seems that there was both a climate of support for such inter-agency initiatives, and a belief that an experimental project such as this would require buy-in from across the spectrum of interested agencies. Interestingly, perhaps, in light of this, there appears to have been no attempt to engage representatives of the court in any aspect of the bureau structure, even at management committee level; in Hampshire, by contrast, very close working relationships were established with key judicial personnel, partly at least in order to gain support (and 'credibility') for local alternative to custody projects (Rutherford, 1992).

The bureaux' principal function was to receive notifications ('C69' forms) from the police on all reported juvenile (10–16) offenders where the offence was admitted, and to carry out an assessment of the offence and make recommendations to the police on the action to be taken. In principle, it was open to the JLBx to recommend any of the range of available responses, from no action through to prosecution. In the very early stages, uncertain where they stood, the bureaux proceeded cautiously, and it is noted that in some cases the police actually administered cautions against a bureau recommendation to prosecute (Smith,

1989, p. 102). Nevertheless, it quickly became the norm for bureau staff (all of whom carried the same responsibilities, irrespective of their parent agency) to pursue alternatives to prosecution wherever possible. An early sticking point, for example, was the concern expressed by local police chiefs about second cautions for repeat offenders (Smith, 1989, p. 103). The idea of a tariff of disposals thus continued to exert considerable influence. Despite this, the cautioning rate for those areas with JLBx began to increase significantly, and certainly more rapidly than in surrounding areas. Significantly, the police became increasingly ready to accept the bureau recommendations (Bell et al., 1999, p. 95). As Blagg and colleagues (1986, p. 24) noted, this was one of the first examples of 'inter-agency co-operation where the police agreed to be directly influenced in their decision-making by other professionals'.

The JLBx undoubtedly benefited from the support of successive Chief Constables who held a liberal view of the role of the police, and were fully engaged with the initiative. At a national conference to promote the initiative in 1983, the Chief Constable at the time claimed that:

> Northamptonshire Police had demonstrated its willingness to depart from its traditional stance and to recognise that its own professional ideology needed to change. I would claim that is justly made out by the decision to do everything possible to keep juveniles out of the criminal justice system.
>
> (Buck, 1983)

The momentum created led quickly to the establishment of a third JLB in the county town, in 1984, and the effect was felt immediately, with the cautioning rate for young offenders in Northamptonshire increasing from 49 per cent in 1981 to 84 per cent in 1985 (Bell et al., 1999, p. 93). By now, the aims of the JLBx had been clearly articulated and established as the common basis for intervention across the agency spectrum. These were:

1. To divert young people, wherever possible, away from the penal and welfare systems into informal networks of control, support and care.
2. To avoid the imposition of those forms of penalties and welfare intervention which tend to aggravate the very problem they seek to reduce.
3. To enable the agencies to respond to delinquent behaviour in ways which will reduce re-offending and enable young people to become responsible adults.
4. To encourage the normal institutions of society to tolerate adolescent behaviour and to respond constructively to it.

(Hinks and Sloper, 1983)

It was clear from this that the bureaux had based their approach on a considered analysis of prior evidence and theoretical insights, which had raised concerns about net widening and 'labelling' (Bell et al., 1999, p. 92). In this sense, then, they were not naïve, and were well aware of the potential risks of becoming over-interventionist, and drawing into the system children who would not previously have been subject to formal action.

In light of this, the Northamptonshire JLBx began to develop additional strategies to support their objectives, sensing perhaps that there were risks in allowing practice to become routinised, or merely a paper exercise. There was a concentrated effort to pursue a policy of diversion from diversion, in recognition that even a caution represented a formal and recordable disposal, and in many cases informal or even no action would further the overall objective of decriminalising children wherever it was feasible. This was argued to be consistent with the agreed aim of promoting positive responses by informal networks around young people, without resorting to a citeable caution.

In addition, the bureaux themselves did initiate short-term interventions of one kind or another, utilising the flexibility afforded by the informal disposal to address the specific circumstances of the offender and offence (Bell et al., 1999, p. 97). Welfare needs could therefore be addressed directly, but outside formal agency processes, and arguably guarding against the risks of drawing young people into the net unnecessarily. In addition, the offence-focused nature of the bureaux' work also encouraged them to begin to develop offence resolution strategies (Blagg, 1985). The idea of dealing quickly with the offence in its own right prompted consideration of reparation, or other means of making amends for any harm caused. Of course, reparation and reconciliation have since become associated with the by now well established idea of restorative justice, but for the JLBx this represented one means of ensuring that an offence was acknowledged and responded to in a way that met the needs of those involved and satisfied expectations that something would be done in response to the act of wrongdoing. Blagg's detailed account of the reparation practices of Corby JLB acknowledges some of the inherent complexities in managing the process carefully so that it does not adversely affect the parties involved, and underlines the bureau's insistence on maintaining a spirit of voluntarism, rather than imposing reparation as a form of extra-legal punishment.

Here, though, some of the challenges of introducing a new model of intervention and innovative practices are crystallised. The JLBx could be viewed as extending the scope of punitive interventions into the realm of minor and inconsequential offending; they could be seen, too, as distorting due process and failing to represent the interests of either victim or offender fairly; they could be viewed as no more than a bureaucratic device for managing system demands; or, they could be seen as a means simply of letting off young troublemakers who needed to experience the full weight of the law.

Diversion in the ascendant: exciting the critics

The Northamptonshire initiative was not the only attempt to extend the scope of diversion during the 1980s. Similar schemes were reportedly developed in Exeter, Rochdale, Merseyside and Essex, according to Blagg (1985, p. 267); and certainly, as we have seen, the national picture was one of a dramatic upsurge in the use of police cautioning for young offenders. This, in turn, prompted a considerable level of attention, much of it critical. Northamptonshire itself was the focus of much critical comment, although in many cases this was used as the basis for more generalised claims about the merits or otherwise of diversionary practices of the time.

Corby JLB was subject to an extensive evaluation (Blagg et al., 1986), and certainly this exposed some uncertainties about the direction of travel. Finch (1986, p. 102), for example, commented on the evidence of 'widely different' understandings of what diversion actually meant to 'professionals in the various agencies'; and this point was underlined in the course of my own investigation into Wellingborough JLB (Smith, 1989), where, again, differing working assumptions were to be found across the range of agency representatives. Others, by contrast, tended to see the JLBx as much more cohesive, although this was not necessarily viewed in a positive light. Pratt (1986, p. 229), for instance, expressed concern at the 'corporatist tendencies' represented by the bureaux, and the associated risk that a uniform and mutually agreed administrative decision-making model could 'be seen as further extending the orbit of delinquency decision-making, helping it to reach out to points even further away from the juvenile court than before' (Pratt, 1986, p. 228). Here, fears of net widening are linked with the loss of access to due process and rights which could simply result in the production of 'a new regulatory field over minor delinquency' (Pratt, 1986, p. 230).

Similar concerns were raised by Davis and colleagues (1989), who carried out a detailed study of Northampton JLB. For them, the JLB's practices betrayed a lack of interest in the wishes of parents or victims, which were simply over-ridden by the procedural demands of the administrative mechanism for processing cases and achieving a pre-determined outcome. In this case, though, the focal point of their concern was not the extension of the machinery of social control, but the bureau's failure to pursue sufficiently robust action in cases where stakeholders demanded a response:

> It is a serious weakness of the JLB approach that they operate a closed system of justice which takes no account of.... the reactions both of parents and victims.
>
> It can be argued, therefore, that there are certain criteria – most obviously, visibility and accountability – against which the JLB suffers in comparison with the juvenile court.
>
> (Davis et al., 1989, p. 234)

Like Pratt, they also wondered whether the focus of the bureaux on minor offending might mean that this had 'encouraged police action in respect of pranks?' (Davis et al., 1989, p. 234) And, in the face of the bureaux' stated aims of promoting informal responses to offending they reflected on whether 'increased notification' might actually undermine 'family and community control over young people' (Davis et al., 1989, p. 234). It is perhaps worth noting at this point that there is some irony in the JLBx being subjected to this kind of criticism, since their original aims had been precisely to build in stronger safeguards against the encroachment of arbitrary state intervention into children's lives without proper justification. And yet, within a few years of being in operation, they were in turn subject to challenge on precisely the same grounds.

In these cases of critical comment, and elsewhere (Finch, 1986; Smith, 1989) it is also of note that the idea of a tariff of disposals was found to remain embedded in the assumptions bureau and agency staff were making about how to approach their assessments and recommendations. Thus, for Davis and colleagues, it was the need to acknowledge the notional tariff which prompted some of the arguments put forward by bureau staff, as in the case of one young person where previous offences are rationalised as being 'relatively insignificant' (Davis et al., 1989, p. 223). And, in keeping with this, the Northampton JLB's achievement in extending the range of informal disposals available is viewed as part of a deliberate strategy of extending the tariff in order to 'delay resort to the court in individual cases' (Davis et al., 1989, p. 222). In a similar vein, there was also observed a tendency on the part of some bureau team members to continue to rely on conventional judgements about culpability, remorse and personal difficulties, presumably as potentially contributing to arguments for mitigation (Smith, 1989, p. 301), even though these also seemed to be at odds with the pursuit of 'pure' diversion.

There did appear to be some continuing resistance to the bureaux amongst other groups as well, with both social workers and magistrates apparently concerned about some young offenders receiving too many cautions (Cheetham, 1985, p. 8, quoted in Smith, 1989); and at the same time, the JLB initiative did not seem to have shaken the understandable belief of a range of other professional interests that punishment should play a legitimate part in the treatment of juvenile offenders (Cheetham, 1985, p. 15, quoted in Smith, 1989).

Persistent concerns were also expressed from a legal perspective, too. Here again, the issue seemed to be to do with the substitution of administrative for criminal justice, and the consequent effect on principles of fairness and proper safeguards:

> Diversion from prosecution in Britain is increasing. The absolute discretion of police prosecutors has allowed growth to be uncontrolled and ad hoc. … Whether diversion is good for suspects and victims, however, is another matter entirely, and one which also demands close attention.
>
> (Sanders, 1988, p. 513)

Acknowledging that informal and unofficial action to deal with minor crime had 'always been' taken, Sanders went on to raise a series of concerns about the effect of formalising these forms of intervention by way of diversion schemes. First, he reiterated the fear that they could contribute to net widening by extending formal disposals such as cautions into terrain where previously no further action would have been taken by the police. Second, he identified examples of cases where offenders had been cautioned in the absence of a full and unambiguous admission of guilt.

With no opportunity to test the evidence, alleged criminals could thus have been induced to accept a formal disposal and thus incur a citeable criminal record, where they may well have been legally innocent. In some cases, he argued, this might be attributable to a form of calculation by offenders that this might be preferable to taking the chance of going to court and possibly being convicted; or, it may be that they simply did not realise that they had any say in the matter, as in the case of a number of young offenders dealt with by a mediation scheme in Sandwell: 'He [the police officer] sort of said "Pay for the damage and you won't have to go to court," and I thought I'd better pay it because it would be better than bringing my parents to court' (from Young 1987, quoted in Sanders, 1988, p. 516).

Aside from these procedural issues, Sanders also expressed concern about variability and extent in the use of diversionary measures. He referred again to the acknowledged geographical variations in cautioning rates, attributing this, in part, to policy differences between police forces; as well as to regional disparities in the perceptions of appropriate thresholds between what were considered minor or more serious offences. He suggested, too, that this might also lead to the incorporation of unequal treatment on demographic grounds, such as class differences, with certain 'middle-class' crimes such as fraud being seen as less problematic, for example (Sanders, 1988, p. 517). So, disparity in enforcement by criminal justice agencies would lead inevitably to variations in diversion rates, partly as a result of the proliferation of different schemes for dealing with offences out of court.

Sanders (1988, p. 517) also expressed concerns about proportionality, and the possibility that 'the conditions or reparations that diverted offenders submit to sometimes exceed what is justifiable in relation to the offence … again, with no guarantee of independent advice for the offender'. As Sanders observed, this was a similar concern to those expressed by others such as Cohen (1985) about the extension of excessively demanding expectations into alternatives to custody, precisely to guarantee their credibility as suitable substitutes for the rigours of a prison sentence.

Sanders' final concern was the victim's interests, which at that point were only, in his view, given 'an ambiguous weight' in determining the decision whether or not to prosecute the alleged offender (Sanders, 1988, p. 517). With what he believed to be an obvious resurgence in interest in the rights and participation of the victim in the justice process, further pressure would be put on agencies and practitioners to make even-handed decisions on whether or not to divert offenders from the justice process. In his view, giving a true measure of control to victims would probably lead to the imposition of more demanding conditions on offenders as the price of a caution. Once again, the concern seemed to be about diversion leading to inappropriate or excessive intervention without the safeguards offered by an effective legal framework. The 'root of the problem is low visibility and low level exercise of discretion. Policing the police's exercise of discretion has fundamental difficulties…' (Sanders, 1988, p. 518).

Notwithstanding the breadth of his concerns, Sanders (1988, p. 524) also continued to argue for increased use of diversion. It was not so much its place within the justice system that concerned him as the unstructured and unregulated forms in which it was then being implemented. The call here was for consistency and transparency, and a new decision-making structure to regularise practice. In this instance, the logic of the argument was that the police should be relieved of the responsibility of the decision as to whether or not to prosecute, given their investigatory and accusatory role; but nor should they retain a partial interest as in the Northamptonshire model, where diversion was said to still take place 'on police terms within a retributive ideology' (Sanders, 1988, p. 527). Instead, the only feasible solution would be to introduce a new independent body (analogous to the Crown Prosecution Service) to consider recommendations from all interested parties and then make the decision. Sanders (1988, p. 529) concluded that the prevailing climate did not provide many grounds for optimism for the 'possibility of reducing punitiveness through diversion', noting that the 'window of opportunity is only present at all because of financial pressures to reduce government spending'. Here, though, one encouraging possibility was apparent; that some of the 'soft-end projects' (Cohen, 1985, p. 257) perforce taking the place of prosecution might actually turn out to be beneficial to those currently coming within the remit of 'the soft machine'.

The golden age of diversion? The 1980s in retrospect

Despite the doubts expressed, diversion had become a success story by the end of the 1980s, and there was a considerable mood of optimism amongst what night be termed the youth justice community about what had been and might still be achieved. Indeed, some of the sternest critics of 'net widening' in earlier years were now persuaded that diversion could be an effective route towards minimising the harmful effects of the justice system on children and young people.

This was partly as a consequence of the kind of model of intervention developed in this period, which was grounded in notions of systems management, informal service provision and minimum intervention, informed by the ideas of Schur (1973) who had coined the term 'radical non-intervention' and others (Thorpe et al., 1980). Whilst there were undoubtedly variations in practice (as between Corby and Northampton Juvenile Liaison Bureaux, for example; Smith, 1989), areas of common ground were much greater.

In a decade which had begun with widespread concern about the encroachment of formal systems of welfare and justice into the lives of children and families, and which concluded with landmark measures to protect children's interests and promote their rights (the Children Act 1989 and the UN Convention on the Rights of the Child), perhaps a corner had been turned, and there was evidence of a new commitment to the 'rights-bearing child'.

On the other hand, the same developments could be viewed through a different lens as evidence of the progressive withdrawal of the state from its former proactive role in shaping and controlling children's lives, especially in working-class communities.

Whilst either of these interpretations of diversion in the 1980s might well hold water, a more cautious observer might point to certain continuities with previous eras, such as the persistence of a tariff of disposals, albeit extended and modified; and certain assumptions about the need to make amends for wrongdoing, even where informal disposals were to be administered. Debates persisted, for instance, on the question of how far cautions should be conditional on compliance with some form of amends making. Similarly, repeat cautioning remained contentious, and although children could certainly expect more than one 'second chance', limits were still embedded in the working assumptions of most diversion schemes.

Thus, even in an era where there appeared to be a substantial degree of consensus about the direction of travel, and there was considerable evidence of progressive change in youth justice practice at all levels of intervention, there remained a number of persistent residual beliefs, and notional limits to the scope of diversion still applied in the minds of most stakeholders. In effect, what remained in place in youth justice was the conceptual edifice of criminal justice, framed around ideas of individual responsibility, children's developing capacities, blame, culpability and proportionate sanctions; even the most radical forms of diversionary practice were constructed, rationalised and legitimised against this backdrop, using many of the same forms of justification. This, for example, emerging restorative practices still utilised ideas of taking responsibility, accountability to offence victims and 'atoning' (Thorpe et al., 1980, for instance) for one's wrongdoing. At the same time, the pattern of disposals also showed that age still had a lot to do with the level of responsibility for actions attributed to children and young people.

5 Diversion, dangerousness and the 'risky child'

Before the storm

In many ways, the end of the 1980s saw the peak of optimism as far as those associated with youth diversion were concerned. There had been a major shift in the balance of disposals for young people reported for crime, and this was supported by a policy environment which offered endorsement for the direction of travel. Minimum intervention had become the accepted starting point for decision-making and action in youth justice; and beyond this, there were signs that this principle had also begun to shape thinking about the treatment of adult offenders. It is certainly worth noting significant parallel developments such as the substantial reduction in the adult prison population over the same period.

The responsiveness of a series of liberal-minded government ministers was also a distinctive feature of the criminal justice landscape at the time, and although they maintained the protective cloak of tough rhetoric, this often contrasted with the substance of policy development. So it was that the proposals to extend 'Punishment in the Community' caused some initial concern, but in fact led to an increasing emphasis on non-custodial means of dealing with offences.

In the context of diversion, too, perhaps practitioner concerns tended to overlook the extent of prior achievements. Whilst any apparent attempt to restrict the scope of pre-court disposals was seen as problematic, this was perhaps to underplay previous successes, crucially in shifting the agenda. Debates did not concentrate on whether informal action short of a caution was acceptable, for example, but more narrowly on the circumstances and scope of this kind of intervention. Legitimacy for a range of non-citable, voluntary disposals had been established, and up to this point opposition had been muted.

Critics had identified potential flaws in the diversionary 'project', but these had similarly been confounded by the evidence. Perhaps one of the unacknowledged features of this period of considerable significance was the close attention given to monitoring practices and outcomes, associated with the more general argument for active systems management. Thus, it was relatively easy to show that there had been no evidence of net widening, with some areas being able to declare themselves as 'custody free zones' and others rendering the juvenile courts more or less redundant (as in Wellingborough, for example; Smith, 1989).

So perhaps there was some justification for the rather complacent view that we were well on the way to establishing a broad and sustainable commitment to minimum intervention in youth justice, based on underlying assumptions about the normality of much errant behaviour in the young, and the primacy of children's rights to a 'normal' childhood as the starting point for any decision about how this behaviour should be viewed and addressed. Similarly, though, the idea of non- or very limited intervention also found echoes in more conventionally right wing arguments of the time which criticised what was believed to be over-zealous state intervention in the family (see Mount, 1982). Parents should be left to deal with their children's misdemeanours, rather than being undermined by excessive interference by the 'nanny state', according to this line of argument.

Within this wide-ranging consensus, however, were a number of embedded difficulties, or unacknowledged inconsistencies, which, as it turned out, proved to be its undoing. Firstly, by their nature, as we have already observed, diversion and other 'alternatives' to conventional disposals, effectively accept their provisional and subordinate position, acting as a kind of counterweight to the accepted rationale(s) supporting the administration of justice, but not offering a direct challenge. Unlike more directly 'abolitionist' arguments (see Mathiesen, 1974, for example), diversion offered no fundamental challenge to the punitive logic of individual responsibility and the importance of paying for one's crimes. Indeed, some of the practices associated with pre-court intervention actually appeared to endorse the principle of children being held to account, at least consistent with their level of maturity, and acquiring a greater sense of personal responsibility through the agreed response to the offence. So, being told off in no uncertain terms by irate shopkeepers might be seen, not least by children themselves (Blagg, 1985), as part of a predictable and easily recognisable process of reasserting dominant patterns of authority and control.

In this respect, diversionary practices, whatever the extent to which they modified previous patterns of 'excessive' intervention in children's lives, could not offer a truly radical alternative in the ways in which proposals to raise the age of criminal responsibility, to replicate the Scottish children's hearings system in other parts of the UK, or to replace penal mechanisms with alternatives grounded in restorative principles could all perhaps claim. As Goldson (2005, p. 238) has observed: 'Diversion by way of cautioning [falls] short of rejecting penal sanctions in their entirety'; whilst, on the other hand, decriminalisation 'proposes that the scope of the criminal law should be substantially narrowed, and that *civil* as distinct from *criminal* sanctions should be sought'.

The inherent problem for those committed to a diversionary approach was thus that they were open to direct challenge on the basis of applying penal logic inappropriately, that they were simply allowing young people to 'get away with it'; and thus encouraging irresponsible and unlawful behaviour rather than putting a stop to it. Even if the evidence tended not to support this final claim, this was not essentially a practical argument so much as a moral one: wrongdoing should simply not be condoned, or treated lightly. Of course, in order for such arguments to gain purchase a series of contextual alignments had to be achieved; so, in order to justify a more interventionist approach, for example, understandings of childhood and the family also needed to undergo something of a transformation, or at least a significant adjustment. The prevailing assumptions of the previous period about childhood misdemeanours being 'normal' would not be consistent with reasserted claims that wrongdoing should be taken very seriously and dealt with accordingly. A new narrative of childhood was therefore required, and as we shall see, the 1990s saw the emergence of the 'risky child'.

Persistent doubts: the limits of consensus

By the beginning of the 1990s, the strengthening alliance between policy makers and professionals seemed to be on the point of achieving a further consolidation, with the publication of a fresh White Paper, *Crime, Justice and Protecting the Public* (Home Office, 1990b). here, for example, the idea of 'punishment in the community' had been translated into proposals that effectively entire categories of offences should be dealt with in non-custodial settings; and that only 'serious' crimes such as those involving violence, domestic burglary or sexual offences could in future be subject to prison sentences. In the eyes of some commentators, this represented a unique expression of the principle of 'just deserts' as the overarching philosophy of the justice system, subsequently translated into law in the form of the Criminal Justice Act 1991: 'Arguably the CJA 1991 represented the first time that a British government clearly enshrined in a piece of criminal justice legislation a single coherent sentencing philosophy and policy' (Haines and Drakeford, 1998, p. 77).

In parallel with this systematisation of criminal justice policy, the Home Office (1990a) had also continued to develop policy specifically in relation to diversion. Importantly, it seemed, the guidance issued by the Home Office at this point endorsed existing practice and sought to extend its reach, if anything. There was certainly encouragement for the extension of the use of cautions more widely across all age groups, consistent with the wider policy objective of differentiating between serious and less serious offences which could be dealt with outside court. At the same time, the view was also buttressed that diversion should be a multi-agency project, with a wider range of interests represented, and by implication a dilution of the role of the police and their criminal justice priorities.

The vestiges of resistance were evident in the reluctance of the official guidance to give positive endorsement to repeat or 'inappropriate' cautioning (Home Office, 1990a), and this was almost certainly influenced by feedback from police and magistrates who believed that diversion was going too far and their authority was being eroded. As Lee (1998) has observed, resistance manifested itself in a number of ways, from the police 'canteen culture' which consistently viewed cautioning as a vehicle for allowing children and young people to evade taking responsibility for their actions; through to magistrates who were fulminating at the drying up of work, as out of court disposals inevitably caused a sharp reduction in the number of juvenile cases they were hearing: 'in Northamptonshire the de-escalating approach of the JLBs had reduced the juvenile court population from

1395 in 1980 to 86 in 1991' (Lee, 1998, p. 71). As Lee found, too, in her study of pre-court intervention in one police area, these concerns were voiced in familiar terms: 'It is clear that out authority is being undermined.... I think most of us feel that part of our role is being eroded.... We have years of experience, and we are trained' (Juvenile court magistrate, quoted in Lee, 1998, p. 70).

For another respondent, the deterrent effect of the courts was being dissipated: 'The official bit of coming to court... might stop them [offending].... When youngsters are cautioned that many times, they'll come to court a year or two older... and by then they are more sophisticated and confirmed criminals' (Juvenile court magistrate, quoted in Lee, 1998, p. 70).

Of particular concern to the magistrates interviewed by Lee seemed to be the use of repeat cautions, but underlying this was certainly the belief that their own place in the criminal justice process was at risk, certainly in respect of children who offended. Of course, perversely, their own direct experience may have appeared to confirm their fears, because effective diversionary schemes were actually taking minor offenders out of the system, leaving the courts to deal only with those at the 'heavy end' and creating perhaps a distorted perception of contemporary trends in youth crime.

Magistrates were also known to be expressing concern about the encroachment of diversion on their domain in other contexts, too (Jones, 2012). Apart from a series of articles and letters featuring in their 'house journal', Justice of the Peace, more formal action was also initiated, with the 1987 Annual General Meeting of the Magistrates' Association calling explicitly for limits to be placed on the use of cautions. This, in turn, was supported by more extensive arguments about the consequences of a de facto transfer of decision-making power away from the judiciary. Savage (1988), for example, provided a lengthy list of concerns, observing that:

1 Society actually wants more punitive sentencing
2 Retribution, deterrence, public protection and reparation... were not given sufficient recognition by diversionary schemes
3 Police were being persuaded to use cautions against their own better judgement
4 Cautioning is class biased
5 Admissions of guilt are extracted from young people on the basis that they will avoid trial
6 Caution plus involving sanctions should only be approved by the courts
7 The number of cautions an individual receives is unlimited
8 Alternative courts have taken the place of criminal courts, who should be assigned the power to administer cautions (adapted from Savage, 1988).

Others writing in the same publication also conveyed the message that they felt that things had gone 'too far' (Smith, 1989, p. 51). So, the extension of cautioning at one end of the scale appeared also to represent a challenge to the use of custody, which was not acceptable:

> I recognise and applaud the remarkable and effective local initiatives which in some areas have not only reduced the numbers of juveniles brought before the court and committed to custody but which also have not led to any apparent increase in the rate of offending. *But* (my emphasis) it seems to me that the argument for the elimination of custody has not yet been concluded....
>
> It is not only the political, but the social and cultural, climate which requires of sentencers a recognition that punishment is appropriate for bad behaviour....
>
> (Browning, 1987, p. 215; p. 216)

Another commentator of the same ilk, argued that:

An offender should not be permitted too easily to avoid prosecution or a stiff sentence by an apology, a mere apology... (Samuels, 1989, p. 183).

Here then, the critique was extended to incorporate developments associated with the evolution of diversion, including restorative practices. Ironically, perhaps, the message here seems to be that victims' interests or preferences should be subsumed under the requirements of formal judicial processes and the holding of miscreants to account.

In parallel with magistrates' concerns, Lee's investigation, undertaken between 1990 and 1992, also revealed that many police officers seemed to share their fears, even those with roles in juvenile liaison: 'There's this sort of softly softly approach to young criminals these days that I think is wrong. I get fed up with people saying, "these kids have only nicked a Mars Bar", well that's still theft to me and the small shopowners are still the victim' (Police chair of juvenile liaison panel, quoted in Lee, 1998, p. 81).

Here, Lee notes, there is also evidence of an increasingly strong position taken by the police as defenders of victims' interests, as well as those of the wider public: 'We have to demonstrate to the criminals that the society would not tolerate such behaviour; we have to be seen by the public as doing something' (Police chair of Juvenile Liaison Bureau, quoted by Lee, 1998, p. 81).

And, in case we should assume that the only voices of opposition to the extension of cautioning were to be found amongst those with vested interests or perhaps attributed with a particular perspective associated with their role in the justice process, allies were to be found amongst those generally thought to take a more lenient view of young offenders. So, writing in *Social Work Today*, Andrews (1987, p. 28) argued that agencies had gone too far 'in their heroic quest to enshrine the rights of children in general' and 'forgotten about the growing band of hooligans who violate the system'. Others, too, in the process of carrying out field research into the effects of diversion schemes had found that there was actually quite a wide-ranging body of opposition to their 'more radical implications' (Smith, 1989, p. 312). Cheetham (1985, p. 8), for example found that, as well as magistrates, there were social workers who were unpersuaded of the merits of the Northamptonshire Juvenile Liaison Bureaux; expressing concern that young people were receiving too many cautions and the bureaux were usurping their function and operating as an alternative 'social work scheme'.

Further evidence that even in the area where cautioning schemes were 'at their most advanced' (Jones, 2012, p. 212), there was considerable residual hostility amongst magistrates and police officers was provided by Evans (1991).

Meanwhile, similar sentiments were being expressed in quite a different forum as the Criminal Justice Bill 1990 was debated in parliament (Windlesham, 1993). Although the Bill itself was described as something of a landmark, in that it aimed to set out a 'coherent statutory framework for sentencing' for the first time (Windlesham, 1993, p. 404), its subject matter provided another opportunity for influential opponents of the liberalising trends in criminal justice to express their views. As Windlesham observes, this groundswell of opposition was not encouraged by many of those in positions of potential influence, such as the senior members of the judiciary, lobby groups or political opponents. It can thus be seen to represent a deeper and more persistent undercurrent of distrust, perhaps. In fact, the early stages of debate on the Bill were overshadowed by the events surrounding the resignation of Margaret Thatcher; which may itself be significant, since, paradoxically it seems that her reputation as a strong leader may actually have facilitated the liberalisation of the justice system under her tenure as Prime Minister (Smith, 2003).

In response to perceived threats of internal dissent, the government undertook a 'subtle process of toughening up the Bill' (Windlesham, 1993, p. 451), reflecting a lack of confidence both in the support of its own members and in public opinion. As the issue of crime and justice became more visible, in this case particularly around a significant piece of proposed legislation, so it became more exposed to political manoeuvring, and more debates became more obviously sensitised to the climate of opinion. At this time, for instance, there appeared the early signs of the Labour Party repositioning itself on the issue of crime, and going 'on the attack' on an issue which had long been seen as a vote loser for them. By 1991, for example, there were reported to be: 'opinion polls that suggest that we are ahead of the Conservative Party. In relation to "Law and Order" there is a background which the Tories will find difficult to defend: crime has doubled since they have been in office' (Barry Sheerman, MP, Labour Spokesman on Home Affairs, quoted in Windlesham, 1993, p. 415).

There was, thus, at this point a sense in which the problem of crime and how it was perceived was beginning to become more politicised, and less clearly an issue simply to be managed by government and those responsible for the administration of criminal justice. For those who had perhaps come to view the achievements of the 1980s as a progressive product of enhanced 'systems management' (Jones, 2012), these rumblings of discontent were unhelpful indicators of what was to come.

Pushing things too far? The backlash and the 'punitive turn'

By the early 1990s, there appeared to be a coherent approach to diversion in place, and despite some persistent regional variations, the trends were all in the same direction (Jones, 2012). In 1992, with the number of arrests still in decline, the percentage of young offenders cautioned had reached over 71 per cent even for males aged 14–16. There was widespread satisfaction at the achievements of the previous decade, and diversion seemed to have achieved the double of both demonstrating effectiveness on a number of indicators, including re-offending, and attracting positive endorsement from influential figures (Goldson, 1999, p. 45).

The apparent solidity of the consensus around these developments had been further emphasised with the publication of the 1990 Home Office Circular (see previously), restating the centrality of cautioning in dealing with youth crime (Home Office, 1990a). This guidance was issued partly in response to continuing evidence of inconsistency in the use of out of court disposals (cautions and informal action) across different police areas (Lee, 1998, p. 63). Here, the emphasis was on extending collaboration between police and other agencies, both to establish common policy objectives and to enhance the quality of decision-making. In addition, the broad expansionary tone of the circular also seemed to underline the sense of a settled direction of travel: 'The expectation… that the consultative arrangements used with juveniles would be extended to all age groups, particularly to young adult offenders, also led to a general mood of optimism at the time' (Lee, 1998, p. 63). Here, perhaps significantly, was implicit evidence of the extension of the 'normal childhood' argument to a slightly older age group, who could now also be seen as less than fully responsible in adult terms, and therefore capable of 'growing out of crime' (Rutherford, 1992).

The circular continued to refer to the use of the courts as a 'last resort' (Jones, 2012, p. 212), and it was recognised as a response to 'very positive support for cautioning' from key organisation such as the Association of Chief Police Officers, and now, the Magistrates Association (Jones, 2012, p. 212), notwithstanding the disquiet of some of the association's members. As Jones (2012, p. 213) points out, this widespread support continued to make itself heard at the turn of the decade, as cautioning found strong endorsement from the House of Commons Home Affairs Committee, which in turn quoted the Metropolitan Police, the Crown Prosecution Service, NACRO and the Howard League as favourably disposed as well.

The principles which seemed to underlie the extended use of cautioning were also to be found in key aspects of the Criminal Justice Act 1991, which sought to enshrine the 'just deserts' principle into law systematically, in the way indicated by Windlesham (1993, p. 404). In effect, the Act appeared to offer something of a trade-off, with tougher community sentences put in place to offset the restrictions on the use of custody which it clearly intended to apply. Offences were to be dealt with in their own right, and the antecedents of offenders were to be given less weight, suggesting again a degree of consistency with diversion policies which allowed for repeat cautions and interventions based solely on the principle of responding to the reported offence in isolation, rather than taking into account the offender's history, background or needs.

Significantly, too, the 1991 Act introduced the youth court, and removed 17-year olds from the adult criminal jurisdiction. Here, criminal justice procedures for young offenders were effectively aligned with the international definition of childhood (0–18), building on the emerging rationale for treating the crimes of the young as being at least partly attributable to their non-adult status, and relative lack of maturity.

In effect, the Criminal Justice Act 1991 offered recognition and legitimacy to trends which were already well established. As Jones (2012, p. 219) points out, by 1990 the number of young offenders (under 17) sentenced to custody had continued to fall significantly during the latter part of the 1980s, at least partly reflecting diversionary efforts both at the entry point to the justice system and the sentencing stage. By 1992, there were fewer than 1,500 admissions of juvenile offenders to custody, and on 30th June 1989, there were just 590 young offenders under the age of 17 in prison department institutions (Jones, 2012, p. 219).

These trends had encouraged the government actually to abolish detention in a young offender institution altogether for 14 year olds in 1991, and there was no doubt that these successes were being attributed directly to the achievements of practitioners and strategic managers in cementing diversionary practices at the heart of their work. Some were less willing to attribute positive outcomes simply to the work of committed staff, though, pointing out, for instance, that the reductions in formal processing and custodial sentencing of juveniles also coincided with a fall in the relevant population, and declining levels of police resources and capacity (Jones, 2012, p. 225). Subsequent analysis, though, has suggested that the picture is actually quite complex, with youth population falls partly responsible, whilst changing government policies and diversionary practices could all be identified as contributing to the end result of a reduction in the use of custody (Graham, 2010, p. 106). Morgan and Newburn (2007, p. 1,027) agree on this point, acknowledging the substantial drop in the numbers of 14–16 year olds in the general population, but noting, too, that this would not account for the similarly substantial fall in the proportion of that age group being sentenced to custody. They also conclude that, one of the key reasons for this, 'crucially… was diversion from court. This was central to the significant decline in the number of juveniles prosecuted in the latter half of the 1980s…' (Morgan and Newburn, 2007, p. 1,027).

There were, however, limits to this story of steady progress. We have noted the continuing murmurings of disquiet amongst those who did not accept either the outcomes associated with diversion, or the underlying philosophy which relied on toleration, negotiation and management of problematic behaviour instead of punishment. We have also noted that, however progressive, diversionary initiatives operated within and according to conventional understandings of deviance, responsibility, blame and gravity. Much practice, for example, was grounded in strategies to mitigate guilt or provide exculpatory explanations for young people's behaviour. Although 'normalisation' may have been an underlying principle of diversionary schemes, this was found to be modified in the real life task of negotiating the lowest level of intervention achievable. Davis et al (1989, p. 224) describe one example of this form of reasoning from a practitioner at the Northampton Juvenile Liaison Bureau, as follows: 'Having completed an assessment visit, Carol [JLB worker] discusses her recommendation [to the police], which is for informal action. She goes through Melvyn's previous offences, arguing that each offence in itself is quite minor'.

In a sense, then, despite the demonstrable achievements of youth diversion to this point, it was still grounded in a form of justificatory argument based on making individualised cases for exceptional treatment. And therefore, diversion remained susceptible to counter arguments that might question the grounds for making such exceptions. And, referring back to our initial discussion of the alternative conceptual frames for understanding children and youth justice, these arguments could similarly claim that our prior understanding of childhood had been misconceived; or that diversionary practices were simply insufficient as a means of holding children to account.

Here then, the conceptual and operational weaknesses in the diversion project were subject to the consequences of unexpected events and concerted opposition. Alternative narratives were readily at hand to justify a quite different approach to dealing with youth crime. The 'punitive turn' (Muncie, 2008) was literally just around the corner. The reasons for the rapid about turn in criminal justice policy in the early 1990s are probably several, although there has certainly been a tendency to view one particular event as pivotal, namely the killing of James Bulger early in 1993 by two other boys, aged 10 and 11 (Jenks, 1996; Pitts, 2001, for example). This was certainly one of the most publicly prominent factors contributing to the changing climate, but it was certainly not the only one; and it is by no means certain that it would have had the same effect if it had occurred at a different point in time.

By then, certainly there had also been signs of a groundswell of opposition to the reforms of the Criminal Justice Act 1991, as well as a number of other perhaps less dramatic 'trigger events'. Firstly, as already noted, there had been a change of Prime Minister, and the newcomer to the role may well have felt that he needed to prove himself as 'tough' in order to secure legitimacy. Certainly, he was prepared to say that 'Society needs to condemn a little more and understand a little less', whilst also criticising what he saw as unduly lenient treatment of young offenders by the courts: 'They are nervous, it is the first time. They go again, they are less nervous. They go a third time, they say: "Well, who can do anything to us?"'(John Major, interview, *The Independent*, 21 March 1993).

In addition, the early 1990s had seen renewed outbreaks of rioting, notably in Cardiff, Blackbird Leys in Oxford and Meadow Well in North Shields. These areas had predominantly 'white' populations at the time and so it may have been more ideologically coherent to attribute these outbreaks of unrest to 'criminal' rather than political motivations or social causes.

Furthermore, the police had begun at that time to take a more active interest in what they saw as 'persistent offenders', with the Chief Constable of Northumbria spearheading the campaign and drawing attention to a number of high profile offenders in or near his area, including a young person who became demonised as 'Rat Boy' (Smith, 2003). More reasoned support for their concerns was provided by the police to the Home Affairs Select Committee in 1993, when they provided evidence of a substantial increase in youth crime between 1980 and 1990.

In the same way as certain elements of the police had consistently resisted the liberalisation of the 1980s, so the courts, too, had at best shown ambivalence to these developments, and especially what they saw as their own marginalisation in the justice process. There was also considerable hostility amongst sentencers to the restrictions on their powers incorporated into the 1991 legislation (Hudson,

1996). They disliked, in particular, the constraints on their ability to take account of previous offences when making sentencing decisions, since these went against the deeply ingrained belief in the sentencing tariff, and the perceived need to respond with greater force to repeated breaches of the law.

And, finally, the justice system became the focal point for a sustained bidding war between the leading political parties as to who could appear toughest on crime. This is commonly associated with the appointment of Tony Blair as Shadow Home Secretary, and his determination to demonstrate that Labour could be 'tough on crime, tough on the causes of crime' (*New Statesman*, 29 January 1993). Opposite him, Kenneth Clarke, who might normally have been thought of as a social liberal, rose to the challenge, stating that: 'the courts should have the power to send really persistent, nasty little juveniles away to somewhere where they will be looked after better and where they will be educated' (*Daily Mail*, 22 February 1993).

Rapid steps were taken, within the context of this newly forged political 'consensus', to toughen up the treatment of young offenders. Within months of the abolition of custody for 14-year olds, Clarke was announcing the creation of 200 new custodial places in what were to be called Secure Training Centres, and two further pieces of legislation (the Criminal Justice Act 1993 and the Criminal Justice and Public Order Act 1994) followed swiftly to restore broader sentencing powers to the courts and to expand the range of custodial options available.

By this time, Michael Howard had become Home Secretary and he had coined his own notorious soundbite: 'prison works' (speech to the Conservative Party Conference, 6th October 1993) on taking on this role. Unlike Clarke, his punitive credentials were certainly not in question, and his influence was certainly felt in the next revision of cautioning policy, which came in the form of Home Office Circular 18/1994. This guidance effectively reversed some of the assumptions which had become well established in diversion practice. Age was no longer to be viewed as a factor in its own right to influence cautioning decisions, and so, effectively a new set of assumptions about children's criminality and levels of responsibility was being incorporated into policy. In addition, the circular actively discouraged the administration of repeat cautions. Again, this represented a shift from an approach grounded in assumptions about growing out of crime and the nature of that particular process to a much stricter tariff-based model of intervention, suggesting a renewed commitment to a belief in the deterrent value of prosecution. And, furthermore, Circular 18/1994 modified the expectation that cautions should be the preferred disposal for young offenders in all but the most serious cases. Here, too, it seemed that historic assumptions about the meaning of justice, grounded in culpability, control and desert, were reasserting themselves, with the active encouragement of politicians with an eye to their election prospects.

As we have observed over the course of time, practice and policy do not usually coincide neatly. Often, indeed, it has seemed that changes in practice either anticipate or even prompt policy change, rather than the other way around. In this instance, however, there does seem to have been a fairly direct effect, as cautioning rates for young offenders went rapidly into reverse. Whilst it seems from the available figures that crime rates were stabilising, the new tougher policy regime produced immediate results, with cautioning declining in use quite sharply, both in absolute terms and as a proportion of those young offenders dealt with formally (that is cautioned or prosecuted). Across all sub-groups of the 10–17 age range and for both males and females, cautioning rates fell over the course of the decade 1990–2000, but the sharpest and most consistent decreases occurred after 1994. Thus, for example, the proportion of 15–17 year old males cautioned fell from 56 to 43 per cent over this period; whilst for females in the same age range, the equivalent fall was from 77 to 63 per cent.

In keeping with the more punitive spirit of the time, these changing patterns were mirrored by substantial increases in the use of the most severe penalties available to the courts. Whilst virtually no 12–14 year olds were sentenced to custody in 1994, the new tougher sentencing options available to the courts had been taken up actively by 2000, and 6 per cent of 12–14 year old convicted males were sent to custody in that year.

The changing pattern of disposals did generate interest and not a little concern amongst commentators, and there were a number of attempts to try and set what was happening within a broader criminological context. Goldson (1997) was one of those who saw the events of the early 1990s as representing a dramatic about-face in both dominant ideas and practices in dealing with the crimes of young people, commenting that 'a reactionary U-turn was launched which rapidly dismantled the successful practice of the previous decade [the 1980s] and set a harsh new tone in relation to state response to children in trouble' (Goldson, 1997, p. 79).

For others, though, there were discernible indications of continuity, and if anything a sense that the 'gains' of the 1980s had been somewhat illusory in that they had opened the way for a new, more procedural approach to intervention geared simple around calculating and managing the risk of further offending. Hudson described the emerging forms of practice as representing 'actuarial regimes', whose procedural basis offered no place for decisions grounded in ideas of leniency or normalisation. For Muncie, too, there was evidence of continuity, grounded in what seemed to be an increasingly prevalent corporatist approach, informed additionally by a tendency to continually copy 'punitive measures from America' (Muncie, 1999a, p. 298). Pickford (2000) also suggests that part of the explanation for the change of direction was simply to do with improved techniques in applying the principles of 'bifurcation'; as it became easier to distinguish between low and high risk offenders, so apparently, it would become easier to justify more intrusive measures of control for those posing the greatest future threat.

Institutionalised practices: the 'managerial turn'

The alarmist rhetoric of the 1990s had certainly contributed to the establishment of a new and more controlling mood amongst policy makers and criminal justice agencies. With dangerousness now established as a possible feature of (problem) childhoods, serious challenges appeared to present themselves for the state's management of their delinquencies. As Jenks (1996, p. 130) puts it:

'alongside the positing of innate evil and depravity as ways of accounting for why children commit violent crimes, other accounts struggled to explore the particularity of the social contexts, like dysfunctional families, which might foster, in the child, the ability to perform adult-like actions'. How would it be possible to distinguish between children whose upbringing and circumstances underpinned their wrongdoings from those who were just plain wicked? As Jenks (1996, p. 131) observes, there certainly remained a body of opinion which sought explanations for children's behaviour in their own experiences and social and moral conditioning, suggesting perhaps that there were still grounds for attempting to distinguish between those who could be reformed and whose needs could be addressed, and those for whom measures of stricter social control were the only feasible option. What was taking place at this point, in Jenks' (1996, p. 131) view, was 'the redrawing of the traditional boundaries of childhood'. So, for example, better resources to provide for 'disturbed children' (*The Guardian*, 27 November 1993) were called for, at the same time as more watchful and rigorous measures were put in place to control their behaviour: 'Truancy Watch, launched in autumn 1993, is designed to encourage the public policing of children' (Jenks, 1996, p. 133). Here, Jenks also identifies two other developments which were significant in changing the way in which the state intervened to deal with children and their behaviour at this point in time – a point in time when the economy was doing reasonably well, and there was scope, perhaps, for state expansionism. In effect, there was a reassertion of the principle of 'public accountability for children', which represented a revival of the idea of the child as 'public property', in whom the state had an interest in investing for the collective benefit (Jenks, 1996, p. 134). Additionally, though, there appeared to be evidence of a twin-track approach, with tighter control of children's freedom of movement and expression, on the one hand; but, on the other, increased support for interventions to meet their long-term needs and support pro-social behaviour, for instance in calls for 'earlier sex education' (Jenks, 1996, p. 134).

Within a context of increasing emphasis on effective management of state services and criminal justice interventions, then, the idea of improving mechanisms for distinguishing between young offenders on the basis of the level of threat they represented was an attractive one. In practical terms, the search for better and more effective solutions translated itself into a substantial and highly influential (for several reasons) inquiry conducted by the Audit Commission (1996). Although ostensibly established to review the question of whether or not the youth justice in England and Wales represented an efficient use of public money (Pitts, 2001, p. 42), the scale of the commission's inquiry was wide-ranging and included a considerable amount of material relating to the causes and nature of youth crime as well as the effectiveness of current or potential interventions. The existing youth justice system was described as 'inefficient and expensive, whilst little is being done to deal effectively with juvenile nuisance' (Audit Commission, 1996, p. 96). Everyone, it seemed, was being failed by a failing system, including 'young people – who are not being guided away from offending towards constructive activities... victims – those who suffer from young people's inconsiderate behaviour, and from vandalism and loss of property from thefts and burglaries… waste, in a variety of forms, including lost time… lost rents… lost business, as people steer clear of troubled areas; and waste of young people's potential' (Audit Commission, 1996, p. 96). Here then, with the combined authority of financial experts and informed criminological researchers, we had what seemed to be a definitive statement of a system in crisis, with cataclysmic collateral consequences; and this might perhaps be understandable given the limited time that had elapsed since the dramatic events of the early 1990s. Nonetheless, couched in this sort of formal language, of course the commission's findings came across as much more authoritative, but also compellingly urgent, and it represented a strong steer to politicians.

Despite its claims to authority and undoubted influence, *Misspent Youth* came in for substantial subsequent criticism (Jones, 2001). Nonetheless, it had a significant bearing on policy development in relation to juvenile diversion and early intervention. The commission was reporting in the later stages of the Conservative government's term of office with John Major as Prime Minister; and, in effect, it was addressing the incoming administration (due to take office in 1997) as much as the current government. So, its support for cautioning was significant, and 'fascinating', according to Jones (2001, p. 371). The Audit Commission evidently supported 'the concept of cautioning, as being low cost and effective', observed Jones, but at the same time he felt that the commission had significantly failed to understand current practice. Thus, for example, the report seriously underestimated the achievements of existing diversion schemes in terms of reported re-offending rates; and at the same time, overstated the merits of intervention in the form of prosecution for repeat offenders, a claim which was subsequently effectively challenged (Kemp et al., 2002). This effectively created a logical space for the Audit Commission to advocate a new form of disposal, and to follow this up subsequently with a stronger endorsement of this model of intervention (Audit Commission, 1998a). Here the combined goals of economic efficiency and effective crime prevention were neatly aligned, with the commission arguing that a 'cautioning plus' model could realise very substantial savings to the justice system (Audit Commission, 1996, p. 47). As Jones (2001, p. 372) observes, these suggestions were first aired in 1996 without a hint of irony, despite the fact that at this point 'there was a very clear Home Office policy discouraging the use of caution plus'. Nonetheless, the commission's reasoning appeared to provide a sound justification for the development or extension of models of intervention based on 'targeting' young people at risk of offending, or re-offending. Multi-agency working was also believed to be at the heart of effective practice, along the lines of the collaborative diversion scheme developed in Northamptonshire and examples from elsewhere in Europe: 'Youth justice services in all areas without multi-agency "caution plus" schemes will have to develop them rapidly in order to manage young people' (Audit Commission, 1998b, p. 8).

Once again, Jones (2001, p. 373) questions the basis of the commission's conclusions, suggesting that they represent a selective reading of 'noncomparable studies'; but, importantly, the source of the conclusions drawn was widely viewed as impeccable, with good practice apparently backed up by good economics. And, at the same time, the broader framing of the problem fitted well with the worldview of the incoming New Labour government. Indeed, it is hard to escape the suspicion that the *Misspent Youth* initiative was undertaken by the Audit Commission with just this eventuality in mind, especially as one of the lead contributors to this work went on to become the first Chief Executive of the newly formed Youth Justice Board (see Jones, 2001, p. 376).

Significantly, though, at no point in this major exercise in reviewing the youth justice system did the dramatic reversal of the early 1990s in policy and practice come under the microscope. The challenges were framed simply in terms of efficiencies and effectiveness, in a manner which appeared to reflect wider preoccupations with managing services better, almost in place of principled policy objectives. It was quite striking at the time that one of the famous 'pledges' made by Labour in its pre-election campaign in 1997 was simply to 'speed up' the delivery of justice for young people, rather than to achieve other perhaps more worthy sounding aims such as promoting fairer and more socially just forms of criminal justice intervention. The more detailed manifesto for that election made a commitment to replace 'repeat' cautioning with a system of 'warnings' with the clear implication that persistent offending would not be tolerated. Still fearful of appearing soft on crime, Labour took the initiative by claiming it as one of the party's key issues, and taking a tough stance on tackling the problem. This, in turn, limited the incoming government's room for manoeuvre. Pitts (2001), for example argues that the White Paper *No More Excuses* and the Crime and Disorder Act 1998 which followed it were the product of a 'rush' by the new government to prove itself; and, indeed, to prove itself on political terrain which had previously been seen as the property of the Conservative Party:

The political message was clear. And it was, pre-eminently, a message to the Conservative voters who had defected to Labour in 1997. It said, 'we will keep our promises, we will fulfil your expectations, we will assuage your fears and confound your enemies and because of this, you will re-elect us' (Pitts, 2001, p. 38).

So, the technicist project of improving the system (by reducing 'delay' amongst other things) would be aligned with a greater degree of certainty about the outcomes of the justice process and the consequences of offending. Here, the whole tone of developments was to generate mechanisms for intervention which would calibrate risk and ascertain the correct level of response to address the identified problem. This kind of formulation of course fitted neatly with a more conventional and well established belief in a progressive tariff of interventions. Here, then, is the space where the arguments for greater efficiency find themselves in tune with deeper seated desires for stronger and more effective forms of control and punishment. And so, the whole tenor of youth justice policy turned towards a preoccupation with the levers of control, as I argued at the time, likening the Crime and Disorder Act 1998 to a model of criminal justice associated with Foucault (1979):

> We should, perhaps, be unsurprised to find a preoccupation with surveillance, assessment, measurement, scrutiny and behaviour management. In other words, we can expect there to be a policy-led concentration on quasi-scientific techniques of control and behavioural change.
>
> (Smith, 2001, p. 17)

Building on the proposals of the White Paper, *No More Excuses* (Home Office, 1997), the Crime and Disorder Act 1998 established a new framework for diversion, dispensing with the previous terminology, also as a symbolic marker of radical change (although some considered it rather as simply radical repackaging; Smith, 2003). So, cautions were to be dispended with, and along with this step, the new legislation created a statutory basis for out of court disposals for the first time; previously, cautioning had been steered in policy terms by formal guidance rather than being prescribed in law.

In place of cautions, young people who offended were now to be subject to a 'reprimand' for a first offence, and almost without exception a 'warning' for a subsequent offence, subject to certain qualifications in terms of seriousness and length of time since an earlier offence. As time went on, the warning became more commonly known as a Final Warning, with the obvious implication that it should be seen as the last chance for a young person before a court appearance in the event of a further offence. With the implementation of the 1998 Act, it also became clear that the gradation of disposals was also to be mirrored by a gradation of interventions, and the Final Warning was expected to be accompanied by some sort of structured assessment and supervisory programme, going well beyond the 'telling off' that was essentially envisaged for the reprimand. Here, then, the idea of the 'caution plus' was to be found reconfigured. As Goldson (1999) points out, the new regime for administering final warnings appeared to be considerably more systematic and rigorous than the arrangements which had preceded the proposed legislation. New *National Standards for Youth Justice* were highly prescriptive as to the procedures to be followed; and within ten working days of the administration of the Final Warning, an assessment of the young person was to be carried out, comprising as a minimum, interviews with the young person and her/his parents or carers, discussions with agency partners and a review of any previous reports on the young person (Goldson, 1999, p. 38). Should this assessment reveal the need for further rehabilitative work, it would be the responsibility of the multi-agency Youth Offending Team (also established under the 1998 Act) to construct a tailored intervention programme to address: the factors contributing to the commission of the offence; the contribution of parents or carers to achieving the programme objectives; the needs of the victim of the offence; and, the potential for the young person to make amends, or to develop better insight into the effects of criminal activity (Goldson, 1999, p. 39).

For Goldson, this raised serious concerns about the 'interventionist priorities that underpin the Final Warning', and the corresponding implications for the potential lack of proportionality between offence and response. Additionally, of course, there would be concerns about the potential effects of excessive early attention and intervention in terms of 'undue criminalisation and labelling' (Goldson, 1999, p. 39); fears which have, in fact, been given greater substance as a result of detailed empirical investigation of the adverse and criminalising consequences of 'system contact' (McAra and McVie, 2007). For some, the prospect of the re-emergence of the questionable practices of earlier decades was alarming. Without the protection of children's rights to fair and appropriate treatment or minimum intervention: 'It is also conceivable – no inevitable – that the concept of proportionality will be stood on its head with more intrusive interventions being provided on the basis of pre-court warnings for less serious offences than those disposals that are the sole prerogative of the court' (Bell, 1999, p. 203). And, at the same time, argued Bell, there would be an increase in the number of young people going to court, often for 'minor infringements' with the imposition of a binding limit on the number of out of court disposals available to any individual child. The ratcheting up of young people's criminalisation would also, in Goldson's (1999, p. 39) view, be compounded by the provision of the Crime and Disorder Act for any previous reprimands or warnings to be cited in court, unlike informal disposals under the previous arrangements. Here, then, was further evidence of the consequences of New Labour's 'tough on crime' stance. And, yet further, the Crime and Disorder Act 1998 precluded the administration off a conditional discharge by the court where a young person had previously been in receipt of a Final Warning. The 'consequences… are clearly to "up-tariff" children', Goldson observes (1999, p. 40). I previously described the effects of these measures in combination as an 'intensification' of the justice system, with children and young people being progressively subject to more substantial and more demanding interventions at each point in the spectrum of disposals.

Muncie concluded, too, that any: 'assessment of the [1998] Act's impact on young offenders must acknowledge that it represents a marked expansion of the legal means through which young people's behaviour can be circumscribed.... What marks out Labour's initiatives is the emphasis placed on "nipping offending in the bud"' (Muncie, 1999b, p. 169). Here, then, we are confronted with what amounts to a policy of 'institutionalised intolerance' (Muncie, 1999b, p. 171). This mood of intolerance was arguably fuelled additionally by the flurry of legislative and policy activity concerned with tackling 'anti-social behaviour', notably associated with the introduction of the Anti-social Behaviour Order in 1999, and the subsequent addition of a further array of associated interventions such as the Acceptable Behaviour Contract. Here, the same logic and forensic approach to intervention were being applied under New Labour to what was merely pre-criminal behaviour, but effectively extended the net even further, precisely calling to mind the idea of 'wider, stronger and different nets' set out so presciently by Austin and Krisberg (2002).

In terms of outcomes, perhaps it is surprising that there was not a greater expansion of the system following the implementation of the 1998 Act and other related reforms in youth justice. In fact, what was evident was a much greater level of continuity than might have been expected, either from the political rhetoric, or from the development of a much greater array of options for intervention under a government with a great propensity for micro-management. Bateman (2006), for instance, argued that, despite the legislative upheaval, patterns established well before 1998 had remained unaltered. Thus, for example the rate of diversion of young offenders (with cautions now replaced by reprimands and final warnings) had continued to decline from a peak in 1992 (73.5 %) to 55.9 % in 2003. The same time period had seen a 55 per cent increase in the imposition of custodial sentences for those under the age of 18, maintaining the position of England and Wales amongst the highest users of custody in Europe (Bateman, 2006, p. 74).

Diversion and the 'risky' child

The culmination of this period of closer control and tighter systems management was perhaps predictably a narrower space for the exercise of diversion; and at the same time there was a redefinition of diversionary practices to involve a greater level of risk-based 'preventive' intervention. As I have also noted elsewhere (Smith, 2011), the focus had shifted over this period from the offence and its context, to the offender and her/his characteristics. Diversion was by now much less concerned with resolving the offence and achieving closure, and much more about changing the offender's behaviour or, at least, reducing the risk that s/he would reoffend:

> Intervention is increasingly reserved for children and young people perceived to be *facing risk* (normally code for those at the sharpest end of the child protection system) or *posing risk* (potential or actual 'anti-social', 'disorderly' and/or offending children and young people) (*his emphasis*).
>
> (Goldson, 2010, p. 169)

Youth justice had by this point become infused with a logic of 'actuarialism' (Smith, 2006), operating at all points in the system. This was supported by a machinery of risk assessment and risk management, epitomised by the development of tools such as ASSET, geared towards identifying a whole range of criminogenic risk factors for young people, and using this as the basis for informing interventions, even at the pre-prosecution stage. Thus, a shortened version of the ASSET form was adopted for use in the case of final warnings, with the aim of tailoring interventions to identified problem areas associated with the likelihood of re-offending. However, this construction of the approach to assessment appeared to have the potential merely to focus on 'problems' and thus to provide confirmatory evidence to justify additional interventions. With a focus on scoring highly subjective indicators such as 'thinking behaviour and attitudes, "soft" information becomes quantifiable, offering a seemingly authoritative basis for significant decisions about state intervention with children and young people' (Smith, 2006, p. 97). And, in turn, the potential for such impressionistic 'evidence' to support processes leading to institutionalised discrimination should perhaps also be a matter of considerable concern. May et al (2010, p. 84) note the tendency for black young people to score more highly on ASSET assessments than their white peers. Here again, the 'inclusive' potential of systematic and apparently objective processes is noteworthy:

> Of course, the scope for negative assessment based upon appearance, attitude, or simply 'being in the wrong place at the wrong time' is enormous, with associated implications for the institutionalisation of oppressive practices and discrimination.
>
> (Smith, 2006, p. 97)

6 Another 'U' turn?

Diversion and community justice

The road to excess

Much has been written about the period of New Labour government and its legacy, and much of that has been critical, not least from the present author. It would perhaps be tempting to repeat much of that criticism here, but this would possibly be to misrepresent the dynamics of diversion to some extent. As has become increasingly clear over the course of this account, government intentions, changes in policy and major reorganisations of delivery mechanisms only bear a tangential relationship to changes in the organisation and delivery of diversion in practice. So, the spirit of interventionism and micro-control which certainly exemplified the period from 1997–2007 could perhaps account for some of the trends associated with that era; but in sustaining an intrusive and ultimately punitive approach to the crimes of young people, it could also be said to be simply extending the punitive shift of the early 1990s into the new millennium.

Paradoxically, as Bateman (2015, p. 6) has observed, the wider context is one of 'a long term decline' in both officially (police) recorded crime and population-wide crime surveys, although these measures do probably underestimate the extent to which much crime may now have shifted online. Depending on whether the police statistics or the Crime Survey for England and Wales figures are used, the falling crime trend can be dated from 1992 or 1995. Whichever is the case, the overall picture of a steady and sustained pattern of reductions in offending rates seems to be crystal clear. Although it is virtually impossible to disentangle youth crime specifically from the overall figure, Bateman (2015, p. 7) argues that there is no reason to believe that the trends for this age group should be different from those for adult offenders, and: 'Indeed, given that children are more likely to engage in relatively unsophisticated criminal activity, in public places' (Bateman, 2015, p. 7), their crimes are actually more likely to come to public and police attention. There is therefore correspondingly less likelihood of a massive volume of hidden offending by younger offenders distorting the overall pattern. Further, more recent, confirmation of the increasingly law abiding nature of children and young people is offered by the substantial reduction in police recorded incidents of anti-social behaviour, according to Bateman (2015, p. 6), although he does acknowledge the subjective and inconsistent nature of the data in this context.

It seems, and given all that we know this is perhaps unsurprising, changes in the nature and extent of out of court intervention with children do not readily map onto wider trends in offending and victimisation. Explaining change here, as elsewhere in the social policy arena, probably requires an approach grounded in an appreciation of the multiple levels at which influencing factors operate, at the same time as recognising that such factors themselves are diverse and, of course, unpredictable. Muncie (2002), for example, saw the raft of New Labour initiatives on taking power as representing just such an amalgam of competing and sometimes contradictory dynamics and ideologies. By this point (the early 2000s), he argued, youth justice could be seen as a complex amalgam of: just deserts; risk assessment; managerialism; community responsibilisation; authoritarian populism; and restorative justice (Muncie, 2002, p. 156). So, he argued, New Labour's reputed modernisation of youth justice had meant that innovations had simply been 'added into existing youth justice discourse', keeping 'authoritarian, responsibilisation and remoralisation discourses firmly in place' (Muncie, 2002, p. 158). Of course, though, as both Foucault (1979) and Cohen (1985) have observed, there is an inexorable logic at play when the object of intervention policy and practice is to exert greater control and extend social order; this is essentially a logic of expansion as the possibility of extending mechanisms of monitoring and compliance further and further into the domain of the social seems to become more viable. The certainty offered by increasingly sophisticated assessment tools, and finer and finer gradations of intervention according to the offender profile persuades us that such objectives are, indeed, achievable and thus worth pursuing.

The problem, though, is that just at the point where certainty appears within our grasp we become aware of the limitations of our knowledge and the mechanisms at our disposal, much in the way that Beck (1992) predicts. Continual expansion in search of perfect knowledge and predictable outcomes brings its own pitfalls, illustrated well by the anti-social behaviour initiative, launched by New Labour shortly after coming to power. Here, children and young people were targeted for 'diversion' from crime, but on the basis of 'nuisance' behaviour, rather than the commission of offences. The standards of evidence were relaxed for action to be taken, and there was a rush, at least in some parts of the country, to put the new powers afforded to local agencies into practice; and this was further supported by government ministers (both Straw and Blunkett as successive Home Secretaries), who continually exhorted local authorities to make greater use of the Anti-social Behaviour Order (ASBO):

> The anti-social behaviour of a few damages the lives of many. We should never underestimate its impact. We have seen the way communities spiral downwards once windows get broken and are not fixed, graffiti spreads and stays there, cars are left abandoned, streets get grimier and dirtier, youths hang around street corners intimidating the elderly. The result: crime increases, fear goes up and people feel trapped.
>
> (Blunkett, 2003, p. 2)

All this at a time when crime rates were actually falling, according to the figures available, and presumably of interest to the Home Secretary!

As has been widely reported, the results of this expansionary approach to the problem behaviour of the young were hugely concerning (Burney, 2005; Squires, 2008). Particular injustices were experienced by children whose 'problematic' behaviour was associated with other conditions, such as the effects of brain injuries or recognised learning difficulties (Smith, 2014, p. 52). Where ASBOs were breached, and despite the diminished evidential requirements for the making of an order, many of those concerned were then made subject to custodial sentences, creating a net widening, 'tariff- jumping' effect, which led to an 'artificially steep and slippery slope into custody' (Squires and Stephen, 2005, p. 109).

Reviewing New Labour's 'scorecard' on youth justice, the Centre for Crime and Justice Studies conducted an audit of achievements over the period 1997–2007, which similarly identified expansionary tendencies, but little evidence of tangible achievements. Between 2000/01 and 2006/07, for example, youth justice spending had increased in real terms by 45 per cent (Solomon and Garside, 2008, p. 9). At the same time, however, the authors of this report found little evidence to support claims of success in reducing youth offending or re-offending, where patterns of decline simply reflected wider trends (Solomon and Garside, 2008, p. 37). Equally worrying from their perspective was that increased spending on the scale identified had produced unacceptable results, according to the government's own targets, in terms of improvements in provision to meet the welfare needs of children in the justice system.

As Goldson (2010) has put it, the combined effects of an array of interventionist, expansionary and 'tough' policies on youth crime was both harmful and wasteful; and at the same time, these developments seemed to fly in the face of what was 'known' about best practice in addressing youthful infractions.

The wheel turns again: policy reversals and 'innovations'

One further expansionary initiative of the New Labour government had quite dramatic consequences for young people on the margins of the justice system; and ironically this could well have been one of the eventual drivers of a more positive approach to diversion from about 2008 onwards. In a move which combined several of the worst features of New Labour, managerialism, faux 'toughness', populism, short termism, rejection of expert advice and disregard of potential unintended consequences, the government introduced a new target for the police, the Offences Brought to Justice (OBTJ) or 'sanction detection' target (Kemp, 2014) in 2002. This was intended to improve police detection rates, but had an immediate net widening effect as a result of the perverse incentives associated with this target which encouraged the police to deal formally with offences which would previously have been dealt with by way of informal or even no action at all. This type of offence, which typically involved nuisance and minor criminal behaviour by young people (low hanging fruit), was easy to identify and detect, with what should perhaps have been predictable consequences. In fact, the police comfortably exceeded the ambitious OBTJ target, but essentially this was achieved by drawing in a greater number of young people at the fringes of the justice system. Thus, as Kemp (2014, p. 2) notes, the number of 'out-of-court disposals' increased by 135 per cent between 2003 and 2008; whilst Bateman (2015, p. 11) notes that the number of 'first time entrants' to the justice system rose by almost a third between 2002/03 and 2006/07; whilst the total number of disposals pre- and post-court administered to young offenders increased from 168,673 to 216,011 (Solomon and Garside, 2008, p. 40). Perversely, over the same period the percentage of young people cautioned as a proportion of all disposals actually increased, whilst the Youth Justice Board had in place at the time (from 2005) yet another target, to reduce the number of first time entrants by 20 per cent. Bateman (2015, p. 32) is certain that:

> Large numbers of minor offences, that would previously have been dealt with informally, were drawn into the formal youth justice process so that the use of reprimands and final warnings grew more rapidly than convictions. The increased use of pre-court measures is accordingly evidence of net-widening rather than demonstrating that children were less likely to be prosecuted.

Kemp's research into the subject revealed the extent to which policing practices had been skewed in response to the OBTJ target, quoting a number of police respondents expressing frustration at the kind of tasks expected of them. For example: 'You get a fight in a school playground – a nothing job. In the old days we would have taken them home and interviewed them in front of their parents but now they are brought into custody' (Police Inspector, quoted in Kemp, 2014, p. 4).

Although this state of affairs was allowed to persist for five years, opposition to the OBTJ target was consistent and voiced in a number of influential quarters. Perhaps as the first signs of an economic downturn began to make themselves felt, there was concern amongst those responsible for policing policy that rather too much police officer time was being concentrated on formal interventions which were simply unnecessary and were solely being driven by the dominant performance culture of the time. A major review of policing was commissioned in 2007, and one of its early conclusions was that:

> An emphasis on sanction detection levels has undoubtedly to a degree produced the unintended effect of [police] officers spending time investigating crimes with a view to obtaining a detection even when that is clearly not in the public interest.
>
> (Flanagan, 2007, p. 10)

This view was loudly echoed by the outgoing chair of the Youth Justice Board (YJB), Rod Morgan, and it was the intransigence of government on this and other issues which prompted his resignation from that position in January 2007:

> During my tenure at the YJB there has been a 26% increase in the number of children and young people criminalised. A key driver of this trend is the government's target to increase the number of offences brought to justice annually to 1.25m by spring 2008. The government boasts that the current achievement—at 1.4m offences brought to justice per annum— is well ahead of target. But how is this figure being achieved? Not by prosecuting and convicting many more serious offenders. On the contrary, the number of convictions in court has been flat-lining. The big increase has almost entirely been achieved by handing out on-the-spot fines or formal cautions for relatively minor offences.
>
> (Morgan, 2007b)

Morgan also pointed out rather stridently that this focus on less serious offenders was diverting police and other justice agencies' time and effort away from dealing with more serious and entrenched offending, combining both wastefulness and effectively greater rather than reduced risk to the public.

Even the Youth Justice Board noted in its 2007 annual report that changes in policing behaviour were having consequences in terms of the numbers of young people coming into the justice system, acknowledging the tendency for minor and easily detectable offences to be disproportionately committed by young people.

These concerns, expressed more publicly than was comfortable for government, seem to have prompted an urgent rethink, and a gradual climb-down, with the revision of the OBTJ target to concentrate on more serious offences, followed by its eventual abolition with a change in government in 2010 (Kemp, 2014, p. 2).

Certainly this seems to have been the point at which the criminalising tendencies of the previous fifteen years in youth justice policy were put into reverse. Concerted efforts were now made to stem the flow of young people into the system, and to give real substance to objectives such as the reduction in the number of first time entrants. Whilst still somewhat hesitant, government policy documents began to make more explicit commitments to this goal, as in the case of the 2008 *Youth Crime Action Plan* (HM Government, 2008). Despite retaining the by now mandatory veneer of toughness, this plan tried to incorporate both a more liberal tone, and strategies which might support a de-emphasis of formal processing of children and young people in trouble. The vehicle for this approach was a 'triple-track' strategy, which would combine 'enforcement and punishment where behaviour is unacceptable, non-negotiable challenge where it is most needed, and better and earlier prevention' (Smith et al., 2008, p. 1). Ostensibly, this appeared to combine the same robust and interventionist approach as previously associated with New Labour, but probably deliberately buried in the detail of the plan, and falling under the heading of 'prevention', there was a statement of a 'desire to see an improvement in the support services to children in, or at risk of entering the youth justice system… underpinned by Public Service Agreement… objectives to reduce new entrants to the youth justice system and to reduce overall offending' (HM Government, 2008, p. 11). At the same time, though, the government claimed credit for 'stopping repeat cautioning to ensure that prolific offenders go to court' (HM Government, 2008, p. 17).

New initiatives were launched, however, with the proposal to pilot the 'Youth Restorative Disposal' which would constitute an innovative approach to dealing with what were described as 'low level first time offences' (HM Government, 2008, p. 21); although for those who had been involved in restorative diversionary practices some twenty years previously (Blagg, 1985) this perhaps did not seem to be quite as much of an innovation as was claimed for it.

Within the *Youth Crime Plan* it was proposed also to pilot the idea of a 'youth conditional caution' (with the option of requiring some form of reparation to victims) for 16–17 year olds whose offending did not necessitate immediate prosecution, but who might have exhausted the options afforded by reprimands and final warnings. Certainly, there did appear to be a change of tone, as represented by this plan and its immediate predecessor, the *Children's Plan* (Department for Children, Schools and Families, 2007). Young offenders were now being treated as part of a wider cadre of 'disadvantaged' children (Department for Children, Schools and Families, 2007, p. 115), and the complexity of their lives was also now acknowledged: 'Young victims and offenders can be the same people subject to the same problems and risk factors' (p. 137). The promotion of restorative interventions was also perhaps confusingly elided with a concern for the needs of offenders: 'The Youth Restorative Disposal aims to prevent re-offending through a more rehabilitative approach' (p. 139). There would also be a focus on improving education provision for young offenders 'in custody and the community' (p. 141). Despite the renewed interest in addressing the underlying welfare needs of children who offend: 'For some young offenders custody will be right and necessary' (p. 140). The overall impression conveyed in this omnibus package of proposed reforms is of a much more disparate approach to youth justice policy than had been pursued immediately preceding the launch of these major 'plans'. Here, then, the interventionist tone of the Labour administration was not diminished, but the policy agenda was becoming more diffuse, and perhaps permissive, in the sense of encouraging a range of differently framed 'pilot' projects and recognising the need to account more sensitively to the complexities of young people's lives. At least implicitly, perhaps this also represented a tacit acknowledgement of the 'diverse meanings of diversion', and the challenge of accommodating these within a unified policy framework (Kelly and Armitage, 2015, p. 119). Further support for the suggestion of a degree of diversification in diversionary policy and practice was provided by yet more 'pilot' programmes, albeit this time grounded in more conventional understandings of risk and need. The Youth Justice Board initiated a 'Triage' scheme in 2008, with the aim of providing a more systematic framework for calculating the appropriate form of intervention at the point where young people came to the attention of the police; and the Department of Health established a pathfinder Youth Justice Liaison and Diversion programme in six areas ' to enhance health provision within the youth justice system and facilitate help for children and young people with mental health and developmental problems, speech and communication difficulties and other similar vulnerabilities' (Haines et al., 2012, p. 7).

Before moving on to the practice implications of this new permissive mood in the policy arena, it is important first to consider the impact of the next phase of the unfolding political story, with the transfer of power to, first a Conservative-led coalition (from 2010) and then a fully-fledged Tory administration (2015).

A rehabilitation revolution?

It is perhaps somewhat ironic that the minister responsible for criminal justice under the new government in 2010 was the self-same Kenneth Clarke who had contributed significantly to the initiation of the 'punitive turn' in youth justice in the early 1990s (see Chapter 5). Perhaps it was guilt, or just a more permissive leadership which encouraged him to reassert his liberal credentials at this point in time. Clarke set the tone by announcing that he found the current prison population (in 2010) of 85,000 as an 'astonishing' figure, which would have been 'ridiculous' (*The Guardian*, 30 June 2010) to predict at the time when he had previously held the office of Home Secretary in 1992–3 (when the comparable figure was around 44,000). He began to speak of a 'rehabilitation revolution', and argued forcefully for an end to the competitive bidding war between the leading political parties as to who was toughest on crime. Predictably, perhaps, he met immediate opposition from his Labour counterpart, Jack Straw, who was not so ready to give up such posturing, claiming in effect that the provision of extra prison places by Labour had itself contributed to a fall in crime (*Daily Mail*, 30 June 2010). As a sharp reminder that one speech alone could not transform the terms of the justice debate, though, this was indicative of what was to come, with plenty of opposition from within his own party directed towards Clarke. Former Home Secretary Michael Howard (of 'prison works' fame; Chapter 5), stated that he was 'not convinced by [Clarke's] speech. Serious and persistent criminal need to be put in prison' (*The Guardian*, 30 June 2010).

Clarke responded forcefully, in a determined attempt to break down what was clearly an established political consensus. In his next public move, a speech to the judiciary, he turned to the evidence (again, a surprising move for a politician, it might seem), and pointed to the absence of any clear correlation between prison use and crime rates. Crime, he observed, had fallen 'throughout most of the western world in the 1990s', irrespective of the prevailing approach to sentencing in any particular country (*The Guardian*, 14 July 2010). Significantly, too, his colleague, then Home Secretary Theresa May joined him in an attack on New Labour's obsessive interventionism, especially at the lower end of the scale. May opted to turn her fire on the Anti-social Behaviour Order, suggesting that Labour had compiled a 'ludicrous list' of sanctions to deal with such behaviour, which were, she said, poorly understood, even by professionals, and inconsistently applied in different parts of the country. Such measures were both 'complex and bureaucratic' and at the same time 'they too often criminalised young people unnecessarily, acting as a conveyor belt to serious crime and prison' (*The Guardian*, 28 July 2010). Excessive use of harmful interventions at the lower end of the justice system was thus explicitly associated with the failings of the previous administration, helping to establish a clearly defined break in the policy narrative, at least in rhetorical terms. Like Clarke, May was beginning to speak of measures that would be rehabilitative and 'restorative' rather than 'criminalising and coercive'. Aligning excessively punitive measures with the claims of over-government frequently associated with Labour administrations enabled these ministers to dismiss them on the grounds of wastefulness, which perhaps played better than a straightforward claim to liberal sentiments, which were by no means associated with the Tory faithful. Clarke was clearly aware of this, and threw them a bone or two at his party's conference in the same year, stating that: 'career criminals and violent, dangerous criminals should be in prison… not roaming our streets' (Clarke, 2010). This intervention is redolent of previous attempts to establish a clear distinction between those offenders who represent a real danger, and the great majority whose misdemeanours amount to little more than nuisance value – a form of 'bifurcation' (Bottoms, 1977). The process of 'organising consent' for this change of approach and the challenge it represented to Tory instincts was supported by careful marshalling of evidence from sympathetic sources such as the Centre for Social Justice, recognised as a right leaning think tank, which produced a series of reports on the theme of criminal justice, and youth offending in particular. Here, again, the core arguments were framed around the wastefulness of over punitive approaches to intervention, and the importance of pursuing policies to promote the reintegration of those identified as offenders.

The new agenda for criminal justice was set out in detail in the major policy document *Breaking the Cycle* (Ministry of Justice, 2010), where claims of a new approach to young offenders were strongly expressed. Here, there was an explicit commitment to tackling the unnecessary escalation of young people up the tariff at the early stages of offending:

> Under the current system of out of court disposals, young offenders are automatically escalated to a more intensive disposal, regardless of the circumstances or severity of their offence…. We believe that this rigid approach can needlessly draw young people into the criminal justice system, when an informal intervention could be more effective in making the young person face up to the consequences of their crime, provide reparation for victims and prevent further offending.
>
> (Ministry of Justice, 2010, p. 68)

Instead, a clear commitment was made to enhancing and supporting the use of discretion by police and other agencies in their localities:

> The police, working in partnership with other local agencies, will have more freedom to determine the most appropriate response, depending on the severity of the offence and the circumstances of the young offender. This could involve reparation or interventions such as a referral to mental health provision to tackle offending behaviour.
>
> (Ministry of Justice, 2010, p. 69)

It would be linked to the newly proposed mechanism of payment by results giving 'providers the freedom to innovate, paying them according to the outcomes they achieve and opening up the market to diverse new players…' (Ministry of Justice, 2010, p. 38).

So local innovation was to be encouraged, and the examples given suggested, too, that a variety of approaches would be acceptable, spanning welfare-based interventions, restorative programmes, or even in some cases the use of simple penalty notices. This was further expanded upon by the minister for policing and criminal justice, Nick Herbert, who stressed the value of reinstating 'professional discretion', eradicating the prevailing 'top-down culture', promoting 'partnerships with the public' and re-emphasising the 'responsibility of the offender' (Herbert, 2011). The administration of criminal justice would, in effect, be taken out of the 'narrow confines of the justice system' and restored to the community.

There was, indeed, a close alignment between these sentiments and wider priorities of the new Conservative led coalition, including the articulation of the concept of the Big Society and a strong emphasis on localism and freeing communities from top-down control to develop their own creative solutions to problems understood better by them than remote government officials. The culmination of the reform programme initiated by Kenneth Clarke was the Legal Aid, Sentencing and Punishment of Offenders (LASPO) Act 2012. Whilst the act was believed to represent something of a modification of the lofty ambitions of *Breaking the Cycle*, and came in for some criticism for its more punitive features (National Association for Youth Justice, 2011), some aspects of the legislation clearly represented a continuing commitment to rehabilitative principles, such as new measures to curb the use of custodial remands for children (Smith, 2014, p. 71).

Importantly, too, the LASPO Act replaced reprimands and final warnings with the former terminology of cautioning; and at the same time, provided explicitly for the use of repeat cautions and an end to the fairly rigid progressive tariff represented by the previous model of pre-court disposals. Just as was the case in 1991, a right-wing government chose to introduce a modification to the tariff, this time by providing both for the repeat use of out of court disposals, and also on occasion for the use of a lesser sanction (a simple or a conditional caution) even in respect of a young person who may have a previous conviction. So here again was a shift of emphasis from focusing on the offender's characteristics, or the measurable level of risk associated with her/him, and back towards finding local solutions for the problems associated with the offence. Restorative practices would actually sit much better within this kind of decision-making framework than strict tariff-based requirements, at least in principle.

These new out of court provisions were accompanied by detailed operational guidance from the Youth Justice Board (Walker and Harvey-Messina, 2012). The guidance specified a threefold repertoire of disposals available to agencies, highlighting that the approach taken should be offence based, rather than being determined principally by offender characteristics or offending history. The alternative options were to be: Community Resolutions, Youth Cautions and

Youth Conditional Cautions; and the option taken should be determined by the specific circumstances of the offence, with the offender's history and victim's views also to be taken into account. Flexibility was encouraged in determining the specific content of the disposal chosen, and the guidance also made clear that:

> Disposals may be used in any order even for those who have a previous conviction.... The minimum appropriate disposal should be used and should include a restorative justice element (their emphasis).
>
> (Walker and Harvey-Messina, 2012)

For once, this did seem to be a significant revision of the policy framework, providing considerable scope for an extension of informal and diversionary disposals for young offenders:

> The new framework for out-of-court disposals is a real opportunity to reduce the unnecessary criminalisation of children.
>
> (Hart, 2012, p. 4)

Even though the frailty of bold policy moves was further underlined with a new, more right-wing Justice Secretary, Chris Grayling announcing a further review of out of court disposals as early as April 2013, there was certainly a sense of possibilities being opened up by the legislation which was not immediately dampened by this prospect.

New agendas: reinventing diversion?

Once again, it is important to restate the degree of discontinuity between policy and practice. Undoubtedly the LASPO legislation represented a significant endorsement of a more open-ended, diverse and non-interventionist approach to diversion; but, at the same time, many of the innovations heralded by the 2012 legislation and accompanying policy documents were already in place, and some were already well-established. Community Resolutions, for example, were very similar in nature to the Youth Restorative Disposal (YRD), introduced several years previously (Bateman, 2015, p. 27). Certainly, it appeared that there was considerable continuity between the array of initiatives launched in the late 2000s and those in place following the changes associated with the LASPO Act, despite the coalition government's claim that its policies represented a dramatic break from the past. This assertion, though, 'is unsurprising', as Bateman (2014, p. 417) comments, 'as that is what politicians do'.

Certainly, by 2008 there was clearly a mood change, and one which sought actively to promote a range of innovations in diversionary practice. This was nonetheless expressed in rather cautious terms with a series of 'pilot' projects, framed in terms of relatively modest goals and scope. The YRD, for example, was designed to be administered summarily by the police, and it was expected that it would be available only once to young people found to be responsible for 'low-level, anti-social and nuisance offending' (Rix et al., 2011, p. 2), and only where the young person had not previously received a reprimand, final warning or caution. Other agencies would be notified of the use of the YRD, but its use was to remain entirely at the discretion of the police. In effect, then, the YRD was envisaged very much as an equivalent form of intervention to the forms of informal action which had pre-dated the introduction of reprimands and final warnings. As its description suggests, the Youth Restorative Disposal was intended to include a 'restorative' element where this was appropriate. An early evaluation of the YRD pilots found that this element usually took the form of an apology, although compensation and other reparation arrangements were utilised in some cases. Apologies might be immediate (that is, offered on the spot) in the case of some offences such as shoplifting; or they might also involve a more formal arrangement such as some form of meeting with offender, victim and parents/carers present (Rix et al., 2011, p. 26). The initial evaluation found that there was some level of agreement amongst youth justice practitioners that the YRD represented a 'good mechanism for dealing with young people and reducing FTEs [first time entrants]' to the justice system (Rix et al., 2011, p. 27).

As in the case of the YRD, 'Triage' schemes initiated by the Youth Justice Board in 2008 also incorporated a two-pronged strategy of combining diversion from 'formal sanctions' and some form of restorative arrangement (Institute for Criminal Policy Research, 2012, p. 4). However, the Triage model was slightly more refined, in that it provided for responses to young people's offending to be geared towards a range of possibilities, of which restoration was just one. In particular, there was an expectation that the welfare needs of offenders might also be identified and addressed through the diagnostic process implied by the medical-sounding term. Triage would therefore involve an initial assessment of the young person reported for the offence, followed by the adoption of a suitably framed response, depending on the nature and intensity of intervention indicated. At Level 1, the young person would be diverted straightforwardly from the youth justice system; at Level 2, there might follow 'a referral to supportive interventions'; and at Level 3, the result would be 'fast-tracked progression through the system' in order to ensure a swift and suitable response to the offence. The appropriate level and substance of the intervention would be determined according to specified criteria, including offending history and 'gravity' of the current offence. And, unlike the summary nature of YRD responses, decisions grounded in the Triage mechanism would be reached following consultation between specialist project staff and police officers (Wood et al., 2011). So, in conception, the Triage model appeared to be much more intensive, even at the point of first contact, and more obviously 'interventionist' than the YRD, with a greater level of practitioner input across a range of agencies; and with the capacity to initiate further, more intensive intervention on the basis of apparent need or future risk. In practice, though, Triage was initially found to operate variably by area; in only two of the pilot areas was a Level 3 service made available for instance, indicating, perhaps the resource issues which were beginning to make themselves felt at this point. At Level 2, similarly, practice was uneven, with young people not being diverted from the justice process in some cases, even where they were offered service involvement in parallel with this; whilst at Level 1, much practice under the banner of Triage was very similar to the YRD format, consisting of 'restorative approaches such as letters of apology' (Institute for Criminal Policy Research, 2012, p. 6), in response to a similar range of offences, including 'theft, violence, criminal damage and public disorder'. Triage, then, seemed quickly to become a kind of catch-all term (much like 'diversion', perhaps) which encompassed a range of early intervention strategies, with a variable impact in terms of both criminal justice outcomes and agency service provision:

> Triage came in a variety of shapes and sizes, having been implemented to meet local needs. However, most commonly schemes focused on the diversion of first time offenders from the youth justice system.
>
> (Institute for Criminal Policy Research, 2012, p. 7)

Clearly, in some areas, there was a merging or overlapping of Triage and YRD-type responses, and where initial actions were taken by police in the form of a YRD, this was believed to have a dampening effect on the use of Triage methods, pre-empting their application, and thereby potentially deflecting attention from the 'specific needs' of 'vulnerable young people' (Institute for Criminal Policy Research, 2012, p. 31). On the other hand, for many of those involved with the Triage model, it 'was highly valued for its early intervention and diversionary approach' (Institute for Criminal Policy research, 2012, p. 30).

Interestingly, both innovations (Triage and YRD) could, under certain circumstances, have provided a logical justification for intensifying the level of intervention with young people on the fringes of the justice system, and hence widening the net of informal social control. That this outcome did not transpire, though, cannot be seen as an inherent or inevitable feature of either scheme. Rather, it seems, both began to act as legitimising vehicles for the underlying strategy of increasing the rate of diversion from the justice system of first time entrants.

Alongside these initiatives, the aspirational Youth Justice Liaison and Diversion (YJLD) pilot scheme was also introduced in 2008, but with a rather clearer orientation towards addressing the welfare needs of young people at the threshold of the justice system. The YJLD was inspired by the findings of the Bradley Inquiry (Department of Health, 2009) into the mental health needs of offenders, and this certainly gave the initiative its distinctive flavour. Interestingly, too, the YJLD scheme was sponsored by the Department of Health as part of a wider programme of work to address concerns about inadequate mental health services; and so the scheme focused on developing opportunities to divert 'vulnerable' children and young people with mental health needs and/or learning difficulties: 'away from the YJS [youth justice system] towards mental health, emotional support and welfare systems' (Haines et al., 2012, p. 24). A caveat was issued, however, to the effect that diversion could only take effect on 'taking into account proportionality, public interest and risk management issues'. Six sites agreed to take part in the YJLD pilot, but with its strong welfare and interventionist orientation the scheme did appear to run into some difficulties, encountering police resistance in a number of the selected areas, apparently because of the potential effect on detection rates (still a sensitive area even after the relaxation of the Offences Brought to Justice Target, as Kemp (2014) observes).

As they were implemented, the pilot operations appeared to be sensitive to local pressures and conventions, so referral routes varied between them, and, as a result, timing issues meant that some were better placed than others to offer a genuinely diversionary response. In some areas, police were effectively pre-empting the work of the YJLD team:

> Although a desired objective within each site, diversion away from the YJS has been a difficult aim to achieve.... Whilst there is evidence that some pilot sites have established a more systematic pathway for diverting away from the YJS (still limited to low level offending), the other sites implemented a more ad hoc approach to diversion.
>
> (Haines et al., 2012, p. 60)

Ironically, perhaps, at a time when diversion rates in general were increasing, some of these project sites with a particular target of increasing the range of out of court options were apparently unable to make use of the opportunities available to achieve this objective.

Alongside these wide-ranging national programmes, it is also clear that there was considerable local activity under way in this period to extend the use of diversionary disposals, with initiatives such as the Durham Pre-Reprimand Disposal (PRD) amongst these (Smith, 2014). Here was an example of a deliberate attempt, crossing agency boundaries, to circumvent the constraints imposed by the rigid reprimand/warning/court framework. The PRD scheme was implemented for 10–13 year olds in 2008, and extended to cover the full 10–17 age range in 2009. The scheme was explicitly geared towards reducing the number of FTEs (first time entrants), but it was also explicitly 'restorative' in its practice philosophy: 'Indirect restorative work is undertaken with *every* PRD through victim awareness sessions, including on occasion letters of apology to victims' (Eshelby, 2011, p. 3).

A very similar sounding approach was adopted in Hull, but this time utilising a Triage model of intervention to support a reduction in 'unnecessary formal criminal prosecutions and thus [to] reduce the numbers of children and young people entering the youth justice system' (Hull Youth Justice Service, 2010, p. 2). In this case, diversion would be complemented by a 'Challenge and Support' intervention which would 'always include a restorative element' (Hull Youth Justice Service, 2010, p. 4). In Hull, this initiative was reported to have achieved a 48.7 per cent reduction in the number of FTEs over just one year (Hull Youth Justice Service, 2010, p. 5); whilst in Durham the comparable figure was a 71 per cent reduction over two years (2007/08 to 2009/10; Eshelby, 2011, p. 2).

A more widely known diversion project was also established in Swansea at around the same time, grounded in the principle of 'children first, offenders second' (Haines et al., 2013, p. 5). In this case, the objective of achieving diversion 'from' the youth justice system was complemented with the goal of diverting young people 'into' services which would promote well-being and prevent further problems arising, it was reported (Haines et al., 2013, p. 5). Here, too, impressive results were achieved, with 70 per cent fewer FTEs reported in 2011/12 as compared to 2008/09 (Haines et al., 2013, p. 9).

These schemes are of interest for several reasons. Firstly, they illustrate the continuing or perhaps growing capacity for local diversionary schemes to be developed according to local priorities, as opposed to following what had previously seemed a rather restrictive model of intervention prescribed by central government. Secondly, and partly as a consequence, they all appeared to adopt slightly different priorities and working models. Thirdly, despite this, all were strongly committed to diverting children and young people from court as a central and perhaps overarching priority.

These emerging patterns of changing practice have also been highlighted elsewhere, with Kelly and Armitage (2015, p. 125) commenting on the findings from their study of diversion in two areas that both were hailed by their managers as 'significant innovations'; and both appeared, in fact, to pre-empt subsequent national policy changes encouraging the expansion of diversionary programmes. At the same time, the two schemes identified appeared to differ noticeably in their emphasis and approach, with one adopting a 'Triage' style approach, utilising a detailed assessment to identify welfare and other needs of the young person; whilst the other prioritised restorative interventions – here the focus was very much on making amends and meeting victims' needs rather than those of the offender. Kelly and Armitage (2015, p. 130) argued though that it would be too simplistic to suggest that these models were completely different; and that, in fact the continuing influence of earlier reforms was still evident in their practice, especially in the elision between 'diversion from the youth justice system' and 'diversion from youth crime'. They conclude nonetheless that the period following 2008 and in particular the coalition government's reduced emphasis on centralised direction and austerity enforced 'diversification of local authority' delivery arrangements have resulted in an obvious '*diversity of practice (their emphasis)*' (Kelly and Armitage, 2015, p. 130). If this is the case, then the current period may possibly manifest a greater variation of practice models, and operational philosophies, than had been the case previously. This is certainly a question to be considered further (see Chapter 7).

Outcomes: the changing shape of diversion

In parallel with a considerable amount of developmental activity as described above, the period from 2008 onwards also saw a considerable change in the pattern of processing, decision-making and outcomes in youth justice, inspired in all probability by the dual drivers of a change in policing targets and the increasing pressures of austerity. Paradoxically though, the same influences do not appear to have had the same kind of effect in the adult criminal justice sphere – they may be necessary, but not sufficient causes, perhaps.

As Bateman summarises particularly well:

> The youth justice system in 2015 is substantially smaller than it was a few years ago. Since 2008, there has been a sharp fall in the number of children receiving a formal youth justice sanction; a decrease that is explained, in large part, by a reduction in the number of children who enter the criminal justice for the first time… (FTEs)'.
>
> (Bateman, 2015, p. 2)

As Bateman goes on to point out, the relationship between the actual incidence of what might be defined as crime and criminal justice processes is by no means straightforward or coherent. So, in terms of what are described as 'substantive youth justice disposals' (both formal out of court disposals and court sentences), there was a decrease of 71 per cent in this figure between 2008 and 2014 (Bateman, 2015, p. 3); but this does not necessarily reflect changing patterns of behaviour or criminal activity. There are factors in the wider social environment which might contribute to such a fall, such as changing (declining) numbers of young people in the general population, as well as shifts in policing priorities and detection rates.

Interestingly, though, similar patterns are also evident in relation to another area of 'out of court' criminal justice intervention, namely, anti-social behaviour. Bateman (2015, p. 6) again acknowledges the sharp decline of 48 per cent in police-recorded incidents of anti-social behaviour between 2007/08 and 2013/14. Although this period coincides with a very substantial reduction in police resources, Bateman does conclude that this does support 'other evidence indicating a reduction in unlawful and other forms of problematic behaviour' (Bateman, 2015, p. 6).

Partly, then, we might surmise that the reduction in formal processing of young people does reflect some shifts in their patterns of behaviour, alongside a decline in the resources and (perverse) incentives to take action against them. Despite this, however, substantial numbers of young people do still come to the attention of the formal youth justice system, and, of course, a response is necessitated in such cases. Bateman concludes that the changing pattern of responses to reported youth offending is not simply a reflection of changes of behaviour amongst young people, but also suggests substantive shifts in practice and policy, whether explicit or implicit. In many areas, then, Youth Restorative Disposals were adopted, going well beyond the specific pilot locations established by government. Durham, for example, initiated the 'Pre-Reprimand Disposal' precisely to provide greater flexibility of response, and to slow down the incorporation of young people into the justice system via reprimands and final warnings. This, in turn, undoubtedly contributed to the county's very rapid reduction in first time entrants mentioned previously. The rapid rise in community resolutions meant that they very rapidly came to represent a significant proportion of police case disposals, which 'coincided with [a] sharp fall in child arrests' (Bateman, 2015, p. 27). This certainly seems to suggest that more informal disposals were being substituted for formal interventions, by this point (around 2011), although regional variations were apparent. Post-arrest, too, there seems to have been some indication of an independent effect of diversionary measures, with the proportionate reduction in the number of first time entrants exceeding the comparable figure for child arrests over the period 2007/08 to 2013/14 (80 per cent as compared to 68 per cent). Bateman, in turn, attributes this pattern to: 'further diversionary mechanisms [that] are at play once children are arrested. From the available evidence, it is apparent that evolving youth offending team practice has proven pivotal in expanding considerably the number of cases involving children at the police station that are resolved without the requirement for a formal pre-court sanction or prosecution' (Bateman, 2015, p. 28). Partly, and perhaps fortuitously, these developments have been further sustained by the subsequent reduction in post court caseloads. Despite a substantial reduction in the available funding for Youth Offending Services, progressive decriminalisation of young people has enabled youth justice practitioners to concentrate more fully on their extra-judicial 'preventive' activities. Here, too, positive official encouragement of a more open-ended preventive approach seems to have prompted the development of a variety of informal interventions (Walker and Harvey-Messina, 2012).

Similar possibilities are signposted elsewhere in official policy documents, too, with the guidance on out of court disposals beginning to incorporate the language of 'community resolution' (Ministry of Justice and Youth Justice Board, 2013, p. 8). This guidance, too, features examples of 'good practice' from Durham and Surrey which appear on the face of it to be quite dissimilar, with one focusing on developing comprehensive assessments and interventions delivered by way of a 'team around the family' (Ministry of Justice and Youth Justice Board, 2013, p. 11); and the other based on delivering a 'youth restorative intervention' (Ministry of Justice and Youth Justice Board, 2013, p. 36). Much is made of the responsibilities of local partnerships to determine their own priorities and monitoring frameworks:

> Police services and YOTs should draw up a joint protocol setting out locally agreed practice with regards to the out-of-court disposal system and agree a suitable means of joint decision-making. Consideration should be given to …the provision of information on the impact of the scheme, including completion and reoffending rates.
>
> (Ministry of Justice and Youth Justice Board, 2013, p. 11)

At the same time, evaluations of diversion schemes were coming to the conclusion that re-offending rates alone were an insufficient criterion for judging success:

> YJLD [Youth Justice Liaison and Diversion] is not a panacea for addressing the offending behaviour of vulnerable young offenders[,] however it can be immensely useful in addressing and rectifying the causes rather than merely the symptoms of offending behaviour if appropriately targeted.
>
> (Haines et al., 2012, p. 134)

There were some indications from the evaluation of YJLD that the scheme had been successful in ensuring that children with additional needs had been able to gain access to appropriate services without being further criminalised (Haines and Case, 2015, p. 198).

In similar vein, the Swansea Bureau initiative was predicated on the fact that diversionary programmes should apply a 'Children First, Offenders Second' (CFOS) philosophy to their interventions. Although, paradoxically, reduced re-offending rates still seemed to feature prominently in reports of the bureau's achievements (Haines and Case, 2015, p. 213), these were nonetheless presented as something of a by-product of the schemes underlying focus on promoting '*inclusion, engagement* and *participation*' (*their emphasis*) and effective involvement of parents in supporting their children's upbringing. Here, then, narrow definitions of positive outcomes are simply inapplicable:

> the Bureau model has delivered a CFOS approach to diversionary practice that is holistic, child friendly and available to all children at all stages of the youth justice process, child appropriate in nature (more so than minimum necessary intervention per se), constituting diversion from the formal YJS [youth justice system] and into external support services where appropriate.
>
> (Haines and Case, 2015, p. 216)

The emerging picture of local variations in youth justice practice is underlined by Kelly and Armitage (2015), who do attribute responsibility for this development to the relaxation of central government oversight in a context of austerity, and 'the removal of many of the mechanisms for standardized youth justice practice' (Kelly and Armitage, 2015, p. 130). Whilst noting the persistence of some unwelcome aspects of previous managerialist tendencies, Kelly and Armitage do suggest that there is concrete evidence of the consequences of this apparent relaxation of centralised control. Here, perhaps, there was evidence of practitioners adapting 'existing, already "approved" ways of working' (Kelly and Armitage, 2015, p. 127), to the new opportunities which seemed to be presenting themselves. However, at the same time, the evidence seemed to suggest very different practice models emerging, described by Kelly and Armitage as, on the one hand needs led and on the other, principally restorative.

Thus, whilst alluding to both models as *novel* practices what they describe as the New Intervention was seen principally as a restorative disposal comprising an 'agreed contract with the young person regarding appropriate reparation for their offence, either to the victim or community' (Kelly and Armitage, 2015, p. 124). The New Disposal, practiced at a different location, was identified as being more akin to the 'triage' model, relying on an 'ASSET-style assessment focusing on the welfare needs of the young person', backed up by a programme of interventions to support the young person and address offending behaviour (Kelly and Armitage, 2015, p. 123). Here, then, at the level of practice, models of intervention were informed by the differing orientations of the Youth Offending Team or Service in operation in the two areas; where: 'Site A had a traditional Youth Offending Team made up of seconded probation officers and social workers. Site B had subsumed the YOT into a broader "young people's service" (YPS) including other agencies, such as youth work and Connexions' (Kelly and Armitage, 2015, p. 123). As we have identified elsewhere (Smith and Gray, forthcoming), there is an apparent alignment between the structural configuration of youth offending services and their modes of intervention, with a clear distinction between those which have retained a children's needs frame of reference, and those which are organised around more specifically criminal justice-led priorities. Thus, in Kelly and Armitage's formulation, Site A had adopted a more inclusive welfare orientation, whilst Site B concentrated more narrowly on matters to do with the offence in question. Site A, then, was characterised as representing a consensus amongst managers and practitioners 'that pre-court work including the New Disposal was a way in which to get young people and their families "the help that they needed" (Site A Report)'; on the other hand: 'Site B considered themselves highly restorative in general practice' (Kelly and Armitage, 2015, p. 124).

Both sites, though, shared common ground when it came to their claims about innovation and success. Each emphasised the originality of their own programme, although there was also a difference of emphasis in their success claims: 'they're not re-offending' (Site A); 'not criminalising kids unnecessarily, and getting them out of the system' (Site B). The evidence from these examples was sufficiently persuasive to lead the authors to claim that diversion had gone through yet another transition, and that: 'we are witnessing a distinct form of "interventionist diversion" that differed from (at least some of) the models previously observable in England and Wales and from the forms of early intervention which had preceded it' (Kelly and Armitage, 2015, p. 125). On the other hand, they also observed some continuities, with previous thinking and practice frameworks, including the persistent influence of managerialism, the continuing emphasis on assessing and managing risk, and the belief of practitioners in the value of preventive intervention.

Diversion at the crossroads?

The emergence, then, of innovative, creative and quite diverse approaches to out of court disposals for young offenders, sits alongside a persistent backdrop of well established rationalisations and embedded assumptions, suggesting perhaps a reshaping of the landscape of diversion rather than a radical transformation. As I have observed elsewhere (Smith, 2014, p. 118), 'several distinct rationales' are in play, including 'needs-based arguments', 'restorative principles' and 'the idea of minimum intervention'; and whilst these are not necessarily incompatible, they do point towards rather different models of practice, and indeed, criteria for judging success. From this rather disparate array of developments and intentions it may be difficult to arrive at a clear formulation of the trajectory of diversionary practices; indeed, it may be that this rather confused picture actually obscures underlying trends of perhaps greater significance in the end. Central government disengagement, the drive towards 'localism', the corresponding relaxation of centrally determined targets and performance standards and the substantial reduction in funding for youth justice might, indeed, have provided the impetus for creative innovations and a non-interventionist zeitgeist. But at the same time, this does leave us with the concern 'as to whether or not there is a more deliberate and intentional process at play in the withdrawal of the state from areas of human life with which it is no longer concerned', such as children's misdemeanours in communities affected by wider experiences of 'disadvantage and state neglect' (Smith, 2014, p. 119).

7 Modelling diversion

Youth justice frameworks

The preceding chapters have presented a structured history of diversion which implies that different periods of time have been associated with substantial variations in the ways in which out of court disposals have been conceptualised and thus implemented. This, in turn, suggests that there have been phases when particular constructs of children and childhood have tended to dominate as well. Whether or not such a neat periodisation of practice developments is sustainable is perhaps a matter of debate, but for the moment, it will be helpful to consider further what distinguishes the various models identified, and what the implications might be for a wider understanding of diversion itself.

The starting point, here, will be the field (in the Bourdieusian sense) of youth justice in general. That is to say, this is the arena within which children and their relationship to law and justice are framed; and this, then, clearly sets the terms for all aspects of administration and delivery of judicial interventions, including those, such as diversion which may in some senses be seen as guided by other priorities, such as welfare or anti-justice. Of course, the field of youth justice, like any other, also imports and responds to wider systemic influences and discourses, but at the same time, it offers a degree of conceptual and substantive coherence which enables us to study, analyse and indeed practice within it, as a recognised entity. This has certainly been the case throughout the modern era, as the previous chapters have implied, being associated with the emergence of an understanding of childhood and adolescence as specific life stages (see Erikson, 1953, for example). So, the interface of this life stage and the constructions of infraction, individual responsibility, due process and sanction which constitute the justice system comes to be resolved in a continuing and unstable outcome in the form of the machinery of youth justice. The specific, concrete resolution of these tensions which predominates at any given time depends, then, on an array of interacting factors and events, some of which have already been outlined here, as in the case of the 'moral panic' (Cohen, 1972) which certainly facilitated the regressive transformation of the early 1990s.

This particular turning point in youth justice suggests that there are certainly to be found alternative bodies of thought and principled beliefs which represent conflicting perspectives on the treatment of young people who offend. These tensions appear to be persistent and only partially resolvable, so that the field itself remains in a continual state of tension and uncertainty. Whilst certain voices and practices might come to dominate, their dominance is only provisional and temporary, with each susceptible to organised and persuasive counter arguments. So it was that only a few years prior to the 'punitive turn', the death of Philip Knight in Swansea Prison in 1990 gave fresh impetus to the alternatives/children's rights lobby, which at the time was actively promoting the abolition of prison custody for children altogether.

Although struggles over youth justice might sometimes be viewed as a straightforward struggle between the forces of liberalism and conservatism, or progressive and regressive practices, what we have already observed suggests that the changing patterns of practice are rather more nuanced than this, and that alliances and common interests often lead to unexpected or counterintuitive outcomes, such as the period of net widening in the 1970s, when, effectively, two alternative youth justice systems operated in parallel, leading to a significant overall inflation in the use of measures of control. Hazel (2008), nonetheless, has argued that youth justice can be seen simply in terms of a recurrent dispute between proponents of welfare and justice, and that other supposed alternatives are simply variations on these two themes. Alternatives to custody, for example, should be viewed simply as an attempt to extend welfare arguments into and against the domain of punitive forms of containment. This position, though, is difficult to sustain, given the evidence of accommodation between these two opposing positions at different times. Indeed, it could be argued that the alternatives movement itself represented no more than an ultimately unsuccessful attempt to find mutually acceptable common ground with those of a more punitive persuasion. Evidence has been provided on a number of occasions to suggest that attempts to offer courts the option of a form of structured and coercive intervention in the community (the Intensive Supervision and Surveillance Programme introduced by New Labour, for example) have been at best only partially successful in replacing custodial sentences (Smith, 2014). As I have suggested elsewhere (Smith, 2005), rather than representing mutually exclusive alternatives, welfare and justice arguments share common ground in certain respects. For example, both adopt an individualising rationale for offending. Both problematise the children concerned (and sometimes their families, too), locating the source of the problem with the young person reported for the offence, as opposed to questioning either the basis on which the system defines certain acts as criminal, or the social conditions within which an offence occurs. Both, too, it could be argued are principally geared towards dealing with the offender rather than resolving the problems associated with the offence, and thus may be viewed as sharing a different orientation to those who promote principles of restoration, reconciliation and offence resolution. In order to illustrate the complexity of the issue, though, it could also be argued that the restorative justice movement has tended to adopt the same responsibilising frame of reference as those who would favour conventional arguments based on the principle of just deserts. Welfarists, though, would not accept this apportionment of blame as the overriding basis for intervention. So it would seem the distinguishing features of differing perspectives on youth justice incorporate a degree of nuance which may helpfully be explored further.

Modelling youth justice

A number of authors have attempted to set out classificatory frameworks which seek to capture the distinctions between alternative positions according to a number of criteria, such as their ideological basis, policy features, and delivery models, including McAra (2010), Cavadino and Dignan (2006) and Winterdyk (1997).

Winterdyk (1997, p. xi) has proposed a six-fold typology of models of juvenile justice, differentiated according to a number of characteristics, including key agency, functions, understanding of client behaviour, purpose of intervention and objectives. Differentiated in this way the typology consisted of the following categories, on what he termed a continuum of approaches: participatory, welfare, corporatism, modified justice, justice and crime control, moving as might be expected from no-controlling to increasingly punitive forms of intervention. Notably, for example at this point in the late 1980s the system prevailing in England and Wales was identified as corporatist (Pratt, 1989). Here, then, we can conclude that rather than seeing youth justice perspectives as simply in opposition, the idea of a continuum suggests a much more fluid and, indeed, complex analytical framework.

Cavadino and Dignan (2006, p. 201) have more recently set out a five-fold typology, which again could be said to reflect a notional continuum: minimum intervention; restorative justice; welfare; neo-correctionalist; and justice, linked in turn to particular ideological and theoretical perspectives. Hazel (2008), as we have noted, does not agree, suggesting that it is the persisting dichotomy between welfare and justice perspectives which permeates all aspects of youth justice, and that these should be seen as extreme poles for the purposes of 'mapping, and charting, the movement of systems and policies' (p. 23). He concludes that 'every other model that has been developed in the literature can be traced back to variations of these two basic types of approach' (p. 24). However, he also seems to confuse his argument by specifying variations on these themes and yet conflating clearly distinguishable theoretical positions; for example, his association of neo-correctionalism with the justice model seems quite contentious, given their rather different approaches to the principles of sentencing.

McAra (2010), in turn, does not agree with Hazel's approach, claiming that it is an over-simplification of the 'myriad principles shaping both policy discourse in contemporary western societies [not to mention other national contexts] and the core imperatives that underpin international conventions (such as the Beijing Rules 1985)' (p. 287). It is evident, for example, that justice based approaches can be seen to differ significantly in their realisation, despite their common rhetorical basis. Arguments for justice for children (Morris et al., 1980) in the 1980s had a strong flavour of children's rights about them, and were invoked to support the liberalising movement of that time; whilst due process principles were likewise championed by influential interests during the 1990s with very different consequences (Smith, 2003).

McAra, following Muncie (2002), emphasises that there is likely to be a disparity between the overarching goals and intentions of any given youth justice system, its infrastructural and organisational implementation and its precise impact and outcomes at the point of delivery. Thus, the implication is that any given analytical framework must be alert to this and avoid an undue emphasis on neat and pure constructions of 'messy reality'. Nonetheless, attempting to articulate models at system level does appear to serve a purpose in her view in that it captures the sense of purpose which shapes specific jurisdictional approaches, and also offers some clues as to how youth justice cultures and practices may be shaped by the prevailing institutional ethos: the spirit of the age.

McAra (2010, p. 288) claims that four:

> paradigms...arguably, have come to dominate youth justice discourse: just deserts; welfare; restoration; and 'actuarialism'. Each of these offers a different solution to the problem of balancing the needs of the vulnerable offender with the needs of society',

which is identified as the central problematic of 'all youth justice systems'. These paradigms are said to be differentiated across three dimensions, namely, concepts of personhood and social relations, and models of intervention. Children are viewed as holders of rights and responsibilities to a greater or lesser extent, depending, of course, on associated conceptualisations of childhood; their natural qualities are differentiated; and accordingly, judgements of the appropriate balance between controlling and enabling interventions also vary. Important distinctions are thus drawn between the rights which might be ascribed to children and young people, who are also deemed to be individually responsible for their actions under a just deserts model; and, on the other hand, the entitlements owed to them by state and community under the welfare model, in a context where they are not viewed as fully responsible (not least because their needs have not been met). Paradoxically here, the just deserts model applies the principle of proportionality in setting limits to the level of intervention justifiable in light of the specific responsible action of the young person; whereas needs based approaches do not. For them the level of intervention is implicitly justified by what is deemed to be required to compensate for or eliminate whatever deficit or disadvantage which the child may be experiencing. McAra (2010, p. 291) argues that the actuarial model is similarly unconcerned with the child as a rights bearing rational actor, but rather views him/her as a source of calculable risk (see Smith, 2006) which is capable of being managed, and which should be controlled in the interests of the wider society. 'Expert involvement is crucial to the assessment of risk' (McAra, 2010, p. 291), and the nature and level of intervention are determined simply by what is required to ensure public protection and reassurance. It is only the restorative paradigm that attempts to integrate assumptions about children's entitlements and rights, and to recognise the social dimension of offending: 'Under a restorative paradigm the aim of intervention is to support victims, restore the harm caused and reconnect the offender to the community' (p. 291). Although the assumption of children's rationality is complemented here by an acknowledgement of the social context of their crimes, it is perhaps less clear that a restorative model is inherently concerned with meeting their entitlements, particularly as the model is typically constructed as being principally focused on the offence alone, at the expense of the 'connections between the child and their wider social situation' (Haines and O'Mahony, 2006, p. 121).

Despite potential quibbles about the precise characteristics of the paradigms outlined by McAra, they do provide a systematic basis for subsequent reflection, not least concerning the fundamental questions of how we assess their various merits and determine how to intervene in light of them (McAra, 2010, p. 291). As she acknowledges, though, attempts to articulate global encompassing frameworks for juvenile justice have themselves been fraught with complexity and contradictions. International conventions have proved unable to resolve inherent conflicts, particularly between 'just deserts and welfarist perspectives'. In highlighting the tensions inherent in the Beijing Rules, for example, she observes that:

> Juvenile justice institutions are charged with the requirement to meet the needs of the child, protect his or her basic rights at the same time as meeting the needs of society.... Procedures should protect the rights of the child..., promote participation (including that of parents) and decisions should be in the best interests of the child'.
>
> (McAra, 2010, p. 291–2)

Unsurprisingly, perhaps, the practice arena is also characterised by inconsistencies, with 'elements of each of the... four paradigms... embedded in almost all western systems' (p. 292). In England, it is observed, restorative measures such as the referral order sit alongside risk-based assessment mechanisms and rehabilitative interventions (such as the Youth Rehabilitation Order itself); whereas in Scotland, it seems that the longstanding welfare led system has now been modified with the inclusion of restorative schemes, punitive anti-social behaviour measures and the emergence of the risk factor discourse in the policy domain. McAra concludes, though, that even obvious inconsistencies may not be unduly problematic, in a functional sense, if they offer a pragmatic basis for compromise; acting, in effect, to provide reciprocal legitimation for competing positions (p. 293). Of course, it remains important to consider the practical consequences of interactions between different paradigms, and their relative degrees of influence, as youth justice systems themselves develop and change. The emergence of the restorative justice perspective, for instance, appears to have been relatively recent, and yet also seems to have changed the penal landscape quite significantly over a relatively short period of time (see below). It is also subject to specific localised influences however, and McAra (2010, p. 312) reminds us 'that the capacity of governments (or, indeed, individuals or agencies) to effect youth justice reform is likely to be constrained by the broader cultural context...'.

Modelling diversion

Within the broad framework of youth justice, it could reasonably be expected that diversion reflects many of the same characteristics and is shaped by the same contributing influences. And at the same time, preceding chapters of this book have tended to present different phases in the development of diversion as substantively different, and compatible with the notion of alternative or competing models, located within the context of wider trends and changes in youth justice. It may then be helpful to articulate these postulated models here in greater detail in order to shed more light on their distinctive qualities and their relationships both to each other and to other fields of inquiry, such as the conceptualisation of childhood. In keeping with the approach taken by McAra (2010) and others in relation to youth justice more generally, I shall seek to distinguish these proposed models of diversion according to a number of relevant criteria; namely, their assumptions about childhood, their modes of practice, their organisational arrangements, and their success criteria. On this basis, I shall try to develop a schematic framework for understanding the differences between the four models implicit in the preceding narrative: welfarist diversion; rights based diversion; risk-based diversion; and, finally (and most speculatively), responsibilising diversion.

Welfarist diversion

As we have seen, the heyday of the welfare state in the UK also saw a substantial expansion in the provision of support services for families, alongside a similar growth in the range of responses and facilities available to deal with the crimes of children and young people. This was a period of great optimism and belief in the capacity of state services to resolve all the problems encountered by citizens experiencing difficulty, and this naturally extended to cover children in trouble with the law. The increasing use of cautioning and other means of dealing with the early offending of some young people (such as Intermediate Treatment) thus made sense as a vehicle for extending the offer of help and support to those whose behaviour clearly appeared to demonstrate a need for it. As we saw previously, this mindset certainly contributed to the parallel developments of care and justice systems which led to the problems of net widening documented during the 1970s (Thorpe et al., 1980).

Underpinning these developments lay an understanding of childhood grounded in notions of vulnerability, developmental challenges, social inequality and disadvantage, which, for some children might lead to a range of problematic outcomes, of which offending would be just one.

Given these underlying assumptions about the factors contributing to children's problems, the logical consequence for diversionary practice would be to frame it as a means of anticipating and preventing what might be worse outcomes and difficult lives for those identified as vulnerable. Thus, the basis of intervention would be diversion into alternative forms of provision, as opposed, say, to simple diversion from the justice system. Here, then, those programmes, such as Intermediate

Treatment (IT), which were developed to offer positive programmes for pre-delinquents fitted exactly with this sort of practice philosophy. As Lee (1998, p. 48) puts it, the opening up of this area of practice was partly a consequence of the non-implementation of the Children and Young Persons Act 1969, which meant that Intermediate Treatment practitioners were not able to undertake the work envisaged for them, so:

> IT practitioners had to work with clients who were available. As a result much IT activity in the 1970s was undertaken for preventive reasons or directed at young people who were low on the tariff, including those cautioned by the police.
>
> (Lee, 1998, p. 49)

This was a logical consequence of the confluence of contemporary events of that era and the principled belief that young people did need help to deal with the range of problems facing them. Lee (1998, p. 48) comments wryly on the paradoxical consequences of this development in terms of the increasing number of juveniles coming to be labelled as delinquent.

The substantive content of the help offered to young people was often rather unspecific, it seems. Intermediate Treatment, for example, was often activity based, grounded perhaps in assumptions about the benefits of healthy, character building pursuits, as well as the intrinsic benefits of being given access to otherwise unaffordable experiences. With the benefit of hindsight, it is perhaps unclear how this type of intervention would be expected to offer longer term benefits to young people directly relevant to the day to day circumstances of their lives.

Beyond this, we might expect diversion initiatives to focus on reintegrating children into conventional services or normal social institutions, notably schools. Specific examples of this kind of engagement include the closer working between police and schools initiated from 1968 onwards, according to Pratt (1986); closer ties between education and other services in the management of juvenile liaison; and the particular practices with which the present author was directly involved in Corby Juvenile Liaison Bureau, where negotiating re-admission of young people to school was a recognised element in our diversionary repertoire.

The organisational arrangements supporting welfare based diversion might perhaps be expected to comply with a view that effective support depends on close collaboration between different service agencies, and a common commitment to shared objectives. Social services departments might well be viewed as the most appropriate source of the kind of welfare intervention indicated by this model. Indeed, most Intermediate Treatment schemes were located within social services, or commissioned from welfare oriented voluntary organisations. However, as indicated above, and as subsequently criticised for its corporatist flavour by Pratt (1986), juvenile liaison management structures also came to reflect a multi-agency commitment during (and beyond) this expansionary period in the 1970s. Here again, the underlying assumption appears to have been that the normal institutions of society had a shared obligation to address and resolve the range of problems encountered by disadvantaged young people, reflecting a common view that offending should be seen as a symptom of wider problems. The designation of Intermediate 'Treatment' is thus no coincidence, but was a direct reflection of the dominant assumptions about the nature of social problems which prevailed at this time.

Welfare led diversion schemes would be expected to define their success criteria according to a broader range of indicators than simply reduced re-offending rates. Here, for example, alternative signs of positive outcomes would also be taken as vindication of the chosen intervention. Successful reintegration into school following a period of exclusion would thus be viewed as an effective form of diversion into mainstream social activities. Similarly, resolution of family conflict would also be seen as a legitimate practice goal for diversion workers.

We can thus posit a coherent diversionary ethos, organised around the principles of compensatory intervention to address shortcomings in provision for children and young people whose offending has alerted services to their vulnerability. From these assumptions stems the organisational framework, grounded in a collective (corporatist, according to Pratt, 1989) agency responsibility, with a shared commitment to investigate the issues underlying the offence, and then taking such remedial action, with families, schools and others, as these initial inquiries indicate. Outcome measures are broadly based and are not specifically restricted to the commission (or not) of further offences.

Although it is undoubtedly the case that the period up to and including the 1970s was perhaps the heyday of welfare based intervention in general, and with young offenders in particular, there have been signs of a similar diversionary ethos in aspects of practice since then. As indicated, the portfolio of responses called upon by practitioners in Northamptonshire included mediation in cases of family conflict, and negotiated and supported readmissions to school. And, more recently, the Juvenile Liaison and Diversion projects referred to earlier (Chapter 6) bear many of the characteristics of the welfare model. Here, for example, we can observe a project funded by the Department of Health, whose rationale for intervention arguably involves a medicalisation of the problems of young offenders. Particular, structured forms of intervention are based on a detailed assessment, which substitutes a deficit model of explanation for the offence for one grounded in blame and responsibility.

Critical perspectives on welfarism have, of course, focused on its net widening tendencies as we have already observed, but there have also been other concerns raised, for example concerning the dilution of diversionary principles through the extension of success criteria and the consequent loss of emphasis on the underlying and fundamental goal of reducing the number of young people being drawn into the justice system. Pratt (1986), of course, is particularly concerned that the eventual consequences of the alignment of welfare goals and social work services with judicial decision-making mechanisms will be nothing more than an extension of the machinery of social control:

> It is not the drive towards progress, nor the motivation of reformers per se that has been the issue.... rather it is the coexistence of radicalism, of all these good intentions, of all the blueprints and plans for the future, with a whole

> range of other social forces which has produced a new regulatory field over minor delinquency.
>
> (Pratt, 1986, p. 230)

The continuing challenge for proponents of welfare based diversion, then, is the extent to which they can justify this as a genuinely alternative approach to the offending of children and young people; as opposed to being an add-on, which only serves to extend the scope of social control, whilst leaving the prevailing logic (and inherent injustices) of the criminal justice system untouched. This, indeed, seems to have been the experience of the Juvenile Liaison and Diversion initiative (Haines et al., 2013); and, indeed, this was arguably only to be expected given the project's initial, rather tentatively expressed rationale and aims.

Rights based diversion

Initially formulated as a direct response to concerns about net widening, it was understandable that the kind of model articulated by proponents of minimum intervention (Morris et al., 1980; Thorpe et al., 1980) emphasised its distance from welfare led diversion. The emphasis was explicitly on children's rights, on proportionality, on minimising the impact of involvement with the justice system, and on diversion from, and certainly not diversion into alternative service arrangements.

Here, then, the underlying principle seems to be one of do no harm (or certainly the least possible harm), based on a consistently critical view of the likely effects of system intervention, whatever its purposes or motivations. Unintended consequences were to be avoided at all costs, and the best way to achieve this would be to do as little as possible. As we have observed previously, Davis and colleagues (1989) captured a sense of this spirit of (non-)intervention in practice in the case of the Northampton Juvenile Liaison Bureau. Interestingly, this also points up one of the aspects of the noted Northamptonshire model, where practices varied between the county's JLBx. Corby JLB, for example, was not averse to additional interventions, whereas in Northampton there was much less readiness to go beyond the minimum necessary to secure a positive decision (to divert) by the police.

The minimum intervention approach is grounded in a conceptualisation of the rights bearing child, who is seen as being entitled to all the entitlements of citizenship, including those, in this case, of not being criminalised unnecessarily, or being subject to intrusive and potentially oppressive interventions on spurious grounds. This line of argument can also be extended to encompass the importance of anti-oppressive practice, and the avoidance of institutional discrimination.

According to this perspective, offending by children is essentially normal, and this is exemplified by the evidence that criminal activity tends to peak during the teenage years, and that desistance can be expected as a predictable feature of the transition into adulthood – and this is best facilitated by leaving young people alone, as Rutherford (1992) has argued persuasively. The aim of the justice system should therefore be to hold on, managing the system so that children are allowed the space and time to grow up normally, rather than suffer the essentially damaging consequences of intervention, whether this takes the form of criminal sanctions or welfare based mechanisms of care or control.

Intervention, then, under the rights based model of diversion, is very much grounded in promoting the least intrusive response possible. Here, for example, lies the justification for progressive attempts to move the threshold for intervention upwards, perhaps by way of inserting ever more rungs in the ladder of disposals. Again, this was a conscious element of the increasingly sophisticated approach undertaken by the Northamptonshire JLBx. As cautioning rates increased, and these became accepted as the norm, the bureaux managers then sought to extend the availability of, first, informal warnings, and then no further action, with a considerable degree of success (Smith, 1989; Bell et al., 1999). The added advantage of substituting informal disposals for cautions was that these would not be citeable, and thus young people would not attract criminal records with potentially long term consequences in respect of early offending.

Rather than seeing themselves as welfare professionals, JLB practitioners began to see themselves equally, or even more so, as advocates for young people. In some cases, certainly, this appeared to bring them into conflict with decision makers, especially senior police officers, who might have felt that their own span of authority was itself being questioned and even perhaps eroded. For some practitioners, perhaps, this shift of emphasis was slightly uncomfortable. Previous understandings of the basis of intervention had to be rethought, as they had to come to terms with the uncomfortable realisation that excessive, albeit well intentioned, involvement with young people might actually be counter-productive. Becoming an advocate and preparing for regular confrontation with decision makers might be difficult for some; whilst others might equally find it difficult to limit their role to a rather one dimensional process of receiving and responding to referrals.

The notional organisational model for a rights based approach to diversion would also, on the face of it, appear rather less extensive than the inter-agency framework upon which welfare oriented models might be predicated. In practice, the emergence of the structures observed during the 1980s appears to have been a rather over-elaborate response to the challenge of achieving minimum intervention. Indeed, according to Pratt's (1986) gloomy prognosis, such top-heavy, labour intensive arrangements could only be expected to seek to extend their remit and maximise the scope of their activities. Instead, it might be thought, it would require independent and relatively narrowly-framed organisational structures to pursue rights based diversion with integrity and clarity of purpose. So for example, a voluntary sector project such as Right Track, established by The Children's Society, seems to have provided just such a vehicle, with a broad anti-discriminatory remit, including diversionary objectives:

> Based in Bristol, the project is run by The Children's Society. It grew from a group originally set up to deal with young people's complaints about the over-use of Stop and Search. It works with young people at every stage – from school exclusions through to young people in prison....
>
> (Home Affairs Select Committee, 2007, p. 231)

Alternatively, of course, under a minimum intervention model, decision-making processes could be routinised, with procedures reduced to a fairly straightforward algorithm, based on conventional calculations of seriousness and persistence of young people's offending. Indeed, this may well be what effectively happened as the very successes of diversion in the 1980s increasingly obviated the need for sophisticated mechanisms to legitimise the arguments for the lowest acceptable level of police response in every case.

In the case of a rights based diversion strategy, too, success is relatively easily measured in terms of maximising the use of out of court disposals. Progressively, this might be further defined by the extent to which increasingly informal forms of police action become the norm; there is no absolute measure of success, then, but a continually moving target of extending the liberties of young people as far as possible. Here, then, we also encounter the crux of the matter for diversionary approaches grounded in principles of least intrusion. If the ultimate aim of such a strategy is the de facto decriminalisation of child offenders, then this is effectively a back door route to raising the age of criminal responsibility. Here maximum diversion encounters the first, and perhaps most predictable, of its criticisms. This is to the effect that it is simply concerned with getting young people off, and thus unconcerned to any great extent with holding them to account, or dealing with the issues surrounding the reported offence, whatever these may be. In effect, then, proponents of minimum intervention are accused of pursuing a rather dishonest, or at last disingenuous, argument, whereby individual decisions are grounded within a conventional criminal justice decision-making matrix, but the cumulative effect is intended ultimately to decriminalise children and young people entirely. In response, then, advocates of minimum intervention may feel that they are forced into the position of accepting that there is a limit to diversion, and thus into a recurrent argument with more punitive voices as to where that line should be drawn. This rather one dimensional argument certainly weakens their position when those voices are in the ascendant, and the prevailing political will determines that the line will be shifted in favour of a more punitive response to youth crime.

On the other side of the coin, there is also scope for criticism of a rights based approach to diversion from those who would favour a direct and unequivocal argument for children to be lifted out of the criminal justice altogether by way of an increase in the age of criminal responsibility, for instance to the levels prevailing in other European countries. As Goldson puts it most succinctly:

> The most effective diversionary strategy, of course, is literally to remove children from the reach of the youth justice system altogether, by significantly raising the minimum age of criminal responsibility.
>
> (Goldson, 2013, p. 122)

So perhaps the debate becomes pragmatic. Is it more likely that maximum diversion will be achieved by working within the established framework which assigns criminal responsibility to relatively young children; or does this actually inhibit more uncompromising principled arguments in favour of a higher age threshold? Perhaps this debate seems less pressing at a point (early 2017) when minimum intervention seems to have re-asserted itself as the governing principle of youth justice out of court decision-making; it is not, however, irrevocably resolved.

Diversion and the 'risky child'

As the punitive turn took hold, and diversion became a political target, the thresholds for formal intervention did, indeed, shift. Cautioning did not disappear altogether, however; and indeed diversion was re-configured under New Labour, under a rather different governing rationale. Here, the model of diversion that applied was much more conditional in its formulation than had been the case previously. Certainly, fears about children and childhood had been heightened, and this prompted a spirit of retrenchment, and a reassertion of the need for control over potentially dangerous delinquents. The imperative, then, was to find effective ways of assessing the level of threat and developing measures to regulate this.

The reawakening of fears about children being out of control in the early 1990s appeared to prompt a renewed emphasis on the need to manage their behaviour. Children were now viewed as a source of potential danger, and of course this inspired a more punitive mood amongst those responsible for criminal justice policy, as we have seen. Progressively, though, this also became a driver for systematic attempts to develop more sophisticated mechanisms of assessment and targeted intervention. Here, the child had become seen principally through the lens of risk management, according to which scientific methods of measurement would be able to determine precisely which finely tuned intervention would be effective in reducing the potential for harmful behaviour. In this case, the preoccupation was with the risky child. Out of this concern stemmed the new mechanisms of assessment (such as Asset) and graded interventions which were perfected by the New Labour government. Here then, the spirit of managerialism and the belief in technical-rational solutions to social problems found its justification in the form of the potential threat presented by children who were out of control. As I've suggested elsewhere (Smith, 2001), these expectations translated into an almost Foucauldian machinery of policies, procedures, and professional alliances designed to identify problems and develop finely tuned, targeted interventions to pre-empt potential future risks.

Out of this confluence of ideological preoccupations, rationales and systemic innovations emerged an array of anticipatory interventions, typified by the provision in the Crime and Disorder Act 1998 that the principal aim if the youth justice system should be to 'prevent offending'. So, the model of diversion associated with his broad goal was understandably grounded in the logic of diversion from crime. On the one hand, this resulted in a recalibration of pre-court decision-making in the form of reprimands and final warnings; and on the other, arguably, it could be said that this particular diversionary ethos also extended its reach into a whole range of other pre-emptive schemes, including the anti-social behaviour initiative, youth inclusion projects, targeted youth work programmes and mentoring schemes (Smith, 2003). As Goldson elaborates, this was very much the ethos of New Labour's youth justice, where: 'Actuarialist logics, a calculus of "risk" and the so-called "scaled approach" premise constructions of early (often intensive) intervention, including "pre-emptive" intervention' (Goldson, 2010, p. 167).

Significantly, for example, the government of the time sought to specify quite closely the forms that interventions would take, with an emphasis on preventive activities. Some concern was expressed, for example, at the limited use of such programmes in tandem with the final warning when it was first introduced (Smith, 2007). Diversion, then, was not expected to result in no action; minimum intervention was definitely not the order of the day. Indeed, the development of a sophisticated array of factors associated with criminality (Communities that Care, 2005) offered a detailed and rational basis for the coordination of tailored interventions with young people. Evidence based programmes could then be devised to address problems such as impulsivity, peer influence, or educational disadvantage, based on their known association with offending behaviour. Thus, in order to 'be effective, preventive programmes may need to target individual children who are low achievers or behave aggressively for remedial interventions' (Communities that Care, 2005, p. 70).

Management and delivery of this kind of anticipatory action would inevitably necessitate a much more extensive institutional structure than diversion grounded in principles of minimum intervention, clearly. Interestingly though, the technicist orientation of the risk management model does not necessarily require an extensive investment in qualities such as professional judgement and use of discretion. Instead, the system becomes the principal driver of practice, and the skills necessary for this purpose are those of effective application of diagnostic tools and operation of pre-determined programmes of intervention. This phase and model of diversion grounded in risk control becomes one of procedural conformity and reliable administration of pre-existing tools. Associated with this was a recognisable process of de-professionalisation, job substitution and de-skilling. Probation training was de-linked from the social work qualification in the mid-1990s; and subsequently a diverse army of new roles, occupied frequently by para-professionals, was put in place to administer various aspects of the new youth justice (Goldson, 1999). The consequences for practice were predictable:

> practitioners are bound more tightly by national standards; the professional 'contract' with children and young people becomes more technical, more unbalanced, more demanding and more subject to breach; practice is increasingly managerialised, target-driven, audit-conscious and performance-indicator oriented; and the interface between child welfare and youth justice is progressively diminished at both central and local government levels.
>
> (Goldson, 2010, p. 168)

In fact, whilst the 1998 legislation purportedly promoted greater collaboration between existing agencies with the establishment of integrated Youth Offending

Services, these quickly developed a distinctive identity and employment structure of their own, with historic issues of boundary-crossing and communication between agencies re-emerging.

Within this organisational and policy framework, diversion became much less a matter of inter-agency negotiation over the exercise of discretion at the doors of the court, and much more about routine and regularised administration of pre-determined procedures and tools. The pre-conditions for the administration of reprimands and final warnings were set down in law, and purportedly removed the risk of inconsistent and potentially unfair and discriminatory arbitrary decision-making. In place of this a range of predictable, practical and supposedly effective processes would be applied in the same way everywhere, with guaranteed outcomes.

The measure of success associated with this targeted risk oriented model of diversion is fairly self-evident, in that it was embedded within an overarching and pervasive ethos of preventing offending. Success or failure, then, resided purely in the level of further offending. This overriding preoccupation certainly became manifest very quickly with the rapid publication of research evidence making significant claims for the achievements of the new diversionary framework (reprimands and final warnings), almost immediately on its implementation (Hine and Celnick, 2001).

Here, though, lie the seeds of criticism of this rather procedural approach to youth diversion. The evidence for its success was, in fact, limited and subject to challenge, both for the inflated nature of its claims, and for its oversight of other risks associated with a strictly applied tariff of disposals, notably the renewed probability of net widening (Smith, 2003). Others, too, have offered more extensive criticism of the 'risk factor prevention paradigm' which underpinned this model of pre-emptive intervention (Case and Haines, 2009). The evidence base is unconvincing, these critics argue, and indeed the framework itself seems skewed in its application, with an over-concentration on some of the risks associated with offending (often personal characteristics and situations) at the expense of other, perhaps less tractable, structural factors. A pre-occupation with the sole outcome of preventing further offending, too, seems to be rather narrow. As with welfare led diversion, this limited focus may not, for example, offer much to assist in resolving the issues surrounding the offence itself; risk oriented diversion is not, of itself, concerned with restoration. Nor does the exclusive focus on offending behaviour provide those involved in programme delivery much latitude to address other issues of concern to the young person or those around them. Again, in common with the welfare model of diversion, the problem resides squarely with the risky young person, rather than with the systems and structures which might themselves be contributing to the process of criminalisation, such as labelling and institutional discrimination, for example.

Diversion from crime might at first glance appear to be the most credible and fundamental objective of any programme of informal intervention to deal with problems of youth offending. In respect of this broader objective, the processes surrounding out of court decision-making become subsidiary considerations, and are only to be judged to the extent that they promote this goal. If this is the case, then the evidence supporting risk based and pro-active interventions has to be evaluated as to the extent that it is plausible and persuasive. But many are not convinced:

> If the extant 'evidence-base' cannot tell us how risk factors work, how these factors may precipitate youth offending or how the programmes they underpin actually reduce offending, subsequent research conclusions and 'evidence-based' policies and practice are built on sand.
>
> (Case and Haines, 2009, p. 302)

If consistently convincing evidence of effectiveness is not available, then this presents real problems for an approach which should expect to be judged in these terms.

Responsibilisation: diverse diversions?

> The solution to your community's problems will not come from officials sitting in the Home Office working on the latest national action plan. They will come from the homes of our citizens, from the heads of our police officers, council employees and housing associations, and from the hearts of our social workers.... We will put power into the hands of our citizens. We will put our trust into the professionals, we expect everybody to take responsibility, take action, get involved....
>
> (Theresa May, Home Secretary, 2010)

Kelly and Armitage (2015) describe an increasingly diverse range of diversionary strategies associated with the change of direction in youth justice originating in about 2008, and this is certainly borne out by previous observations here. On the face of things then, it may be stretching a point to suggest that there is a common strand or consistent set of principles underpinning these developments. Somewhat speculatively, however, I would venture to suggest that what we have seen is an increasing emphasis on self-generated solutions. Here, for example, there would appear to be space for the range of quite distinctive models of practice emerging in recent years. Here, too, there is conceptual space for the ideas associated with the responsibilisation of individuals, families and communities, who are actively invited to devise their own solutions to problems associated with offending. There is even, perhaps, an expectation that the various stakeholders will take the lead in setting agendas and finding opportunities to negotiate mutually determined outcomes. Certainly, principles of victim involvement, restoration and reconciliation fit more readily within this kind of empowering framework than they do with the alternative models of diversion outlined here.

Considerable interest has certainly been generated in models of diversion grounded in notions of community justice and mutual problem solving, as articulated in Northern Ireland, for example. Clearly, Northern Ireland has been characterised by very specific social conditions, and the experience of seeking out reconciliation across communities, but in the process it has perhaps become a kind of test-bed for innovations in addressing youth crime. Doak and O'Mahony (2011, p. 324) conclude that, in that jurisdiction: 'the new restorative youth conferencing arrangements have considerably enhanced levels of community participation in criminal justice'. As a result, they anticipate that the state-initiated:

> Youth Conferencing Scheme will have some role to play not only in restoring individual victims and offenders, but also through restoring a degree of trust among the citizenry in the capacity of the state to address young offenders in a fair and legitimate manner.
>
> (Doak and O'Mahony, 2011, p. 325)

Here, then, are signs that the community becomes privileged over the state as the arbiter of just solutions to the problems of youth crime, and that responsibility can be effectively devolved to the local level to achieve fair and mutually agreeable outcomes.

Acknowledging the more systematic adoption of such approaches in Northern Ireland, Muir (2014, p. 1) also advances a strong case for fostering 'greater community involvement in the justice system', noting the lack of public 'confidence in the courts' ability to deliver appropriate penalties…'. Instead, he argues, the justice system should adopt a principled approach to ensure that 'everyday relationships that are damaged by crime and social exclusion can be repaired and strengthened' (Muir, 2014, p. 1). Restorative justice is highlighted here as a means of enabling straightforward, economic and meaningful solutions to youth offending to be found, and Muir (2014, p. 10) cites evidence of very substantial savings associated with one such initiative in North Wales. Calling for a major extension of the use of restorative justice, Muir (2014, p. 16) also sets out a proposal for this to be delivered in some cases by means of 'a neighbourhood justice panel involving members of the community'. He concludes that: 'community participation represents a huge untapped resource with which we can meet the challenge of promoting desistance from crime' (Muir, 2014, p. 23).

Muir's report on behalf of the Institute for Public Policy Research seemed to capture the mood of the times, and it certainly found echoes elsewhere, with the growing evidence of official support for a range of low level forms of offence resolution, engaging community interests (Walker and Harvey-Messina, 2012). This was seen as a positive step by advocates of more liberal approaches to youth crime, such as the National Association for Youth Justice:

> The key challenge for practitioners at local level will be to establish effective processes for decision-making.
>
> (Hart, 2012, p. 4)

This aspiration was similarly reflected in the arguments of those who felt that returning responsibility to the community might also mean that attention would be turned away from a narrow focus on the behaviour and interests of individuals (offenders and victims), and perhaps towards a concern with 'the environments which promote and sustain offending, particularly in respect of experiences of discrimination and deprivation' (Byrne and Brooks, 2015, p. 8). So, alongside restorative interventions to address the specific contexts of offending and harm, models of practice are proposed which are more about concentrating on potential and possibilities than on risk and damage caused. For example, the service for young offenders in Surrey was restructured, to provide what is described as an integrated service for those in trouble with the law:

> In Surrey the opportunities of 'localism' and expectation of greater integration of youth services… led to the disbanding of the traditional YOT [Youth Offending Team] in 2012 and the incorporation of the functions of the YOT into a wider youth support service (YSS) working with a range of vulnerable young people.
>
> (Byrne and Brooks, 2015, p. 11)

Within this framework, one of the service goals was 'to achieve wide-scale diversion from prosecution and formal pre-court outcomes. This has included the development of the youth restorative intervention (YRI)' which 'focuses on restoring relationships and enabling the young person to make some form of amends…' (Byrne and Brooks, 2015, p. 12).

Similar sentiments are to be found in reports of the development of preventive programmes in Swansea grounded in the 'Children First, Offenders Second (CFOS)' motif. As in Surrey, the aim is to move beyond targeted approaches grounded in the notion of risk and to provide common opportunities for children in and beyond the youth justice system. The CFOS model is described as being anti-risk, moving beyond concerns with negative indicators to 'prioritise *promotion of the positive*: positive behaviours and positive outcomes for children' (Haines and Case, 2015, p. 269). Prevention according to this model 'is grounded in child-friendly principles of universalism, diversion and normalisation'. There is considerable emphasis placed on what are described as distinctive features of the CFOS model, whose 'forward-looking, promotional focus distinguishes [it] from ostensibly similar "positive" models… which remain wedded to reducing risk and promoting the absence of negativity through resilience- and desistance-based behaviours' (Haines and Case, 2015, p. 270). Key features of the model are its commitment to participation and engagement of children and young people. Intervention should be geared to children's particular characteristics and socio-structural status, and 'should be provided through a non-responsibilising, inclusionary model' that works with them to encourage their direct involvement 'in decision-making processes that affect them' (Haines and Case, 2015, p. 271).

Although this practice model clearly aspires to an enabling approach to children and young people at risk of being drawn into the youth justice system, and in doing so, highlights its distinctive characteristics, it could be argued that it is actually quite consistent with the mood of the times. Control and autonomy are devolved to the locality and the constituencies most directly involved in and affected by youth crime; and, they are invited to play a full part in addressing the issues identified and reaching an agreed solution. Even though this may be a non-responsibilising model, in the sense that it is not concerned with the attribution of blame or imposition of criminal sanctions, it does represent a very clear devolution of responsibility to those affected. Here, then, diversionary inclusion strategies as exemplified by CFOS bear some resemblance to post-offending models of restorative practice grounded in similar principles of community led problem solving.

In essence, then, there appears to be an emerging intervention paradigm, which is grounded in the devolution of decision-making power and the organisation of practice from the state, via local agency partnerships to communities and individuals. Whilst there may appear to be quite different driving principles behind alternative approaches to diversion such as triage and community resolutions, they share a commitment to reducing the level of formal involvement of young people in the justice system, and its substitution by informal means of dealing with the problems associated with the reported offence. Thus their apparent differences may actually be of less significance than their shared characteristics and the common features of their eventual outcomes, such as reduced levels of formal processing, on the one hand; but also, more limited direct intervention with young people of any kind, on the other.

Whilst the language of devolved control and greater use of informal mechanisms for resolving the crimes of the young are, of course, attractive, there is also a different interpretation of these trends which offers a much less optimistic view. Here Phoenix and Kelly (2013) offer an alternative and much less upbeat insight into what the process of responsibilisation might mean, in light of these developments. Whilst they criticise models of responsibilisation which treat young people not as social actors 'but as a set of *behaviour effects*' (Phoenix and Kelly, 2013, p. 425), they remain concerned with how young people themselves make sense of and adapt to youth justice interventions. Thus, they recount young people involved with Youth Offending Teams acknowledging their responsibilities for what happens to them, and the choices they make, often in quite bleak terms:

> From their perspective, being responsibilized meant that they understood that they (as opposed to anyone else) were responsible for themselves) as in there was no one else who could effect change in their lives), despite the fact that may of the conditions that shaped their offending were outside of their control to change.
>
> (Phoenix and Kelly, 2013, p. 433)

Thus, taking, or being awarded, responsibility over decision-making in youth justice may not necessarily equate to a subjective sense of increased control and power to determine outcomes in one's own interest; actually this applies here in much the same way that more conventional understandings of responsibilisation have viewed it as a mechanism for shaping consent and promoting self-management of behaviour. Indeed, the constraining factors remain essentially unaltered by the devolution of authority in this one fairly narrow respect. Phoenix and Kelly (2013, p. 434) conclude by raising 'questions about the amount of control young people can exercise over lives characterized by poverty, abuse and social and educational exclusion'. Their study found that whilst some young people did make use of the opportunities to make changes in their lives afforded to them through youth justice services, others were led simply to resign themselves to the limiting constraints which characterised their lives. Being responsibilised in this way did not mean that they were in any sense liberated or enabled to take control.

As a result, the withdrawal of resources associated with austerity needs to be seen as a critical backdrop to the parallel withdrawal of the machinery of the youth justice system from substantive areas of engagement with young people around the system's diversionary margins. As Phoenix and Kelly (2013, p. 435) rather pessimistically conclude:

> responsibilisation is accomplished (perhaps only in a strictly *literal* sense) at the point at which these young offenders come to *know* the absence of support in their lives (despite inequitable and unjust social and material circumstances) and make choices based on that.

Models of youth justice and diversionary practice: a useful analytical tool?

In briefly revisiting the question of whether the models described here represent a helpful analytical device, it is important to note that they are to some extent presented in caricature form, and it is highly unlikely that any era of practice could be said to represent any one philosophy of intervention perfectly. Instead, they are presented to exemplify some of the recurrent practical and analytical challenges and conflicts which appear to re-emerge continuously, perhaps recast in a different form, but often seeming stubbornly intractable. Does this perhaps highlight instead the extent to which youth justice and diversion are themselves bound up with wider debates and social forces, of which they are merely representative, albeit in a particularly clearly defined form? Certainly it does seem that each of the models presented here is in some sense a reflection of the historical period during which it gained prominence; but at the same time, we must also acknowledge that concerns to which interventions respond, such as the problem behaviour of the young, seem to be perennial. Diversion, therefore, has waxed and waned, and taken different forms (caution-warning-caution again, for instance); but it has retained an acknowledged place at the threshold to the justice system despite the long-running argument of whether or not we are too soft on crime. So, perhaps then, we must turn again to consider those fundamental questions of what we mean by childhood, crime and justice with which we started.

8 Diversion and youth justice

Meanings and possibilities

Continuity and change; surface and depth

The preceding chapters have served a dual purpose: providing us with a structured historical account of the development and implementation of diversion in youth justice, on the one hand; and, on the other, articulating an explicit typology in the form of four different, temporally bound, models of diversion, represented in both policy and practice. Inevitably, structuring the account in this way depends on a number of working assumptions, so it is important to take a step back and ask the question of the extent to which the historical phases of diversion reported here are actually distinguishable, and on what basis. Superficial and quite sharp distinctions might be made, for example, whilst deeper structural influences might suggest a greater degree of consistency of ideology and practice than at first appears to be the case. That is to say, alternative interpretations of different eras might concentrate, sometimes for their own reasons, on accentuating their differences rather than digging deeper to explore sustained commonalities between supposedly disparate positions. Major changes in welfare provision may thus be interpreted in terms of their role of adopting the social relations of production to the demands of capital, for example, so sustaining rather than disrupting existing configurations of dominance and exploitation. On the other hand, it can be argued that irrespective of such deeper forces, the social changes wrought by innovations such as the construction of the modern welfare state are of such impact that they outweigh such fundamental concerns about the exercise of power and control. These considerations certainly open up the possibility of multiple interpretations of change, depending on the level of analysis adopted, and the interests prioritised in the conduct of our inquiries. In addition, of course, it is likely that these levels will interact, with the mundane and day-to-day features of our taken for granted assumptions and practices being shaped and modified by deeper lying influences. And at the same time, we too have a part to play in ourselves interpreting these influences and demands and making choices about how to act in pursuit of our own immediate and longer term objectives. Here, we are reminded of the very helpful insights offered by Nicos Poulantzas, whose concept of relative autonomy helps to illustrate how local and contextual interests can, themselves exercise quite different choices within an apparently common operating framework. As he sees it, even apparently monolithic institutional forms, such as capital and the state will inevitably incorporate different and competing interests, which will translate into quite different manifestations of power:

> Condensed within the State are, for example, differentiation within the power bloc and relationships of force among its components; shifts in hegemony from one class fraction to another; changes in… the organization of the working class and its relations with the bourgeoisie. These are all imprinted in the organization of each state apparatus; in the relative autonomy of the State…; in the… form of contradictions within the State; … in permutations in the various functions of the state; and in the organization of State personnel.
>
> (Poulantzas, 1978, p. 159)

This might be one of the key drivers of a complex and confused mélange of policy objectives and practice orientations in youth justice, as suggested by some observers. Fionda (2005, p. 58), for example, has suggested that: 'Contemporary policy attempts to try all approaches at the same time,... in the hope that within the melting pot we will discover that something works'. And, in this formulation, she seems to echo Muncie (2002, p. 159), who also views the field of youth justice as a congested and contested amalgam of a variety of differing positions, including, for example, just deserts, risk management and restorative justice. He concludes that this 'reveals the fundamental contradictions underlying a youth justice system cemented around loosely defined notions of "crime prevention and reduction"'. Immediate and contingent factors such as high profile events, or changes of key personnel, may potentially be located within a wider context of persistent and powerful interests and conflicts which are repeatedly played out, in youth justice as elsewhere, but each time in different configurations, and perhaps with different consequences. We can thus, expect to see aspects of continuity as familiar characterisations and persistent challenges are perhaps reframed but find themselves being played out repeatedly. We may thus, in fact, expect to observe elements of continuity alongside what appear to be dramatic changes in the continuing narratives of youth, crime, justice and diversion; where the interaction between these competing dynamics are both of historical interest and offer distinctive contemporary insights.

In terms of youth diversion, then, certain ever present features may be identifiable, and perhaps in turn linked to deeper ideological currents and conflicting interests within and beyond the criminological sphere. These include: exceptionalism, whereby diverting children from the justice system depends on their status or special circumstances; the tariff of disposals, whereby diversion can only be considered or applied in relation to minor infractions; individualisation, and assumptions about the young offender being the principal object of intervention; guilt, in the sense that a legally sound determination of culpability is necessary to justify intervention; and responsibility, in that the nature and level of blame will determine the nature and level of intervention.

As we have observed previously, these principles are typically brought into play, irrespective of the model of intervention being applied. So, for example, exceptionalism may be found to come into play under different diversionary frameworks, albeit constituted somewhat differently. A welfare model of diversion may thus articulate reasons for exercising leniency in terms of a young person's criminogenic need, whereas a more restorative approach might argue that the young person was specifically willing and able to accept and take responsibility for her/his actions. Similarly, the minimum intervention argument would be advanced on the basis of its relative insignificance or minimal harm caused by the offence; and a risk management strategy would make a case for diversion based on the young person's assessed capacity to modify her/his behaviour by way of a targeted intervention. In each case a specific and individualised argument is made, both identifying the particular scope for redemption of the young person concerned, but also constructing an implicit other who is not capable of accepting responsibility, change or demonstrating desistance.

These observations point towards a number of commonalities in youth justice and diversion which need to be understood, in order to draw out the basis on which change, contradictions and possibilities can be put in perspective, especially if we wish to take stock and sketch out speculative futures for the overarching project of decriminalising children.

Narratives of change in youth justice: Cohen's analytical model

How, then, do we establish a basis for understanding alternative perspectives? How is it that the same developments come to be viewed and depicted in quite different ways? Clearly, youth diversion is characterised by competing paradigms, and unresolved conflicts between different positions. In order to explore these areas of uncertainty and disagreement, it may be useful firstly to draw on an influential attempt to account for the narratives of change which are brought to bear on developments in criminal justice, namely the framework offered by Stanley Cohen in the important and influential book, *Visions of Social Control.* Cohen (1985) suggests three alternative (and competing) narratives of change which can be seen to permeate depictions of patterns and trends in criminal justice (and wider social) policy, namely:

- Uneven (but continual) progress;
- Good (but complicated) intentions – disastrous consequences; or
- Discipline and mystification.

These accounts of the changing nature of the justice system are clearly shaped by very different assumptions about wider processes of social development, governance and social organisation; and, indeed, the benevolence, or otherwise of state-led initiatives to manage social problems.

i). Uneven progress

Thus, for those who subscribe to the notion that all change is essentially positive, and indicative of progress, the key challenges are simply technical matters of how best to calibrate interventions and manage processes to optimise outcomes for all concerned:

> Changes occur when the reform vision becomes more refined and ideas become more sophisticated. Institutions do not so much 'fail' as adapt and modify themselves in the light of changing moral sensitivities, scientific knowledge or social circumstances. Not that this vision is at all complacent. The system is seen as practically and even morally flawed. Bad mistakes are often made.... But in the course of time, with goodwill and enough resources... the system is capable of being humanised... and made more efficient....
>
> (Cohen, 1985, p. 18)

Translated into the youth justice context, this kind of reasoning can, for example, be identified in the continuing attempts to enhance and refine the Asset assessment tool, following its introduction as a key element of New Labour's risk management machinery, and its rather unspectacular initial outcomes. So, for example, the narrative surrounding the use of Asset, even at the 'earliest stage' of young people's offending (Youth Justice Board, 2002), incorporates a number of the elements predicted by Cohen, such as the acknowledged 'scale of the project' (Baker, 2005, p. 108), and 'patchy' implementation. Claims that prescriptive assessment tools such as Asset lead to de-professionalisation are disputed; although it is acknowledged that it could be used inappropriately (Baker, 2005, p. 106). Shortcomings in its application, then, are attributable to poor understanding amongst practitioners; the system is, indeed, flawed, as Cohen would put it, but things can be put right by way of careful adjustment. Better training can be provided to counter 'persisting confusion and uncertainty amongst youth justice staff about the meaning of Asset scores', for example (Baker, 2005, p. 115). This might be supported by clear management guidance in the tool's use; improved use of electronic systems to support implementation; and refinement in its application (Baker, 2005, p. 117). Indeed, looking ahead, it appeared that the insights gained from the early use of Asset would prove an important guide to future developments:

> With the gradual proliferation of assessment tools the issues identified here will have a wider relevance. Lessons learned in relation to the implementation of Asset can be applied to the use of additional specialist tools for use within the youth justice system (e.g. for assessing mental health or literacy needs) and to broader based early intervention frameworks.
>
> (Baker, 2005, p. 118)

In the case of youth diversion, the notion of steady if uneven progress appears to apply comfortably to the extended period of time when the treatment of children was dominated by an exceptionalist and exculpatory welfare ethos. As differential assumptions about childhood became established during the 19th and early to mid-20th centuries, so it was also consistently unproblematic to view children through the lens of vulnerability and diminished responsibility. They were not fully prepared or socialised into the expectations of the adult world, and therefore allowances could be made for this, it was assumed. During this phase, indeed, the very idea of diversion became firmly established as a legitimate component of a fairer, compassionate and understanding system of justice.

Within this frame of reference, interventions could equally be viewed as being subject to a continuing process of evaluation and enhancement, exemplified by the introduction of specific provisions for the treatment of child offenders in the latter part of the 19th century and the dedicated children's legislation of 1908 and 1933, for example. The ethos of continual improvement and progressive change was clearly reflected in policy change. So:

> The Children Act of 1908… was in fact a composite, consolidating measure which synthesised the demands of child-saving philanthropy with those of national efficiency and the criminological programme.
>
> (Garland, 1985, p. 222)

Similarly, the reports of the Molony Committee in 1927, and later the Ingleby Committee of 1960 both accepted diversion as an element of the youth justice landscape, albeit in both cases with clear limits in mind. Importantly, taken alongside initiatives such as the Liverpool Juvenile Liaison Scheme and subsequently many other areas (Steer, 1970), these developments suggested that a consensus had been established around the legitimacy of the use of police cautions, even if the extent of their use and their content remained a matter of debate. Cautioning under this conceptual framework becomes almost a natural application of a common sense approach to minor infractions; and the challenge is thus to ensure that it is applied consistently and effectively to respond to these. So, for example, an established position appeared to be achieved amongst policing commentators:

> It would be foolish to argue that no youngster has a 'bad bit', that they do not sometimes need a tough line. What tends to be overlooked is that minor anti-social behaviour is part of growing up. Most people have been involved in such behaviour at some time in their lives – apple scrumping, petty theft, minor vandalism – we have all done it at some time. Most people grow out of it quickly…. A police warning can sometimes reinforce parental discipline, sometimes take its place and have the desired effect in preventing further offending. To invoke the whole majesty of the law in cases that are very petty… is to make the law look foolish.
>
> (Schaffer, 1980, p. 29)

The parameters of the consensual approach to diversion are also identifiable here: its principal aim is to prevent reoffending; it is to be applied in the case of petty misdemeanours, which are a normal feature of child development (growing up); it aims to supplement family discipline; it is a proportionate use of legal powers; and it sits at a certain point in the tariff of criminal justice disposals. As our underlying understanding of children and their offending improves, and as our experience of interventions is built up, and even as mistakes are made, changes can be made within this overarching framework to enhance the effectiveness of diversionary measures. So when things go wrong, the required solution is necessarily a form of technical adjustment rather than a radical overhaul:

> Good intentions are taken entirely at their face value and are radically separated from their outcomes. It is not the system's professed aims that are at fault but their imperfect realisation. The solution is 'more of the same'.
>
> (Cohen, 1985, p. 18)

The failings of the 1970s, in terms of net widening and the increased institutionalisation of young people on the fringes of the justice system, were nonetheless capable of being addressed effectively, without major organisational or legislative change, as the lead official for the Northamptonshire Juvenile Liaison Bureaux sought to make clear, for example:

> These Bureaux began operating… to try and implement the real spirit of the 1969 Act… to limit Juvenile Court appearances for offences to those of an exceptionally serious nature or where care and control could only be provided by such an intervention.
>
> (Hiscock, 1987, p. 12)

The emergent consensus of this period was further underlined by the steady flow of official documentation which reflected only minor adjustments to the framework and guidance offered to those directly involved in administering out of court disposals, as Goldson (1999, p. 44) acknowledges:

> Diversion was repeatedly affirmed in government documents, including circulars to the police… and in the Code of Practice for prosecutors… even the Association of Chief Police Officers confirmed that the most senior officers had been persuaded that diversion was effective'.

Interestingly, as they developed in the range of their activities and influence and became more firmly established, the Northamptonshire JLBx also became more closely identified with an implicit model of incremental improvement, with partnership working as the basis for 'productive practice' (Bell et al., 1999, p. 107). The message conveyed here is one of incremental progress towards shared objectives, leading to government approval and an apparent commitment to 'integrate' positive aspects of diversion 'within its current legislation' (Bell et al., 1999, p. 107). Here the authors were in fact referring to the proposals incorporated in the Crime and Disorder Act 1998, and the model of intervention based on reprimands and final warnings; although they did highlight concerns about potential unintended consequences should restrictions be placed on the number of out of court disposals available to any one child or young person.

This debate, though, was framed as a technical argument over the efficiency of contemporary diversionary practices, with the Audit Commission (1996) having cited evidence that repeated cautioning becomes progressively less effective in preventing further offending (Smith, 2003, p. 47); and this evidence, in turn, was translated into the limits to use of diversionary disposals set out in the 1998 Act. At this point, though, there appears to have been a degree of tension between the kind of narrative that saw these changes as a refinement of diversionary practices, and alternative portrayals which promoted them as evidence of radical change. Certainly, the recently elected New Labour government was keen to highlight the reported failures of its predecessors, and the radicalism of its own strategy.

Despite this concern with presenting an image of rapid and significant change, there is also evidence of a continuing commitment to the idea of incremental improvement amongst those responsible for delivering diversionary initiatives. So, for example, the language associated with Triage is grounded in such principles, relating current change to the lessons of history. Triage is presented as an approach to youth justice intervention drawing on the principles of multi-agency working and joint decision-making associated with Youth Offending Teams (themselves established by the Crime and Disorder Act 1998). The model fits with the established understanding of diversion, being applicable to the low level offending of inexperienced offenders (Soppitt and Irving, 2011, p. 20), and having the recognised objectives of: reducing levels of 'serious crime'; diverting young people 'into effective interventions to reduce offending; increasing community confidence in the criminal justice system; and promoting targeted and proportionate interventions'. Furthermore, there appears to be some evidence that Triage-based interventions do achieve the objectives of diverting 'lower-level and first time offenders away from the formal justice system' (Muir, 2014, p. 31), whilst demonstrating substantially lower reoffending rates than 'other interventions' (Soppitt and Irving, 2011, p. 55).

According to this frame of reference, there is always the capacity to make change in order to improve the system of intervention, and all such changes represent attempts at making progress towards a better form of provision. There are no negative or dishonest forms of motivation, and any mistakes or unintended consequences are nonetheless born out of good intentions:

> All change constitutes 'reform' (a word with no negative connotations); all reform is motivated by benevolence, altruism, philanthropy and humanitarianism, and the eventual record of successive reforms must be read as an incremental story of progress.
>
> (Cohen, 1985, p. 18)

Thus, even quite substantial shortcomings such as the impact of the Offences Brought to Justice Target of the early 2000s, are interpreted simply as a form of misguided attempt to improve criminal justice practice; and the subsequent removal of that target represented an adjustment which then enabled youth diversion to flourish to an extent which it had not done previously. Similar arguments could be advanced regarding the introduction and then abolition of the short-lived framework of reprimands and final warnings. Whilst on the one hand, this innovation did confirm the statutory recognition of out of court disposals; on the other, it did not appear to offer sufficient flexibility for the exercise of discretion and the application of proportionate disposals. The return to a revised cautioning scheme by 2013 therefore represented a further refinement of the statutory model of pre-court interventions.

From this perspective, then, contemporary achievements in terms of increased use of diversion, and reductions in the numbers of young people entering the justice system represent the culmination of a number of parallel developments, including effective multi-agency working, and suitably framed and targeted practice mechanisms. These can only be achieved through a progressive but inevitably flawed process of trial and error. For Cohen, this is effectively the default position, governing all aspects of policy development and research, typifying the paradigm associated with the notion of evidence-based practice and 'What works?' in criminal justice: 'A modern version of Enlightenment beliefs in progress, this vision represents the mainstream of the rhetoric of penal reform.... As a view of history and a rationale for present policies, it is... taken for granted...' (Cohen, 1985, p. 18).

ii). 'We blew it'

The second of Cohen's narrative frameworks to account for the history of criminal justice is characterised as much more nuanced, with an acknowledgement both of the good intentions of those engaged in the justice system and of the negative outcomes of many of their sincerely motivated attempts to provide an effective response to the problem of crime. Unlike the previous explanatory model, the discourse here does not convey a sense of continuing linear progress, but of advance followed by retreat, and even a complete change of direction, where the consequences of reform are completely unanticipated.

Cohen himself associates this emerging form of analysis with a 'sour voice of disillusionment, disenchantment and cynicism, at first hesitant and now strident... within the liberal reform camp' originating roughly in the mid-1960s (Cohen, 1985, p. 19). There is, however, a case to be made for the argument that there is a much longer record of a cycle of optimism and disenchantment associated with a wide range of penal reforms, such as the much heralded introduction of reformatories for juvenile offenders in the nineteenth century, for instance (Lewin, 1940, p. 45). As Cohen observes, the level of disappointment associated with recurrent major system failures may lead to such a mood of pessimism that 'the reform vision itself [becomes] potentially suspect... The gap between rhetoric and reality is so vast, that either the rhetoric itself is deeply flawed or social reality resists all such reform attempts' (Cohen, 1985, p. 19).

Despite this level of concern, belief in the ultimate goals of reform remains undiminished, and so new ideas are produced, and continuing efforts are made to secure beneficial change that will not be blown off course: 'Things can still be improved' (Cohen, 1985, p. 21). Past experience suggests that choices and outcomes are contingent, and 'an appreciation of how reforms are implemented, shows that the original design can be systematically, not incidentally, undermined by managerial and other pragmatic goals' (Cohen, 1985, p. 21). Systems failures are exactly that; they do not necessarily invalidate the underlying sound principles and strategic objectives. So instead of giving way to despair, it is important to gain a better understanding of the levers of change and the mechanisms that need to be put in place to guarantee success.

It is certainly possible to identify this narrative at play in youth justice practice and policy debates over time; although it may also be important to distinguish between its opportunist use as a political device, and a rather different strand of thinking associated with those directly engaged in research and practice. Examples of the former are to be found at several points in the recent past in youth justice. Thus, for example, the incoming 1979 Thatcher government made much of the failure of its predecessor to address youth crime effectively. The introduction of the 'short, sharp shock' by that government was proclaimed as a testament to the Conservative Party's genuine 'law and order' credentials, capitalising on the mood of unease about the consequences of the liberal reforms of the 1960s, and the evidence of a rapidly rising crime rate:

> the country is now in the grip of the steepest rate of increase in crime this century. The police are understaffed and overloaded.... The prisons are full to bursting; vandalism is growing; in some places people are afraid to answer their doors at night.
>
> (Thatcher, 1978)

Here, despite what some have reported as evidence of an underlying continuity between governments (Kettle, 1980), the clear intention was to stake out the ground to emphasise the failings of previous policies and the potential certainty of outcome offered by the government-in-waiting.

Similarly, positioning themselves as the potential saviours of criminal justice policy from years of Tory incompetence, Labour politicians once again highlighted the then government's record of 'failure' to tackle youth crime effectively in the run up to the 1997 election. This, of course, originated with Tony Blair's now infamous soundbite: 'tough on crime, tough on the causes of crime' (Blair, 1993). Here, again, some very familiar tropes were called into action to convey a sense of the failure of Conservative policy. Blaming their failures on a spirit of unfettered individualism, he argued that:

> The Tories have given up on crime. Not just their policies but their philosophy has failed.... In 1993, there are expected to be close to one million assaults, muggings, rapes and murders.

> But it is not just the daily lurid headlines that are a cause of concern; it is the constant round of abuse, vandalism and petty disorder....
>
> Labour is the only party seriously confronting all the issues connected with crime.
>
> (Blair, 1993, p. 27–28)

Once again, though, commentators later suggested that the policies implemented by the incoming New Labour government from 1997 onwards did not differ as markedly from those of their predecessors as their inflated rhetoric suggested (Pitts, 2001, p. 49, for example).

And, once again, the 'rehabilitation revolution' proclaimed by Kenneth Clarke following the Coalition Government's formation in 2010 was grounded in fervent dismissal of the previous government's policies and achievements. Expressing his frustration at shortcomings of the immediate past, he said:

> We hope to... establish through consultation an effective and honest approach to sentencing and a radical new approach to rehabilitation. We hope it will lead to a coherent package of legislation perhaps in the second Parliamentary session.
>
> So I believe today marks a change of direction; undoubtedly it is a break with the recent past.
>
> In my opinion the failure of the past has been to use tough rhetoric and to avoid taking tough decisions....
>
> (Clarke, 2010)

In fact, as we have already seen, youth justice practice and outcomes were barely affected as a result of the reforms introduced by this particular administration (Triage, the Youth Restorative Disposal, Juvenile Liaison and Diversion projects, and, indeed, conditional cautioning) which came into office just as a series of innovations were being introduced in youth diversion, and these proceeded without hindrance thereafter.

As these examples indicate, there is considerable political mileage in advancing arguments about the failures of preceding administrations and making exaggerated claims about the extent and depth of reform programmes to be introduced. But while 'we (or you) blew it' appears to be a convenient device for making positional claims in the political arena, it is also a characterisation applied to apparent wrong turns in practice. Diversion as a form of intervention has certainly been subject to periodic criticism of this kind, going beyond mere concern over the misapplication of agreed processes to constitute a more fundamental challenge. Thus, for example, strong doubts about the use (and misuse) of police discretion were expressed as soon as diversion became formally recognised as an established feature of operational policing (see Chapter 2), with the Molony Committee (Home Office, 1927) notably objecting to the 'institutionalization of the warning system' as in the example of 'the Superintendent's Court operated by the Glasgow City Police in the early 1900s' (Lee, 1998, p. 21). In this case, the issue was the apparent usurpation of the role of the court by a form of arbitrary justice which could itself lead to significant injustices and unequal treatment; and this criticism itself was substantially echoed by those associated with the 'back to justice' movement of the late 1970s/early 1980s (Morris et al., 1980).

As we have already acknowledged, there was certainly a sense of collective realisation of very significant systemic shortcomings in diversionary practices at this point, associated in particular with the evidence of massive system expansion and the absence of satisfactory safeguards for young people (Thorpe et al., 1980). For example, consistent evidence to support the theoretical concept of net widening had a cumulative effect (Farrington and Bennett, 1981); and, similarly, the consequential effects even of extra-legal processing seemed to demonstrate the concrete effects of labelling, with records even of informal contacts being kept by police, and presumably thereby contributing to future decisions in respect of those young people who had previously come to their attention (Parker et al., 1981). As Cohen observes, it is significant, too, that the realisation that 'we blew it' (in contrast to the oppositional stance typically taken by politicians) suggests an alignment between the evidence provided by researchers and the sense of frustrated goals and distorted priorities experienced by practitioners and agencies: 'There is an implicit identification between the analyst and the… reformers being analysed…' (Cohen, 1985, p. 21). This sense of self-awareness and mutual recognition also, perhaps, encourages a spirit of learning from our mistakes, and renewed confidence that we can put things right, because we can honestly admit when they are going wrong.

Diversion was once again subjected to this sort of criticism in the mid-2000s, when it appeared that the new model of pre-court intervention introduced under the Crime and Disorder Act 1998 was not producing the desired results. Rod Morgan, as the previous Chair of the Youth Justice Board, expressed trenchant criticisms of current practice at the time (see also Chapter 6):

> Criminalising children and young people who could be made to face up to the consequences of their behaviour by other means is criminogenic. Cluttering up courts with minor offenders deflects the system from devoting more attention to persistent, serious offenders whose risk of reoffending is high. We should be spending more on early preventive work with children at risk and their parents. In recent years, the Youth Justice Board has had no option but to spend seven times as much on custody as on early prevention schemes, the cost benefits of which are proven.
>
> (Morgan, 2007c)

Here, again, from his strategic perspective, Morgan's observations were supported by evidence generated through the contemporaneous review of policing (Flanagan, 2007) and messages from academic research (Smith, 2007). It is significant, of course, that in both these instances, in the early 1980s and later 2000s, the emerging consensual view of catastrophic system failure does appear to have contributed to a substantial shift in policy and practice; and this, in turn, appears to represent at least a partial vindication of the view that, there is scope for change based on realistic appraisal of our problems: 'A new type of liberalism unencumbered by the naïve optimism of its historical predecessors still allows room for manoeuvre. Things can still be improved' (Cohen, 1985, p. 21).

iii). 'It's all a con'

Others, though, are unconvinced. For them, the narrative is not one of continuing progress, or even recurrent moments of dramatic realisation, critical insight and renewal. Instead, developments in criminal justice, as in other spheres of social policy, are best explained in terms of the continuing project of establishing and maintaining social control on the part of dominant interests. The goal of this strategy is to maintain dominance whilst at the same time also establishing a sense of the necessity, inevitability and legitimacy of the particular configuration of social and legal relations in place. Thus, any initiative or development in any aspect of the justice system is principally to be explained by the contribution it makes to achieving this objective, irrespective of its surface representation:

> Everything has occurred as ordained by the needs of the capitalist social order. Ideals and ideologies cannot much change the story. Stated intentions are assumed a priori to conceal the real interests and motives behind the system. They constitute a façade to make acceptable the exercise of otherwise unacceptable power, domination or class interests which, in turn, are the product of particular politico-economic imperatives.
>
> (Cohen, 1985, p. 22)

Cohen identifies a consistent model of analysis which has sought to formulate the means and mechanisms by which such forms of control have been established and sustained, identifying the work of Rusche and Kirchheimer (1938), for example as a prototype of this form of reasoning. Thus, the particular point of economic development of any given society is mirrored by its system of justice, whose purpose is simply to support and facilitate the regulation of 'the capitalist market system' (Cohen, 1985, p. 22). Others, such as Quinney (1970) have set out the same kind of argument; and attempts have similarly been made to map out the processes and structures according to which sophisticated mechanisms of control are maintained (Althusser, 1970, for example). Importantly, under this formulation of the logic of control, the formal processes and institutional systems of justice are simultaneously aligned with the underlying task of maintaining social order, but are sustained by their own internal and self-justifying logic. Thus, for example, the decision to impose a particular form of sanction (or not) may be grounded on the one hand in a logic of responsibility and blame; and, on the other, on a need to align this with the expected (normal) role the individual should take in the wider social order. There is therefore behind this a continuing task of readjustment and reconceptualization in order to sustain this natural-seeming equivalence between the ways in which justice is administered and the required forms of socialised behaviour to be expected of conforming and productive citizens. Change should therefore be seen as an integral feature of this project rather than as evidence of its inadequacy or failure. Here, for instance, Cohen draws attention to the work of Foucault, as an illustration of this process of adaptation and realignment, particularly in respect of the re-organisation of institutional practices to accommodate the rapidly changing demands of the nineteenth century economy:

> The 'Great Incarcerations' of the nineteenth century – thieves into prisons, lunatics into asylums, conscripts into barracks, workers into factories, children into school – are to be seen as part of a grand design. Property had to be protected, production had to be standardized by regulations, the young segregated and inculcated with the ideology of thrift and success, the deviant subjected to discipline and surveillance.
>
> (Cohen, 1985, p. 25)

Closer to home, there have been a number of attempts to articulate the implications of this kind of analytical frame for youth justice, and youth diversion. Pratt (1989), for example, argued that the corporate model of intervention which characterised diversion in the 1980s, whilst appearing benevolent and non-interventionist, actually extended the machinery of social control into minor areas of juvenile misbehaviour (see also Chapter 4). For Pratt (1989, p. 236), the emergence of a more justice oriented form of diversion in the 1980s was simply another stage in a continuing process of policy reconstruction: 'Since the 1908 Children Act, the framework of juvenile justice of England and Wales has been periodically redrawn and refurbished to take account of shifts in the prevailing ideological balance'. Thereby, the manifest goodwill of the state agencies demonstrated in the remaking of diversion during the 1980s could also be seen as offering a tacit form of justification for wider expectations of conformity and self-discipline (such as 'programmes that induce changes in behaviour'; Pratt, 1989, p. 249); whilst at the same time maintaining the implicit threat of (justifiable) harsher treatment should these not be maintained. Here the educative function of youth justice intervention appears to be made manifest.

And subsequently, at a different point in time, under changed political and social circumstances, the recasting of policies around youth justice and diversion has been identified as reflecting very similar forms of integrated logic, whereby benevolent objectives are bound up with programmes geared at managing behaviour and promoting an adapted model of conformity (Smith, 2001). Thus, for example, no distinction was made between children's well being and achieving positive behavioural change; by definition this would be in the child's interests:

> the Government does not accept that there is any conflict between protecting the welfare of a young offender and preventing that individual from offending again. Preventing offending promotes the welfare of the individual young offender and protects the public.
>
> (Home Office, 1997, p. 7)

Here, notably, early youth justice interventions conflate welfare and justice, whilst emphasising the role of parents in securing behavioural change. The policy direction signposted by the Crime and Disorder Act 1998 was a concrete example of the emerging responsibilisation agenda, bound up with what appeared to be a progressive move towards establishing a strong statutory basis for out of court disposals. Reflecting Foucault's projection of the finely tuned process of assessment and determination of the appropriate response, each step in the tariff of disposals would be clearly demarcated, and 'in the case of the Final Warning would be accompanied by planned programmes of corrective intervention with the young person concerned' (Smith, 2001, p. 24). As others have acknowledged, of course, this emerging framework sat well with the prevailing and pervasive orientation of child welfare policy towards risk assessment and risk management (Gray, 2009). Here the suggestion was that:

> current youth justice policies and practice, particularly those informed by risk thinking, reflect more than an emergence of a distinctively new approach to the governance of delinquent youth. Such measures offer a novel strategy for articulating class discipline within the context of a reconfigured hegemonic project or style of socio-political and economic leadership.
>
> (Gray, 2009, p, 444)

Here then, quite detailed classificatory mechanisms, evaluative procedures and disposal frameworks are to be seen as the calculated products of a conscious strategy for both rationalising and then exercising control, summarised quite nicely as follows:

> In essence, this process is a reframing of social problems as individual problems. It silences alternative needs claims. Only 'manageable' problems are targeted for intervention. Manageable criminogenic problems are those that can be resolved through behavioural or lifestyle changes that are seen as achievable with a positive attitude and being amenable to normalizing interventions, programs, or therapists who provide tools for change and teach offenders to think rationally and logically. Structural barriers conveniently disappear.
>
> (Hannah-Moffatt, 2005, p. 43)

As with the 'uneven progress' narrative frame, though it becomes more difficult to account for what appear to be abrupt and rapid changes of direction, as was certainly the case from 2008 onwards in England and Wales, as diversion gained renewed impetus (Smith, 2014). As we have also noted, though, models of intervention in place after this point remained reasonably diverse (Kelly and Armitage, 2015), and there no longer appeared to be a clear and prevailing explanatory model, to account for young people's deviant behaviour or rationalise the particular disposals administered. Some attempts have been made to identify a coherent 'story' of diversion at this point (Smith, 2014; Bateman, 2015, for example), but these remain somewhat tentative.

Of course, changing patterns of practice were aligned with a period of economic retrenchment, and it may well be that the upheavals associated with this did affect the sustainability of both existing processes and their underlying justifications. In other words, these became redundant much more quickly than might have been the case if the economic transitions experienced had been less turbulent. In this context, then, perhaps there has been a greater degree of variability than might normally apply of attempts both to re-establish normative explanations of young people's behaviour and to (re-)establish forms and standards of intervention which equate to these. There has been some suggestion that the effective withdrawal of the state associated with very substantial spending cuts at local level represents a wider lack of concern to intervene directly in the lives of young people, and to leave them to the discipline of the market, expressed in the form of insecure low paid (zero hours) jobs. In such circumstances, the disciplines of the justice system are effectively superfluous (Yates, 2012, for example). This withdrawal of the state perhaps equates to emerging models of interventions such as community resolutions (Ministry of Justice and Youth Justice Board, 2013, p. 8); and responsibilisation (Phoenix and Kelly, 2013), which begin to suggest a rationale for this process of progressive disengagement with the criminal activities of young people. Perhaps this in turn suggests at least the scaffolding for an ideological project (whose roots are very well established) which renders young people, their families and their communities entirely responsibility both for their troubles and for taking steps to put things right when they go wrong. Diversion then provides a natural vehicle for the formalisation and legitimisation of this aspect of the wider strategic withdrawal of the state from any form of direct engagement with disadvantaged communities; unless, that is, they pose a specific and identifiable abnormal threat, as in the case of radicalisation (Youth Justice Board, 2013).

Is there another way?

For each of the perspectives Cohen identifies, it would be possible to advance criticisms as to their potential limitations. The idea of uneven progress, for example, may be confounded by evidence of the limited success of each supposed enhancement of the justice process, as in the case of the Youth Justice and Liaison initiative, for example (Haines et al., 2012). The 'we blew it' frame of reference does not account well for the constant features of youth justice systems which may themselves be the source of system failure as much as unsuccessful innovations. And, the problem with the 'it's all a con' explanatory model is that it appears to attribute a level of intentionality and certainty to the authors of system change which is hard to substantiate in the light of messy reality.

In reflecting on the stories of criminal justice he has outlined, Cohen observes that they serve various functions, such as maintaining 'the self-confidence, worth and interests of those who work in the system, [protecting] them from criticism and [suggesting] that they are doing alright in a difficult world' (Cohen, 1985, p. 157). They are therefore informed and influenced by the positions held by those who narrate them. However, they are not necessarily motivated simply by self-interest or self-deception; and they are often derived from a close and insightful understanding of how the system works. As I concluded in reflecting on my research into Wellingborough Juvenile Liaison Bureau, it would be unwise to assume that 'staff… are fundamentally naïve…. Team members were acutely aware of the contradictions and conflicts inherent in their work; and they were prepared to challenge conventional assumptions in various ways' (Smith, 1989, p. 359). Although in Cohen's (1985, p. 157) terms, the stories we tell about our own practice do 'constitute sociological data', this means that we do need to take them seriously, and explore their relationship to their material context, rather than simply dismissing them as illusory. Thus, he argues: 'An informed sociology of social-control talk can afford neither to be deceived by appearances nor to be obsessed by debunking' (Cohen, 1985, p. 156). In practice, a number of often conflicting dynamics are at play, which must render problematic any account which tends to present a unilinear or over-simplified account of complex materialities:

> What should be asked is less whether these theories are correct or not… but how they can be made to work. We must begin neither with a simple congruence… between words and deeds, nor with the existence of abstract forces which will render any such congruence illusory. The best working strategy is to assume… that most of the time there will be anomalies, incongruence, lack of fit, contradictions….
>
> (Cohen, 1985, p. 156)

Phoenix (2016), too, raises concerns about the tendency amongst theorists of youth justice to paint a rather uniform picture, largely informed by the 'discipline and mystification' model associated with Cohen and others. Here, the concern is that 'contemporary responses to youthful lawbreaking have been reduced to and explained away as part of an on-going neo-liberal government project and/or a managerialist revolution that started in the late 1990s' (Phoenix, 2016, p. 123). The issue here is that any aspect of the various reforms of youth justice in evidence can and will be 'co-opted into the service of the on-going neo-liberal revolution', according to this essentially one dimensional narrative. There is, however, a mismatch between this 'gloomy' theoretical reading of the current terrain of youth justice policy and practice and the lived reality, which reflects rather more diversity and a conscious commitment to promoting young people's interests by way of decriminalisation, in her view. To some extent, Phoenix argues, the problem lies in the tendency of theorists of youth justice to seek globalised explanations of a complex and diverse field of practice, grounded in the logic of 'governmentality', which is prone to being 'functionalist and totalizing' in its logic (Phoenix, 2016, p. 126). This results in a readiness to attribute every policy initiative, organisational innovation or practitioner action to an organised process of co-option and alignment of aims and interventions purely in the interests of ruling interests and 'market logics'.

Associated with this is a sense of inevitability and closure about the hegemonic neo-liberal project which 'closes off the theoretical space to analyse the conditions in which change is possible' (Phoenix, 2016, p. 127); and crucially also negates the possibility of dynamic or progressive change emerging from any reconfiguration of practice (whether intended or unintended). Worse still, from Phoenix's viewpoint, proponents of the governmentality thesis have also closed off the possibility of providing a positive account of change by suggesting that any new development or variation of practice is simply an indication of the contingent nature of the social control project. So it is, by definition, impossible to imagine or identify a form of state sponsored policy or practice in youth justice which is capable of challenging the underlying logic or intentions of youth governance. As a consequence of this line of reasoning, it is concluded that 'the only change that is possible is change that functions to extend the grip of government' (Phoenix, 2016, p. 128). This certainly reflects a persistent concern of those involved with the implementation and delivery of diversion, where even initiatives with the record of achievement shown in Northamptonshire were open to the 'cynical interpretation... that collaboration [between agencies] is simply a means by which the control of the juvenile population is extended or refined' (Smith, 1989, p. 348). Thus, even, the apparently benevolent consequences of a greater use of non-criminalising, negotiated out of court disposals can be incorporated within a logic which sees official leniency towards offences deemed as minor as integral to an ideological (and material) project of bifurcation and heightened criminalisation of those who represent a serious threat to the social and moral order. The line is simply drawn more sharply and more efficiently between those whose behaviour can be 'normalised' and forgiven and those whose actions continue to require the full force of the criminal law in response.

Phoenix (2016, p. 131) also challenges the tendency amongst some analysts to portray the youth justice system as a discrete, coherent and monolithic whole, which 'flattens the... complex and highly diverse field of social relations, bureaucratic organizations, social actors and the ways in which power infuses these relations'. Here, not only is the system treated simplistically as a unified entity whose behaviour can be predicted straightforwardly from its formal structure and characteristics; but also, there is no room allowed for the exercise of independent agency and initiative by any of the actors who, together, constitute the 'moving parts' of the system, including, of course, children (see Chapter 1). For her, ultimately, this is a profoundly depressing and self-limiting view of youth justice and the possibilities for imagining change towards 'non-penal' responses to young people's infringements are highly restricted. It does not, in fact, provide us with the tools or resources to consider 'important questions raised by some of the recent changes' in the delivery of youth justice, in Phoenix's view; notably whether the reductions in the levels of formal processing of young people and the associated changes in the 'shape, size and structure of youth justice signify anything beyond small shifts in sentencing practices' and multi-agency relationships (Phoenix, 2016, p. 133). Phoenix concludes that the necessary theoretical steps to be taken involve moving beyond a preoccupation with the fixed and apparently determinant parameters of the youth justice system and adopting a wider frame of reference, characterised in the terms of a 'critical youth penology' (Phoenix, 2016, p. 132). Here, the particular features and practices of the youth justice system (including diversionary schemes) should be distinguished from and analysed in the context of the wider social conditions and experiences which frame childhood and youth and also make possible the forms of intervention and sanction to which they are (differentially) exposed. Thus, for example, institutionally racist outcomes of the youth justice process can only be fully comprehended and addressed within a wider analysis of culture, ethnicity and oppression (Bateman, 2015, p. 25).

Consistent with this line of argument, is it possible, then, to reframe 'diversion' as a form of critical intervention which aspire to some of these wider-reaching objectives, at least in the sense of offering both a theoretical critique of conventional mechanisms of control and some alternative and progressive possibilities at the level of practice? Can we articulate a form of practice which itself represents a realisation of some of the elements of a 'critical youth penality' perspective, perhaps?

Turning first to the historical example of the Northamptonshire Juvenile Liaison Bureaux, refusal to endorse the prevailing penal logic was reflected in the position adopted by practitioners that they would never recommend prosecution, in this sense reflecting the abolitionist (Mathiesen, 1974) stance on criminal justice, at least implicitly. Similarly, the extent to which a through-going diversionary approach does not comply with a notional tariff of disposals is also both an important practice strategy and a challenge to what is a highly important pillar of conventional criminal justice thinking. The modification of the tariff under the provisions of the Legal Aid Sentencing and Punishment of Offenders Act 2012 is potentially of some significance here, even though its origins and motivation may be viewed with suspicion.

Those aspects of diversion which focus on inclusionary responses, where practice perhaps involves a degree of rights-based advocacy (diversion *into*) may also be seen as potentially progressive, where they reduce or obviate the discriminatory effects of being defined (labelled) as problematic. Here, of course, the connection is made between the consequences of criminalisation and the wider and potentially linked systemic effects of marginalisation and differential treatment to which young people may be exposed (Phoenix, 2016, p. 137).

And, finally, diversion (along with more radical interpretations of restorative justice) is capable of developing a coherent model of collective, communal justice, whose focus is on resolving the concerns and issues of all those affected by an offence; as opposed simply to reinforcing an individualised and responsibilising model of blame and shame.

A progressive vision of diversion thus envisages no limits to diversion, or to the potential for reframing criminal justice processes that it pre-figures (Smith, 1989, p. 375). In this sense then, a comprehensive diversionary strategy represents a concrete articulation of the critical analysis which resists the one-sided and harmful criminalisation of children through a variety of institutional forms and rhetorical devices; and instead poses a challenge to these marginalising and oppressive tendencies which are written into conventional ideologies and structures of criminal justice. As Phoenix points out, it is not just a matter of achieving technical or administrative changes in one direction or another: 'giving practitioners increased discretion alone will not necessarily in and of itself, create a less punitive outcome, system contraction or a more compassionate youth justice response' (Phoenix, 2016, p. 132). This kind of initiative only makes sense if grounded in an appropriate '*ethical* and *moral* space', she argues.

Here, then, lies the recurrent challenge for diversion in youth justice. It has to move beyond the kind of calculation which simply judges success (or failure) according to current trends towards greater or more limited use of prosecution; and it should avoid incorporating ideological assumptions which replicate individualising, exclusionary and responsibilising forms of practice. Instead, it should reassert its position as a model for reframing and potentially transforming the ways in which young people are problematised and categorised, principally through the criminal justice system, but also supplemented by other institutional mechanisms at play in education, care and even health systems.

When I first carried out a detailed study of diversion, I concluded along similar lines. Practice (or praxis) is capable of acting as an effective critique of established assumptions and posing alternative ideas and possibilities in dialogue with theoretical inquiry; and from this emerges the prospect, and sometimes even a hint of the reality, of progressive change. As I wrote at the time:

> Translating this into the context of diversion, it might imply certain... principles. One would not expect an acceptance of the value of prosecution..., but rather a commitment to seek alternatives.... Reparation should be based on voluntary and mutually acceptable agreements between offender and victim, rather than contrivance and imposition.... Individualising responses to offending should be avoided (links should be made, for example, between crime and the lack of youth facilities).... Agency practices and policy should be constantly reviewed and challenged... and practitioners should be wary of cooption.
>
> (Smith, 1989, p. 375)

In writing regularly on this subject, I have tried to maintain a balance between articulating and critically analysing the structures and mechanisms of control and the sources of inequality and oppression which are central to the delivery and experience of justice for young people, on the one hand; and, on the other, recognising the capacity for progressive alliances of practitioners and others to make the case for substantive, emancipatory change, essentially through their active engagement with children, and their own work to gain influence and change systems. It is, of course, highly encouraging that other colleagues have also reached similar conclusions about the capacity for principled, theory-informed, participatory, rights-based practice to achieve such goals, as in the following summation of Children First, Offenders Second: 'we have sought to outline... a practical, progressive, participatory and promotional model of evidence-based partnership working.... a positive youth justice that puts *children first*', as Haines and Case (2015, p. 293) put it.

And so diversion in youth justice has a critical part to play in engaging constructively with our understandings of childhood, as a period of learning and evolving capacities and the institutions and structures which seek to shape it. Issues arising from their reported offending should be dealt with in this spirit, and in the spirit of promoting *social,* rather than criminal justice. In the final analysis, youth diversion should be a critical and transformative endeavour above all else, in pursuit of the overarching goal of a better childhood.

References

Althusser, L. (1971) *Lenin and Philosophy and Other Essays*, London: Verso.

Ariès, P. (1962) *Centuries of Childhood*, New York: Vintage Books.

Arnett, J. (1999) 'Adolescent storm and stress reconsidered', *American Psychologist*, 54, pp. 317–326.

Audit Commission (1996) *Misspent Youth?*, Abingdon: Audit Commission.

Audit Commission (1998a) *Misspent Youth '98*, Abingdon: Audit Commission.

Audit Commission (1998b) *Briefing: Misspent Youth '98*, Abingdon: Audit Commission.

Austin, J. and Krisberg, B. (1981) 'Wider, stronger, and different nets: the dialectics of criminal justice reform', *Journal of Crime & Delinquency*, 18, 1, pp. 165–196.

Austin, J. and Krisberg, B. (2002) 'Wider, stronger and different nets: the dialectics of criminal justice reform' in Muncie, J., Hughes, G. and McLaughlin, E. (eds) *Youth Justice: Critical Readings*, London: Sage, pp. 258–274.

Baker, K. (2005) 'Assessment in youth justice: professional discretion and the use of asset', *Youth Justice*, 5, 2, pp. 106–122.

Bateman, T. (2006) 'Youth crime and justice: statistical "evidence", recent trends and responses', in Goldson, B. and Muncie, J. (eds) *Youth Crime and Justice*, London: Sage, pp. 65–77.

Bateman, T. (2014) 'Where has all the youth crime gone?', *Children & Society*, 28, pp. 416–424.

Bateman, T. (2015) *The State of Youth Justice 2015*, London: National Association for Youth Justice.

Beck, U. (1992) *Risk Society*, London: Sage.

Becker, H. (1963) *Outsiders*, New York: The Free Press.

Bell, A., Hodgson, M. and Pragnell, S. (1999) 'Diverting children and young people from crime and the criminal justice system', in Goldson, B. (ed) *Youth Justice: Contemporary Policy and Practice*, Aldershot: Ashgate, pp. 91–109.

Bell, C. (1999) 'Appealing for justice for children and young people: a critical analysis of the Crime and Disorder Bill', in Goldson, B. (ed) *Youth Justice: Contemporary Policy and Practice*, Aldershot: Ashgate, pp. 191–210.

Blagg, H. (1985) 'Reparation and justice for juveniles', *British Journal of Criminology*, 25, 3, pp. 267–279.

Blagg, H., Derricourt, N., Finch, J. and Thorpe D. (1986) *The Final Report on the Juvenile Liaison Bureau Corby*, Lancaster: University of Lancaster Department of Social Administration.

Blair, T. (1993) 'Why crime is a Socialist issue', *New Statesman*, 29 January.

Blakemore, S.-J. and Mills, K. (2014) 'Is adolescence a sensitive period for sociocultural processing?', *Annual Review of Psychology*, 65, pp. 187–207.

Blakemore, S.-J. and Robbins, T. (2012) 'Decision-making in the adolescent brain', *Nature Neuroscience*, 15, 9, pp. 1184–1191.

Blunkett, D. (2003) 'Foreword', in Home Office, *A Guide to Anti-social Behaviour Orders and Acceptable Behaviour Contracts*, London: Home Office, p. 2.

Bottoms, A. (1977) 'Reflections on the renaissance of dangerousness', *Howard Journal*, 16, pp. 70–96.

Bowlby, J. (1947) *Forty-Four Thieves: Their Characters and Home-Life*, London: Baillère, Tindall & Cox.

Browning, P. (1987) 'The elimination of custody – another point of view', *Justice of the Peace*, 151, pp. 215–216.

Buck, M. (1983) 'The police perspective', in Northamptonshire County Council, *Diversion-Corporate Action with Juveniles*, Northampton: Northamptonshire County Council, pp. 35–36.

Burney, E. (2005) *Making People Behave*, Cullompton: Willan.

Burt, C. (1945) *The Young Delinquent*, London: University of London Press.

Byrne, B. and Brooks, K. (2015) 'Post-YOT youth justice', *What is Justice? Re-imagining Penal Policy,* Working Papers 19, London: Howard League.

Cain, M. (1968) 'Role conflict among police juvenile liaison officers', *British Journal of Criminology*, 8, 4, pp. 366–382.

Cain, M. and Dearden, M. (1966) 'Initial reactions to a new juvenile liaison scheme', *British Journal of Criminology*, 6, 4, pp. 421–430.

Case, S. and Haines, K. (2009) *Understanding Youth Offending*, Cullompton: Willan.

Cavadino, M. and Dignan, J. (2006) 'Penal policy and political expediency', *Criminology & Criminal Justice*, 6, 4, pp. 435–456.

Cawson, P. (1985) 'Intermediate treatment', *Journal of Child Psychology & Psychiatry*, 26, 5, pp. 675–681.

Cheetham, J. (1985) 'Juvenile offenders and alternatives to custody in Northamptonshire: the views of magistrates and social workers', unpublished report.

Clarke, K. (2010) 'The Government's vision for criminal justice reform', Speech to Centre for Crime and Justice Studies, *The Guardian*, 30 June.

Clarke, K. (2010) Speech to Conservative Party Conference, 5 October.

Cohen, S. (1972) *Folk Devils and Moral Panics*, London: Paladin.

Cohen, S. (1985) *Visions of Social Control*, Cambridge: Polity Press.

Communities that Care (2005) *Risk and Protective Factors*, London: Youth Justice Board.

Corsaro, W. (1997) *The Sociology of Childhood*, Thousand Oaks, CA: Pine Forge Press.

Cottrell, R. (1979) 'Wellingborough Juvenile Bureau', unpublished policy paper, Northamptonshire County Council.

Cunningham, H. (2005) *Children and Childhood in Western Society Since 1500*, Harlow: Pearson Longman.

Davis, G., Boucherat, J. and Watson, D. (1989) 'Pre-court decision-making in juvenile justice', *British Journal of Criminology*, 29, 3, pp. 219–235.

Department for Children, Schools and Families (2007) *Children's Plan*, London: The Stationery Office.

Department of Health (2009) *The Bradley Report*, London: Department of Health.

Director of Public Prosecutions (1987) *Crown Prosecution Service Annual Report 1986–87*, London: HMSO.

Ditchfield, J. (1976) *Police Cautioning in England and Wales,* Home Office Research Study No. 37, London: HMSO.

Doak, J. and O'Mahony, D. (2011) 'In search of legitimacy: restorative youth conferencing in Northern Ireland', *Legal Studies*, 31, 2, pp. 305–325.

Durrant, R. and Ward, T. (2012) 'The role of evolutionary explanations in criminology', *Journal of Theoretical and Philosophical Criminology*, 4, 1, pp. 1–37.

Erikson, E. (1953) *Childhood and Society*, New York: Vintage.

Erikson, E. (1995) *Childhood and Society,* New York: Vintage.

Eshelby, G. (2011) 'County Durham Youth Offending Service pre-reprimand disposal', *Report to Durham County Council Safer and Stronger Communities Overview and Scrutiny Committee*, Durham: Durham County Council.

Evans, R. (1991) 'Police cautioning and the young adult offender', *Criminal Law Review*, August, pp. 598–609.

Fahlberg, V. (1994) *A Child's Journey Through Placement*, London: BAAF.

Farrington, D. and Bennett, T. (1981) 'Police cautioning of juveniles in London', *British Journal of Criminology*, 21, 2, pp. 123–135.

Feld, B. (1981) 'Justice by geography: urban, suburban, and rural variations in juvenile justice administration', *Journal of Criminal Law and Criminology*, 82, 1, pp. 156–210.

Finch, J. (1986) 'Inter-agency cooperation' in Blagg, H., Derricourt, N., Finch, J. and Thorpe D. *The Final Report on the Juvenile Liaison Bureau Corby*, Lancaster: University of Lancaster Department of Social Administration, pp. 84–103.

Fionda, J. (2005) *Devils and Angels: Youth Policy and Crime*, Oxford: Hart Publishing.

Fisher, C. and Mawby, R. (1982) 'Juvenile delinquency and police discretion in an inner-city area', *British Journal of Criminology*, 22, 1, pp. 63–75.

Flanagan, R. (2007) *The Review of Policing: Interim Report*, Surbiton: The Police Federation.

Foucault, M. (1979) *Discipline and Punish*, Harmondsworth: Penguin.

Fox Harding, L. (1991) *Perspectives in Child Care Policy*, Harlow: Longman.

Fox Harding, L. (1997) *Perspectives in Child Care Policy* (2nd edition), Harlow: Longman.

Garland, D. (1985) *Punishment and Welfare*, Aldershot: Gower.

Garland, D. (1996) 'The limits of the sovereign state', *British Journal of Criminology*, 36, 4, pp. 445–471.

Garland, D. (2001) *The Culture of Control*, Oxford: Oxford University Press.

Goldson, B. (1997) 'Children, crime, policy and practice: neither welfare nor justice', *Children and Society*, 11, pp. 77–88.

Goldson, B. (1999) 'Wither diversion? Interventionism and the new youth justice', in Goldson, B. (ed) *The New Youth Justice*, Lyme Regis: Russell House.

Goldson, B. (2010) 'The sleep of (criminological reason): knowledge-policy rupture and New Labour's youth justice legacy', *Criminology & Criminal Justice*, 10, 1, pp. 155–178.

Goldson, B. (2013) '"Unsafe, unjust and harmful to wider society": Grounds for raising the minimum age of criminal responsibility in England and Wales', *Youth Justice*, 13, 2, pp. 111–130.

Graham, J. (2010) 'Responding to youth crime', in Smith, D. (ed) *A New Response to Youth Crime*, Cullompton: Willan, pp. 104–142.

Gramsci, A. (1971) *Selections from Prison Notebooks*, London: Lawrence and Wishart.

Gray, P. (2009) 'The political economy of risk and the new governance of youth crime', *Punishment & Society*, 11, 4, pp. 443–458.

Haines, A., Goldson, B., Haycox, A., Houten, R., Lane, S., McGuire, J., Nathan, T., Perkins, E., Richards, S. and Whittington, R. (2012) *Evaluation of the Youth Justice Liaison and Diversion (YJLD) Pilot Scheme: Final Report*, Liverpool: University of Liverpool.

Haines, K. and Case, S. (2015) *Positive Youth Justice: Children First, Offenders Second*, Bristol: Policy Press.

Haines, K. and Drakeford, M. (1998) *Young People and Youth Justice*, London: Macmillan.

Haines, K. and O'Mahony, D. (2006) 'Restorative approaches, young people and youth justice', in Goldson, B. and Muncie, J. (eds) *Youth Crime and Justice*, London: Sage, pp. 110–124 .

Haines, K., Case, S., Davies, K. and Charles, A. (2013) 'The Swansea Bureau: a model of diversion from the youth justice system', *International Journal of Law, Crime and Justice*, 41, pp. 167–187.

Hall, S., Critcher, C., Jefferson, T., Clarke, J. and Roberts, B. (2013) *Policing the Crisis* (35th anniversary edition), Basingstoke: Palgrave Macmillan.

Hannah-Moffat, K. (2005) 'Criminogenic needs and the transformative risk subject: hybridizations of risk/need in penality', *Punishment & Society*, 7, 1, pp. 29–51.

Harris, R. (1982) 'Institutionalised ambivalence: social work and the Children and Young Persons Act 1969', *British Journal of Social Work*, 12, 3, pp. 247–263.

Hart, D. (2012) *Legal Aid Sentencing and Punishment of Offenders Act 2012: Implications for Children*, London: National Association for Youth Justice.

Hart, H. (1968) *Punishment and Responsibility: Essays in the Philosophy of Law*, Oxford: Clarendon Press.

Hazel, N. (2008) *Cross-National Comparisons of Youth Justice*, London: Youth Justice Board.

Heller, K. (2009) 'The cognitive psychology of mens rea', *Criminal Law & Criminology*, pp. 317–379.

Hendrick, H. (1994) *Child Welfare: England 1872–1989*, London: Routledge.

Hendrick, H. (2003) *Child Welfare: Historical Dimensions, Contemporary Debates*, Bristol: Policy Press.

Herbert, N. (2011) Speech to Association of Chief Police Officers/Restorative Justice Council Conference, 22 February.

Hine, J. and Celnick, M. (2001) *A One Year Reconviction Study of Final Warnings*, Sheffield: University of Sheffield.

Hinks, N. and Sloper, G. (1983) 'How to divert in practice', in Northamptonshire County Council, *Diversion-Corporate Action with Juveniles*, Northampton: Northamptonshire County Council, pp. 30–34.

Hiscock, K. (1987) 'Juvenile justice: the Northants experience', *County Councils Gazette*, 80, 1, pp. 12–14.

HM Government (2008) *Youth Crime Action Plan*, London: The Stationery Office.

Home Affairs Committee (2007) *Young Black People and the Criminal Justice System*, Vol II, London: The Stationery Office.

Home Office (1927) *Report of the Departmental Committee on the Care and Treatment of Young Offenders (Molony Report)*, Cmnd 2831, London: HMSO.

Home Office (1960) *Report of the Committee on Children and Young Persons (Ingleby Report)*, Cmnd 1191, London: HMSO.

Home Office (1965) *The Child, the Family and the Young Offender*, Cmnd 2742, London: HMSO.

Home Office (1968) *Children in Trouble*, Cmnd 3601, London: HMSO.

Home Office (1970) *Part I of the Children and Young Persons Act 1969: A Guide for Courts and Practitioners*, London: HMSO.

Home Office (1976) *Observations on the Eleventh Report from the Expenditure Committee*, London: HMSO.

Home Office (1978a) 'The citing of police cautions in the Juvenile Court', *Circular 49/78*, London: Home Office.
Home Office (1978b) 'The citing of police cautions in the Juvenile Court', *Circular 70/78*, London: Home Office.
Home Office (1978c) 'Juveniles: cooperation between the police and other agencies', *Circular 211/1978*, London: Home Office.
Home Office (1980a) 'Juveniles: cooperation between the police and other agencies', *Circular 83/1980*, London: Home Office.
Home Office (1980b) *Young Offenders*, Cmnd 8045, London: HMSO.
Home Office (1984) *Cautioning by the Police: A Consultative Document*, London: Home Office.
Home Office (1985) 'The cautioning of offenders', *Home Office Circular 14/1985*, London: Home Office.
Home Office (1990a) 'The cautioning of offenders', *Home Office Circular 59/1990*, London: Home Office.
Home Office (1990b) *Crime, Justice and Protecting the Public*, London: HMSO.
Home Office (1994) 'The cautioning of offenders', *Circular 18/1994*, London: Home Office.
Home Office (1997) *No More Excuses: A New Approach to Tackling Youth Crime*, London: The Stationery Office.
Hudson, B. (1996) *Understanding Justice*, Buckingham: Open University Press.
Hull Youth Justice Service (2010) *Hull Youth Crime Diversion Scheme: Annual Report July 2009-July 2010*, Hull: Hull Youth Justice Service.
Hullin, R. (1985) 'The cautioning of juvenile offenders', *Justice of the Peace*, 149, p. 312.
Hylton, S. (2015) *The Little Book of the 1970s*, Stroud: The History Press.
Institute for Criminal Policy Research (2012) *Assessing Young People in Police Custody: An Examination of the Operation of Triage Schemes*, London: Home Office.
James, A. and James, A. (2004) *Constructing Childhood*, Basingstoke: Palgrave Macmillan.
Jenks, C. (1996) *Childhood*, London: Routledge.
Johnston, H. (2015) *Crime in England 1815–1880*, Abingdon: Routledge.
Jones, D. (2001) 'Misjudged youth', *British Journal of Criminology*, 41, pp. 362–380.
Jones, D. (2012) 'Conditions for sustainable decarceration strategies for young offenders', PhD thesis, London School of Economics.
Kelly, L. and Armitage, V. (2015) 'Diverse diversions: youth justice reform, localised practices, and a "new interventionist diversion"?', *Youth Justice*, 15, 2, pp. 117–133.
Kemp, V. (2014) 'PACE, performance targets and legal protections', *Criminal Law Review*, 4, pp. 278–297.
Kemp, V., Sorsby, A., Liddle, M. and Merrington, S. (2002) *Assessing Responses to Youth Offending in Northamptonshire*', Nacro Research Briefing 2, London: Nacro.
Kettle, M. (1980) 'The drift to law and order', *Marxism Today*, October, pp. 20–27.
Kidner, D. (1985) 'Guidelines on cautioning – a justices' clerk's view', *Justice of the Peace*, 149, pp. 308–309.
Labour Party Study Group (1964) *Crime – A Challenge to Us All: Report of the Labour Party Study Group* (Longford Report), London: Labour Party.
Landau, S. and Nathan, G. (1983) 'Selecting delinquents for cautioning in the London Metropolitan Area', *British Journal of Criminology*, 23, 2, pp. 128–149.
Lee, M. (1998) *Youth, Crime and Police Work*, Basingstoke: Macmillan.

Lee, N. (2001) *Childhood and Society*, Maidenhead: Open University Press.

Lemert, E. (1967) *Human Deviance, Social Problems and Social Control*, Englewood Cliffs, NJ: Prentice-Hall.

Lenroot, R. and Giedd, J. (2006) 'Brain development in children and adolescents: insights from anatomical magnetic resource imaging', *Neuroscience and Biobehavioural Review*, 30, pp. 718–729.

Lewin, Y. (1940) 'The treatment of juvenile delinquency in England during the early nineteenth century', *Journal of Criminal Law and Criminology*, 31, 1, pp. 38–54.

Mack, J. (1963) 'Police juvenile liaison schemes', *British Journal of Criminology*, 3, pp. 361–375.

Martinson, R. (1974) 'What works? – Questions and answers about prison reform', *The Public Interest*, pp. 22–54.

Mathiesen, T. (1974) *The Politics of Abolition*, Oxford: Martin Robertson.

Matza, D. (1969) *Becoming Deviant*, Englewood Cliffs, NJ: Prentice-Hall.

May, T. (2010) Speech at Coin Street Community Centre, *The Guardian*, 28 July.

May, T., Gyateng, T. and Hough, M. (2010) *Differential Treatment in the Justice System*, London: Equality and Human Rights Commission.

May, T., Gyateng, T. and Hough, M. (2010) *Differential Treatment in the Youth Justice System*, London: King's College.

Mays, J. (1965) 'The Liverpool Police Juvenile Liaison Officer Scheme', *The Sociological Review*, 9, S1 pp. 185–200.

McAra, L. (2010) 'Models of youth justice' in Smith, D. (ed) *A New Response to Youth Crime*, Cullompton: Willan, pp. 287–317.

McAra, L. and McVie, S. (2007) 'Youth justice? The Impact of system contact on patterns of desistance from offending', *European Journal of Criminology*, 4, 3, pp. 315–345.

McClintock, F. and Avison, W. (1968) *Crime in England and Wales*, London: Heinemann.

McKittrick, N. and Eysenck, S. (1984) 'Diversion: a big fix?', *Justice of the Peace*, 148, pp. 377–379/393–394.

Merton, R. (1957) *Social Theory and Social Structure*, Glencoe, IL: Free Press.

Michalowski, R. (2016) 'What is crime?', *Critical Criminology*, 24, 2, pp. 181–199.

Ministry of Justice (2012) *Breaking the Cycle: Effective Punishment, Rehabilitation and Sentencing of Offenders*, London: The Stationery Office.

Ministry of Justice and Youth Justice Board (2013) *Youth Out-of-Court Disposals: Guide for Police and Youth Offending Services*, London: Youth Justice Board.

Morgan, P. (1981) 'The Children's Act: Sacrificing justice to children's needs?', in Brewer, C., Morris, T., Morgan, P. and North, M. (eds) *Criminal Welfare on Trial*, London: Social Affairs Unit, pp. 44–67.

Morgan, R. (2007a) 'Rebalancing youth justice' New Developments in Criminal Justice Lecture, Centre for Crime and Justice, 22 March.

Morgan, R. (2007b) 'What's the problem?', *New Law Journal*, March 2.

Morgan, R. (2007c) 'A temporary respite', *The Guardian*, February 19.

Morgan, R. and Newburn, T. (2007) 'Youth justice', in Maguire, M., Morgan, R. and Reiner, R. (eds) *The Oxford Handbook of Criminology* (4th edition), Oxford: Oxford University Press.

Morris, A. and Giller, H. (1987) *Understanding Juvenile Justice*, London: Croom Helm.

Morris, A. and McIsaac, M. (1978) *Juvenile Justice?*, London: Heinemann.

Morris, A., Giller, H., Szwed, E. and Geach, H. (1980) *Justice for Children*, London: Macmillan.

Mount, F. (1982) *The Subversive Family*, London: Jonathan Cape.

Muir, R. (2014) *Everyday Justice*, London: Institute for Public Policy Research.
Muncie, J. (1999a) *Youth and Crime: A Critical Introduction*, London: Sage.
Muncie, J. (1999b) 'Institutionalised intolerance; youth justice and the 1998 Crime and Disorder Act', *Critical Social Policy*, 19, 2, pp. 147–175.
Muncie, J. (2002) 'A new deal for youth? Early intervention and correctionalism', in Hughes, G., McLaughlin, E. and Muncie, J. (eds) *Crime Prevention and Community Safety: New Directions*, London: Sage, pp. 142–162.
Muncie, J. (2008) 'The 'punitive' turn in juvenile justice: cultures of control and rights compliance in Western Europe and the USA', *Youth Justice*, 8, 2, pp. 107–121.
Muncie, J. (2009) *Youth & Crime* (3rd edition), London: Sage.
National Association for Youth Justice (2011) *For a Child Friendly Youth Justice System*, London: NAYJ.
Oliver, I. (1978) *The Metropolitan Police Approach to the Prosecution of Juvenile Offenders*, London: Peel Press.
Parker, H. (1974) *View from The Boys*, Newton Abbot: David & Charles.
Parker, H., Casburn, M. and Turnbull, D. (1981) *Receiving Juvenile Justice*, Oxford: Basil Blackwell.
Parsloe, P. (1978) *Juvenile Justice in Britain and the United States*, Abingdon: Routledge.
Phoenix, J. (2016) 'Against youth justice and youth governance, for youth penality', *British Journal of Criminology*, 56, pp. 123–140.
Phoenix, J. and Kelly, L. (2013) 'You have to do it for yourself'', *British Journal of Criminology*, 53, pp. 419–437.
Piaget, J. (1959) *The Language and Thought of the Child*, London: Routledge.
Pickford, J. (2000) 'Introduction: a new youth justice for a new century', in Pickford, J. (ed) *Youth Justice: Theory and Practice*, London: Cavendish, pp. xxi–lx.
Pitts, J. (2001) *The New Politics of Youth Crime*, Basingstoke: Palgrave.
Pollock, L. (1983) *Forgotten Children*, Cambridge: Cambridge University Press.
Poulantzas, N. (1978) *State, Power, Socialism*, London: Verso.
Pratt, J. (1986) 'Diversion from the juvenile court', *British Journal of Criminology*, 26, 3, pp. 212–233.
Pratt, J. (1987) 'A revisionist history of intermediate treatment', *British Journal of Social Work*, 17, pp. 417–436.
Pratt, J. (1989) 'Corporatism: the third model of juvenile justice', *British Journal of Criminology*, 29, pp. 236–254.
Priestley, P., Fears, D. and Fuller, R. (1977) *Justice for Juveniles*, London: Routledge & Kegan Paul.
Prior, D., Farrow, K., Hughes, N., Kelly, G., Manders, G., White, S. and Wilkinson, B. (2011) *Maturity, Young Adults and Criminal Justice: A Literature Review*, Birmingham: University of Birmingham.
Quinney, R. (1970) *The Social Reality of Crime*, Boston, MA: Little Brown.
Rafter, N. (1990) 'The social construction of crime and crime control', *Journal of Research in Crime and Delinquency*, 27, 4, pp. 376–389.
Rix, A., Skidmore, K., Self, R., Holt, T. and Raybould, S. (2011) *Youth Restorative Disposal Process Evaluation*, London: Youth Justice Board.
Rose, W., Aldgate, J. and Jones, D. (2006) 'Developmental progression' in Aldgate, J., Jones, D., Rose, W. and Jeffery, C. (eds) *The Developing World of the Child*, London: Jessica Kingsley, pp. 163–184.
Rusche, G. and Kirchheimer, O. (1938) *Punishment and the Social Structure*, New York: Russell and Russell.

Rutherford, A. (1992) *Growing Out of Crime*, Winchester: Waterside Press.

Rutherford, A. (2002) *Growing Out of Crime*, Hook: Waterside Press.

Rutter, M. and Giller, H. (1983) *Juvenile Delinquency: Trends and Perspectives*, Harmondsworth: Penguin.

Rutter, M., Giller, H. and Hagell, A. (1998) *Antisocial Behaviour by Young People*, Cambridge: Cambridge University Press.

Samuels, A. (1989) 'Reparation and mediation', *Justice of the Peace*, 153, pp. 182–183.

Sanders, A. (1988) 'The limits to diversion from prosecution', *British Journal of Criminology*, 28, 4, pp. 513–531.

Savage, S. (1988) 'Caution for cautions', *Justice of the Peace*, 152, pp. 85–90.

Schaffer, E. (1980) *Community Policing*, London: Croom Helm.

Scott, E. and Grisso, T. (1997) 'The evolution of adolescence: a developmental perspective on juvenile justice reform', *Journal of Criminal Law & Criminology*, 88, 1, pp. 137–189.

Schur, E. (1973) *Radical Non-Intervention*, Englewood Cliffs, NJ: Prentice Hall.

Shore, H. (1999) *Artful Dodgers*, Woodbridge: The Boydell Press.

Simpson, J. (1968) 'The police and juvenile delinquency', *British Journal of Criminology*, 8, 2, pp. 119–129.

Smith, D. and Gray, J. (1985) *Police and People in London*, Aldershot: Ashgate.

Smith, J., Balls, E. and Straw, J. (2008) 'Foreword', in HM Government, *Youth Crime Action Plan*, London: The Stationery Office, pp. 1–2.

Smith, R. (1989) 'Diversion in practice', MPhil thesis, University of Leicester.

Smith, R. (2001) 'Foucault's law: The Crime and Disorder Act 1998', *Youth Justice*, 1, 2, pp. 17–29.

Smith, R. (2003) *Youth Justice: Ideas, Policy, Practice*, Cullompton: Willan.

Smith, R. (2005) 'Welfare vs justice – again!', *Youth Justice*, 5, 1, pp. 3–16.

Smith, R. (2006) 'Actuarialism and early intervention in contemporary youth justice', in Goldson, B. and Muncie, J. (eds) *Youth Crime and Justice*, London: Sage, pp. 92–109.

Smith, R. (2007) *Youth Justice: Ideas, Policy, Practice* (2nd edition), Cullompton: Willan.

Smith, R. (2010) *A Universal Child?*, Basingstoke: Palgrave Macmillan.

Smith, R. (2011) *Doing Justice to Young People*, Abingdon: Willan.

Smith, R. (2014) *Youth Justice: Ideas, Policy, Practice* (3rd edition), Abingdon: Routledge.

Smith, R. (2015) 'Troubled, troubling or troublesome? Troubled families and the changing shape of youth justice', in Wasik, M. and Santatzoglou, S. (eds) *The Management of Change in Criminal Justice*, Basingstoke: Palgrave Macmillan, pp. 49–63.

Smith, R. and Gray, P. (forthcoming) 'The changing shape of youth justice: models of practice'.

Solomon, E. and Garside, R. (2008) *Ten Years of Labour's Youth Justice Reforms: An Independent Audit*, London: Centre for Crime and Justice Studies.

Soppitt, S. and Irving, A. (2011) *An Evaluation into the Effectiveness of the Early Diversion Intervention 'Triage' as a Mechanism for Tackling Youth Offending in Newcastle Upon Tyne*, Newcastle: Northumbria University.

Squires, P. (ed) (2008) *ASBO Nation*, Bristol: Policy Press.

Squires, P. and Stephen, D. (2005) *Rougher Justice*, Cullompton: Willan.

Steer, D. (1970) *Police Cautions – A Study in the Exercise of Police Discretion*, Oxford: Basil Blackwell.

Steinberg, L., Cauffman, E. and Monahan, K. (2015) 'Psychosocial maturity and desistance from crime in a sample of serious juvenile offenders', *Juvenile Justice Bulletin*, March.,Washington, DC: Office of Juvenile Justice and Delinquency Prevention.

Taylor, L., Lacey, R. and Bracken, D. (1979) *In Whose Best Interests?*, Nottingham: The Cobden Trust/MIND.

Taylor, M. (1971) *Study of the Juvenile Liaison Scheme in West Ham 1961–1965*, Home Office Research Study No. 8, London: HMSO.

Thatcher, M. (1978) Speech to Young Conservative Conference, February 12.

Thatcher, M. (1982) Speech to Conservative Central Council, March 27.

Thorpe, D., Smith, D., Green, C. and Paley, J. (1980) *Out of Care: The Community Support of Juvenile Offenders*, London: George Allen & Unwin.

United Nations (1989) *United Nations Convention on the Rights of the Child*, Geneva: United Nations

Vygotsky, L. (1986) *Thought and Language*, Cambridge, MA: MIT Press.

Walker, S. and Harvey-Messina, L. (2012) *Implementation of the LASPO Act 2012: Key Stakeholder Information*, London: Youth Justice Board.

Windlesham, L. (1993) *Responses to Crime* (Volume 2), Oxford: Clarendon Press.

Winterdyk, J. (1997) 'Introduction' in Winterdyk, J. (ed) *Juvenile Justice Systems: International Perspectives*, Toronto: Canadian Scholars' Press, pp. vii–xxx.

Wood, S., Eckley, L., Stuart, J., Hughes, K., Kelly, D., Harrison, D. and Quigg, Z. (2011) *Evaluation of the Youth Crime Action Plan (YCAP) in Liverpool*, Liverpool: LJMU Centre for Public Health.

Yates, J. (2012) 'What prospects youth justice? Children in trouble in the age of austerity', *Social Policy & Administration*, 46, 4, pp. 432–447.

Youth Justice Board (2002) *Building on Success: Youth Justice Board Annual Review 2001/02*, London: YJB.

Youth Justice Board (2005) *Risk and Protective Factors*, London: YJB.

Youth Justice Board (2013) *Preventing Religious Radicalisation and Violent Extremism*, London: YJB.

Index

www.ingramcontent.com/pod-product-compliance
Ingram Content Group UK Ltd.
Pitfield, Milton Keynes, MK11 3LW, UK
UKHW011016180926
475701UK00004B/766